'This is a fabulous adventure – reckless, insanely ambitious and filled with sweat, tears and laughter. It is irresistible reading for all ages. Thank you so much for letting me read it; and now I have the thrill of the TV version, which will make us all fasten our safety belts as we watch. An immense challenge and a thrilling true story. Bravo, Alex, and bravo to all who were part of this epic tale.'

Joanna Lumley

'Alex Bescoby weaves travel, adventure, history and the contemporary together like no one else. His great gift is to take us on a journey through past and present. By its end we have learned more about the world and ourselves.'

Dan Snow

'Not content to just pay homage to a legendary journey, Alex Bescoby must drive the very Land Rover, complete with GIN and TONIC jerry cans, that made the trip in 1955. Spoiler alert: nothing goes to plan. *The Last Overland* is steered by an indomitable spirit through time, friendships, obsession, doubt and perpetual motion. A book not only for adventurous hearts who want to seize life, but for those who want to interrogate what it is to be human.'

Keggie Carew

'A fantastic piece of travel writing set to become a classic of the genre. *The Last Overland* is an epic journey, epitomizing the spirit of the great modern adventure.'

Levison Wood

'If you thought the Age of Adventure was over, think again. Told with verve, passion and above all a huge amount of fun, this is the real thing. In a madcap escapade, Alex Bescoby sets out to recreate a road journey from Singapore to London first done in 1955 – driving one of the original vehicles, a rebuilt Land Rover Series One rescued from a scrap heap in St Helena, of all places. It's a cracking story. Has the world changed? You bet it has. Is the spirit of adventure still alive? In the hands of Bescoby and his intrepid team, it certainly is. Travelling through some of the most beautiful, fascinating and troubled places on earth, from Thailand and Burma to Tibet and Central Asia, *The Last Overland* is packed with fascinating tales, hilarious encounters, and hair-raising brushes with disaster – with a surprisingly touching ending. Bescoby is a terrific travelling companion, full of insight, sharp observation and enviable sangfroid: just the kind of person you'd want at your side if you are being shot at by rebels in Nagaland or taking your life into your own hands in Tajikistan's Tunnel of Death.'

Michael Wood

'Elegant, wry, indomitable, self-deprecating – a splendid, sparkling addition to expeditions and to travel writing.'

Rory Stewart

'A proper adventure story – a journey halfway around the world with all the scrapes, hiccups, wonderment and exhilaration to be expected from an epic journey in an old Land Rover with a leaky roof. Told with an infectious enthusiasm, passion and compelling verve, this is the story of an overland journey that says much about our ongoing relationship with the planet on which we live, but also the passage of time and an undimmed thirst for adventure.'

James Holland

'The First Overland was an amazing journey, underlining the fact that adventure is always out there for anybody who seeks it. This epic recreation of that trip shows us that whether you're the first or the thousandth, the view from the mountaintop is just as incredible. I know that Alex's Last Overland expedition will inspire other intrepid explorers to ensure that this is definitely not the last – there is always more to see and explore.'

Tony Wheeler, co-founder of Lonely Planet

THE
LAST
OVERLAND

SINGAPORE TO LONDON:
THE RETURN JOURNEY OF THE
ICONIC LAND ROVER EXPEDITION

ALEX BESCOBY

with a foreword by Tim Slessor

Michael O'Mara Books Limited

First published in Great Britain in 2022
by Michael O'Mara Books Limited
9 Lion Yard
Tremadoc Road
London SW4 7NQ

A CIP catalogue record for this book is available from the British Library.

Papers used by Michael O'Mara Books Limited are natural, recyclable products
made from wood grown in sustainable forests. The manufacturing processes
conform to the environmental regulations of the country of origin.

ISBN: 978-1-78929-463-7 in hardback print format
ISBN: 978-1-78929-477-4 in trade paperback
ISBN: 978-1-78929-475-0 in ebook format

1 2 3 4 5 6 7 8 9 10

www.mombooks.com

Designed and typeset by Claire Cater
Maps by Peter Liddiard
Photographs on front and back cover, in plate sections and Last Overland
images in endpapers by Léopold Belanger © Grammar Productions. First
Overland photographs in endpapers © First Overland team.

Printed and bound by CPI Group (UK) Ltd, Croydon, CR0 4YY

'It's one thing to set out to scale Everest and turn back – no one will blame you for that. But embarking on something ridiculous, paradoxically, leaves no room for failure.'

DAN KIERAN, *THE IDLE TRAVELLER*

Contents

Foreword

By Tim Slessor

'An overland drive to Singapore? You're crazy ...!'

It was certainly true that no one had done it before – though it was no secret that a few expeditions had tried or had at least talked about it. Indeed, back in those days – and I'm talking about the mid-1950s – it had sometimes been called 'the still unclimbed Everest of motoring'. Certainly, in our ambition to give it a go, we were reckoned by some of the motoring press to be 'geographically ignorant and politically naive'. But, to us, a bunch of freshly graduated (and rather innocent) twenty-two- and twenty-three-year-olds, that kind of 'advice' was just an added incentive.

We set to work – to raise the financial steam, to research a possible route, to start applying for the myriad visas, permits and licences and, above all, to find two appropriate vehicles. We approached the folk at the Rover Company; amazingly, they seemed to have more faith in us than those media sceptics did, and (again) amazingly, they lent us two brand-new Land Rovers – one painted dark blue for Oxford and the other light blue for Cambridge. Then, no less astonishingly, the BBC – via a young producer called David Attenborough – came good with £300, enough to buy a simple clockwork camera and the film to go with it. With that kind of backing, other potential sponsors now began to take us a little more seriously.

Anyway, against the odds, and to cut very short on the umpteen details of our 30,500-kilometre (19,000-mile) journey, we succeeded. Of course, there were any number of problems, both geographical and political. But the one that had really worried us, and the one that had dissuaded all previous attempts, was a roadless gap between Assam (north-east India) and northern Burma.

Twelve years earlier, during the war, the Americans (under General Vinegar-Joe Stilwell) had built a road across that 450-kilometre (280-mile) gap through the remote and jungly Naga Hills. The aim was to get military supplies into southern China where the Chinese Nationalist Army was fighting the Japanese. But, once the war was ended, the road had no purpose. So, in 1945 it was abandoned. Even in our geographical ignorance we knew that, after ten years of the heaviest rainfall in the world (a monsoonal 370-plus inches a year), the road through those hills would almost inevitably have been washed away. But no one really knew. The challenge was enough. Let's just say that, even though we had some rather hairy moments along the way, were in low gear and four-wheel drive nearly all the time, fording rivers up to our wheel-arches, and that 450 kilometres (280 miles) took three long days (we had allowed ourselves at least a week), we succeeded. Ridiculous – but jubilation!

After six months on and off a variety of roads and tracks, from desert to tarmac, from mud to motorways, two very weary Land Rovers eventually pulled up outside the Rover showroom in downtown Singapore – to a welcoming chorus of congrats, flashbulbs and popping corks. An American journalist put it rather neatly: 'I guess you boys have run plumb outta road.' We guessed we had. And it was most satisfactory. (If, gentle reader, you want to know more, may I refer you to my book, *First Overland*. In some conceit, I'll boast that it is still in print – after six decades and six editions.)

And those two Land Rovers? Well, after a bit of a breather in Singapore, we shipped them back to Calcutta and began the long drive home – via a tranquil Afghanistan and a friendly Iran. Yes, those really were the days. Eventually, back with Rover in Birmingham, they were thoroughly overhauled and then lent to two other expeditions. The Cambridge car went back to Iran, but, sadly, rolled down a steep ravine one night and was mortally wrecked; Oxford went off with a bird-watching expedition to Ascension Island in the south Atlantic and then, a year or two later, found herself shipped even further south – to remote St Helena. There, after a further thirty years of faithful service, the old lady was finally retired and parked in the long grass.

Over the following decades, I used to get occasional phone calls or emails from Land Rover aficionados. Their messages were always much the same: 'I've read your book and I think you'll be interested in a plan we're hatching to bring your old Oxford car back from St Helena' – or words to that effect. In the early days, I was enthusiastic, even excited by what those callers had in mind. But as the years went by and nothing ever seemed to happen, I became increasingly sceptical – to the point of being almost dismissive. Then, one day in 2016, a Yorkshireman phoned. Well, as the rest of us know, there's something special about Yorkshiremen (and women): they don't mess about; they tend to mean what they say. At the very least, one has to take them seriously; one doesn't dare be dismissive. So it was that the rather wonderful Adam Bennett came to the rescue.

Over the next six months and via endless frustrations, emails, and transoceanic phone calls, he eventually managed to bring the old thing back from the long grass. By the time he had paid the actual owner of the wreck, then arranged for it to be shoehorned into a container and finally shipped back to England, he must have spent thousands. Expensive – but wonderful!

I well remember Adam's invitation to join him in York to open the doors on that just-arrived container – to the pop of a bottle or two. Yes, there she was: old Oxford. Sure, she was more than a bit of a wreck. But she was immediately recognizable. Yes, that was the bracket that had held the oversize fire extinguisher; there was the hidey-hole where we kept our passports and cash; there was the leaky roof-hatch; there was the now-faded '1st Overland' that, sixty-one years earlier and a day or two short of Singapore, we had triumphantly painted on the back door.

Memories, memories. I don't normally get emotional over bits of metal, but standing there that afternoon, I don't mind telling you, I found myself just a bit weepy.

Three months later, and meticulously restored by Ben Stowe and his masterly team at York's Blackpaw Motors, Oxford went off to be checked for her MOT. We held our breath … Then the phone went: she had passed! The final touch came a few days later when the DVLA agreed to reissue the old girl's original (1955) licence: SNX-891. And then Adam let me drive her for a few miles. After all those years, not much had changed: no power steering, no synchro-mesh gearbox, no disc brakes, no coil springs and, of course, no air-con. Wonderful.

So, what next? Well, the old thing was almost immediately in demand at various Land Rover gatherings up and down the land. And on the continent too – from Milan to Lisbon and various rallies between. At some point, I suggested to Adam that it was only a matter of time before, maybe, she should hit a really long-distance trail once more. Come to think about it, howzabout London to Singapore?

One of those gatherings to which Oxford was invited was centred on a beach in Anglesey. The place had long become sacred ground to Land Rover worshippers because, according to history, it was here in the summer of 1947 that a holidaying Maurice Wilks, the top engineer at the Rover Company, had scratched, in the sand, the first outline of what he hoped would become Britain's first smallish, four-wheel-drive, go-anywhere car: dare I say it, a sort of British Jeep.

As Alex will tell you in this book, he and his father (both Land Rover nuts) were at that Anglesey gathering, where a fateful meeting took place. It would be true to say that it seemed better to think about reversing the London-to-Singapore idea; Singapore to London would make more sense. But thinking about it was about as far as things had got. But once Alex became involved, it was not long before things began to happen. After all, Adam had a full-time Yorkshire business to run, so he was only too willing to allow Alex to take up the challenge.

A plan began to take shape: if enough sponsorship could be generated, Oxford would be escorted across the 19,500 or so overland kilometres (12,200 miles) from Singapore by two much more modern Land Rovers, and the expedition would probably route itself via Tibet and Central Asia – via one of the highest road passes in the world. Then came the suggestion from both Adam and Alex that I should join the team. I was very flattered, but a bit worried. After all, I was eighty-seven, and the last thing I wanted was to be a liability – either to myself or to the expedition.

But, for now, from me – enough. Indeed, more than … But, for the full story of that epic return, read on. Alex, it's over to you. Take it away!

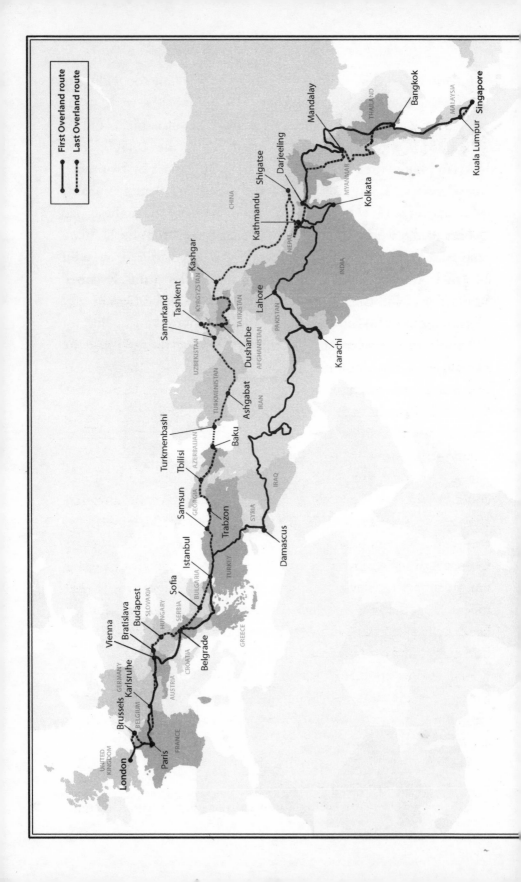

First Overland route

Last Overland route

Prologue

6 November 2019: The Middle of Nowhere

Under a crystal-clear sky, in a country you've probably never heard of, the sand gathered slowly on the ruins of Oxford and of my great and foolish dream.

I knelt with my head in my hands, watching through gaps in my fingers as her vital fluids gushed around my feet. They formed into a little stream, running along a deep gouge in the tarmac that Oxford had carved in her death throes. Slowly, like a tentacle, they crept to where a single tyre now lay flat, still impaled by half an axle pointing stubbornly to the sky.

She – and yes, I had come to concede the 'Grand Old Lady' could be nothing else – had overcome so much. She was a world-conquering heroine, lost to history on a remote, rocky outcrop, then brought triumphantly back to life after six decades in exile. Oxford had been in my care for all of seventy-three days, carrying me safely across eleven countries and 13,000 kilometres (8,000 miles). Together we had seen Mount Everest at sunset, dodged headhunters and the Taliban, half-drowned in monsoon rains, and half-baked in the Southeast Asian sun.

And for her troubles, I had dumped her into a roadside ditch, leaving her bleeding and maimed. There were now three wheels on my wagon, and – contrary to popular myth – I wasn't rolling anywhere.

'Well, I guess this means we'll be late for lunch?' said Marcus, his looming form casting a shadow on my grief.

'Do you ever stop thinking about your stomach?' said a second,

Nat-shaped shadow. I had managed to keep him alive for another day, at least.

'How bad is it, Doc?' I asked, as a third, much shorter shadow appeared.

He paused, looking thoughtful.

'How do you walk with no legs?'

Larry stooped down to give a second opinion, casting his seasoned eye over the damage.

'That's going to take days to fix, if it even is fixable, which I doubt.'

'You have only five days on your visa. After that you must leave,' said our guide Tashmurad, helpful as ever.

I looked back to see our two support cars parked a respectful distance from the crash site, both reassuringly intact. From them emerged Leo and David, cameras rolling as ever. They padded up to Oxford with a rare reverence, as if filming a funeral.

The fog of shock began to clear enough for me to take a silent headcount, which then only sparked a new panic. Seven ... there should be eight? Where was Tibie? Calm down – she's waiting for us in Georgia, of course, after we mislaid her a little carelessly in Uzbekistan.

It felt like the end, but surely it couldn't be? People all over the world were watching and waiting for us to finish, and we still had twelve more countries and 8,000 kilometres (5,000 miles) further to go. I had given this ridiculous endeavour every penny I had, missing births, marriages and funerals of those I loved to see this mission through. Had it all been for nothing?

I felt my stomach churn; it had not been quite right since that volcanic diarrhoea in Nepal. I looked round at my crew, my little family of oddballs dressed in their jumbles of grubby layers, hair unkempt and faces unshaved, all of them lost in private thought. Had I dragged them all the way across the world simply to fail alongside me?

After an hour, a flatbed truck appeared on the horizon, summoned from the desert haze by Tashmurad. For the first time on her epic transglobal journey, all Oxford's remaining wheels left the road. As she was slowly winched into place, the rescue-truck driver shouted to me in yet another language I did not understand.

'He wants to know what you're doing,' translated Tashmurad.

'We're on an expedition,' I said, immediately feeling stupid as he took in my bedraggled, dust-covered form. The driver screwed up his face as if sucking on a lemon. He looked at me hard, then answered, shaking his head. I turned to Tashmurad for help.

'He said: "No one goes on *expeditions* anymore."'

1

Beginnings

22 June 2018: Anglesey, Wales

429 Days Before Expedition (BE)

In AD 61, a Roman legion set off across the stretch of water separating mainland Wales and the tiny island of Anglesey. A roaring band of bearded, black-robed druids stood waiting on the island's shore. They were the last of the free, zealous guardians of the old ways, bravely but vainly defending one of the last bastions of pagan Britain from the forces of the future.

Today, anyone watching the UK's Land Rover Series One Club gather at a disused hangar in north-west Wales might wonder if the Romans ever finished the job. Huge men in dark clothes, some sporting beards you could nest birds in, pitch tents all around. As the sun began to dip on a balmy summer's evening, barbecues and gas stoves flickered to life, like beacons in an ancient army camp. But these men (and more than a few women) didn't worship mistletoe or standing stones. There was only one religion here, and it had four wheels.

'Welcome to Land Rover Mecca,' my dad, Roger, announced as he pulled his beloved 1952 RAF-blue Series I into our reserved pitch, the engine sputtering to silence after a long day's drive. A true believer from birth, he had indulged a lifelong obsession for all things four-wheeled. There was always one 'project' or another blocking up the driveway at our family home in Manchester, yet another crazy purchase that raised the eyebrows of my mum, Pam, in tandem with her blood pressure. But his first love never left him; Land Rover always had his heart.

Like many Land Rover fans, my dad's obsession was inherited from his own dad, Vin, who had died before I was born. Together they had bought their first Series I, and I had no doubt he thought of Vin every time he climbed in his little blue Land Rover.

My dad had tried his best to pass on his passion to my brother Sam and me, but so far with limited success. Sam now drove a Toyota (Land Rover's arch nemesis) round the horse-studs of Somerset where he worked as a vet, and as for me – well, any one of the dashboard lights on my battered little Skoda would send me into nervous sweats, and I still gave thanks every driving day that I had never had to change a tyre on my own.

I was a documentary filmmaker by trade, and had spent the last decade trekking to weird and wonderful corners of the globe in search of great historical stories. Whether up in the Peruvian Andes or in the backcountry of Sierra Leone, my greatest joy was grabbing a thread of the great tapestry of history and tugging on it to see where it led.

But it was Burma – now known as Myanmar – that had captured my imagination like no other, and where I'd made my home for much of the last ten years. Travelling its length and breadth as the country opened from decades of dictatorship, I'd found myself swept up in a movement to dig up a long-dead king, trekking through the Himalayan foothills in search of veterans of the Second World War, and walking in the footsteps of Orwell through the rubble of the British Empire.

My years in Myanmar had been the most rewarding of my life, but had also kept me from my home in the UK and my family for far too long. This weekend in Wales was a long-overdue chance to spend time with my dad, in a place where our two great passions – history and Land Rovers – could conveniently collide.

For my dad and the other devotees of the Land Rover Series

One Club, this visit to Anglesey was a pilgrimage of the same spiritual depth to those taken by the sickle-wielding druids of ancient Britain. It was here in Red Wharf Bay seventy-one years ago, dad explained to me for the hundredth time in my life, that the Land Rover was conceived.

Maurice Wilks, chief engineer at the Rover Company, had owned a holiday home here on Anglesey, right by Red Wharf Bay. Whenever Wilks could escape the Rover factory in Warwickshire, he would thunder around Anglesey in his beloved American Willys Jeep. The Jeep – the world's first mass-produced, four-wheel-drive car – had been used by Allied troops in combat across the globe. Eisenhower called it one of the most decisive weapons of the war.

As much as Wilks loved that Jeep, he dreamed of building better. And it was here in 1947, in the sand of Red Wharf Bay, that he first sketched the design of a car that would bring that dream to life.

By April 1948, that boxy outline would be made real in steel and aluminium, becoming the Series I we were sitting in today. 'It was the first in a long line of Land Rovers spanning seven decades ...' Dad gestured excitedly with a tent peg, reaching his crescendo. 'A motoring icon beloved as much by royalty and popstars as by farmers and fishermen.'

The UK's Series One Club are arguably the most devout believers in a truly global religion – automotive Jesuits who have exchanged cassocks for overalls, holy water for WD-40. There are thousands of paid-up members in sister-chapters spread across forty-eight countries, setting the gold standard in piety for the many millions more Land Rover owners who would describe themselves as at least part-time fanatics of the one true faith.

My dad was in heaven, squeezed elbow-to-elbow with the faithful around a plastic table. As I nudged alongside him into the soup of excitable chatter about floating half-axles and parabolic leaf-springs, a nearby conversation cut through the noise.

'She's here!'

'Have you seen her? Amazing …!'

'Syria … Iraq … Iran …! Can you imagine?'

I tuned in, hearing one word repeating more than the others: 'Oxford'. Intrigued, I left my dad holding court and stepped outside for air.

'Excuse me, mate, but what's "Oxford"?' I asked a round, bearded man cupping a cigarette outside.

He turned, revealing a T-shirt proudly declaring: 'I'M HAVING A DIRTY WEEKEND'. 'Oxford?' he replied, his grin laced with pity at my ignorance. 'It's right over there!'

He pointed into the darkness beyond the pool of light spilling from the hangar. I could just make out the boxy, iconic silhouette of a Land Rover Series I. Little did I know that this inanimate pile of metal and grease would change the course of my life. It looked fit for a museum. Or a scrapyard. Certainly not a road. I flicked on the torch on my phone for a closer look. The first thing I noticed was the paintwork. Oxford's flanks were mottled with three shades of blue, patches of silver peeking through like a rash. The roof, clearly once a bold white, was now speckled grey and pitted with dents.

Unlike its more modern offspring, the Series I's insides are on its outsides – twin fuel tanks both visible and vulnerable under the driver and passenger doors, while wires for the windscreen-mounted fog lamp loop untidily from the bonnet. There were gaps between panels so large they'd surely expose anyone inside to the elements, and a large wad of cardboard was wedged in the passenger windowpanes to halt a rattle.

Around us were all manner of classic Land Rovers, each of which would no doubt earn a small fortune if their fanatical owners were ever desperate enough to commit the sin of selling. On the door in front of me, however, was a clue that even in such distinguished company this Land Rover was something truly special. Semi-legible through the mottled paint, I could just make out:

O–FORD & C–MBRID–E
FAR –ASTERN E–PEDITIO–

Beneath the text was a winged horse – Pegasus – once blood-red but now peppered with white. Two front-mounted jerry cans protruded from the bumper, one labelled 'GIN', the other 'TONIC'. (The driver had their priorities squarely in order.) I followed my torch round the back of the car and stepped back to take in more hand-stencilled text. In bold red-and-white, clearly visible through the blotchy paintwork, were the words:

LONDON –
SINGAPORE

1ST OVERLAND
1955–56

'Can I help?' a melodious voice inquired.

I was greeted by the owlish, stubbled face of Graham Aldous, whom I would quickly learn was something of a high priest in the Land Rover religion. I explained that I was keen to know what all the fuss was about.

'You're looking at the most famous Land Rover of all,' Graham announced, eyes sparkling with evangelical zeal. 'I'm giving a talk about it here in the "GazebOdeon" tomorrow.' He patted the tent he had emerged from. 'See you then?'

The following morning, I sat, notepad in hand, as Graham recounted Oxford's exploits to a small gathering of the faithful in his tent.

In March 1955, six recent graduates from Oxford and Cambridge, barely into their twenties, set off from London in two Land Rovers. Six months later, they made history as the first people to drive 'the unclimbed Everest of motoring' – more than 19,500 kilometres

(12,200 miles) from the English Channel across the entire Eurasian landmass to the tiny island of (then British) Singapore. They departed with the dust still settling on the bloodiest conflict the world had ever witnessed, and ventured forth through the thickening permafrost of the Cold War.

The cars, nicknamed 'Oxford' and 'Cambridge', were painted in the famous dark- and light-blue university colours respectively. Graham – then a schoolboy – had been out shopping in the outskirts of London when the expedition thundered past. He was so captivated by the sight that he had followed the story from start to finish – and had since become the foremost expert on the 'Oxford & Cambridge Far Eastern Expedition', now better known among the faithful as the 'First Overland'.

The expedition were unable to cross much of Eastern Europe, cut off by what Churchill had dubbed the 'Iron Curtain', so skirted south through Yugoslavia and across the Bosporus to Asia. They went sightseeing in Syria, shopping in Iraq, and camping in Iran. They were among the first people ever to enter Nepal by car, and among the last to cross the country then known as Burma on the blood-soaked Stilwell Road.

Other adventurous types had previously reached as far as Bengal, but none had managed the Burma crossing. When the wheels of Oxford and Cambridge finally crossed over from Burma into Thailand, the team knew they had already made history, but they were determined to complete their ultimate objective, which lay at the far-southern tip of the Malay peninsula. Cameras flashed and champagne popped as the expedition pulled into their final stop, the Rover Garage on Orchard Road, Singapore, half a year after setting off from London.

'It was most satisfactory,' the expedition's scribe, Tim Slessor, wrote in understated fashion in his account, *First Overland*. The book has never been out of print since 1956. If such a thing existed, Graham explained clutching his copy, *First Overland* was the bible of the Land Rover religion.

That night, as a symphony of snoring rippled across the campsite, I closed my tent and trawled Google for everything I could find on the expedition, discovering a BBC documentary from 2005 marking its fiftieth anniversary. I watched, captivated, as a much fresher-looking Oxford charged through the deserts of Afghanistan, and kicked up dust in the shadow of the Himalayas.

Of all the people who might have opened the film, I had not expected to see Sir David Attenborough. This was a story of high adventure in petrol-guzzling cars, not the perils of climate change to which they were undoubtedly contributing. Five decades ago, however, the world was very different. Attenborough – then a young producer at the BBC – recalled his incredulity as six young men appeared in his office proposing to drive from London to Singapore.

Attenborough seemed convinced that wars and revolutions had since made the voyage unrepeatable. 'I don't think it would be possible today,' he concluded, 'and certainly not in the gay, happy-go-lucky cavalier spirit that these chaps did it in.' I switched off my phone, the seeds of a reckless idea taking root in my brain.

The next morning, I sheltered my eyes from the sun and scanned across Red Wharf Bay. Land Rovers of every colour and condition covered the hallowed sand, but there was only one I wanted to see. Looking seawards, I spotted Oxford's now unmistakable battered outline.

I approached cautiously from the driver's side. Behind the wheel was a mountain of a man in a loose black T-shirt. Summoning my courage, I tapped nervously on the window.

'Hello?' he growled.

'I've heard all about this car,' I gabbled. 'It's amazing! Is it yours?'

After a calculating pause, a small smile broke his stern veneer. 'I suppose so, given what I went through t' find it!' responded Adam Bennett, the county of Yorkshire made flesh, as he began to unfold his and Oxford's incredible story.

When the cars returned to the UK from Singapore, the mechanics at Rover had judged them to be in fine fettle, ready to hit the road again immediately if needed. While the expedition team began their lives in the real world, both Cambridge and Oxford were quickly off on new adventures.

Cambridge was commandeered for an archaeological expedition in Turkey. This journey was short-lived, however, as Cambridge was driven into a ditch in the darkness somewhere along the Iran–Turkey border. The driver, Terence Bendixson, was dragged half-dead from the wreckage; after recovering, he could never remember exactly where he'd left the road. Cambridge, Adam explained, was lost to history. It would take a braver man than he to go looking for a Land Rover carcass around today's Iran.

Oxford was a different story. 'Where the car landed was never in doubt,' Adam recalled, 'the problem was getting to it.'

Oxford was loaned by Rover to the 1957 British Ornithologists Union Centenary Expedition led by a Dr Bernard Stonehouse, assembled to study birdlife on Ascension Island. Ascension is a rocky South Atlantic fragment, one of the most remote places on Earth at nearly 1,600 kilometres (1,000 miles) from the nearest major landmass.

Once Dr Stonehouse was finished birdwatching in 1959, Rover were not keen to foot the costs of repatriating Oxford. The car was donated to a local named Melvyn Merch. On his retirement in 1977, Merch shipped Oxford about 1,300 kilometres (800 miles) to the (relatively) nearby island of St Helena, another British outpost, on which he'd been born and raised.

Over four decades, Oxford was slowly cannibalized to maintain Merch's two other vintage Land Rovers. By 2017, Merch had even cut Oxford's carcass into pieces to prevent it being bulldozed by a road-construction team. He had always known the car was special, however, and went to great pains to dismantle it in such a way that it could one day be rebuilt, should anyone have the drive and wherewithal to do it.

That person was Adam, who had started collecting Land Rovers with his father aged fourteen and, like my dad and so many others here, could never shake that first love. Now in his early fifties, and with the money to back a mad adventure, Adam's sights were set on the Holy Grail of Land Rover collecting.

Adam's rescue of Oxford was a tale of bloody-minded battles through red tape and baffled officials, who could not understand why he wanted to rescue a pile of scrap from one of Earth's remotest points. After months of work and a 19,500-kilometre (12,000-mile) journey via South Africa, Gibraltar, Rotterdam and Leeds, Oxford's remains finally touched down on Adam's driveway in May 2017. Adam recalled how his hands had trembled as he opened the container to start the most challenging restoration of his life. With expert help, using as many of the existing parts as possible, he revived Oxford in only two months. By the end of the third, Oxford had all its paperwork to allow it to drive in the UK. (Adam had persuaded the authorities that Oxford had merely been on a sixty-year holiday.)

One reason for the rush to get Oxford working was the First Overlanders. 'They're not hanging about,' Adam stated bluntly. Three had passed away, and now only three remained, all in their late eighties.

'This was for them,' Adam said, patting Oxford's dashboard. He recalled how he had reunited the surviving First Overlanders with the car late last year, and seeing them preen lovingly over their old friend had made all his stress worthwhile.

He then divulged his ulterior motive for the restoration. Like me and millions of others, Adam had been captivated by the old footage of Oxford romping across the globe.

'Oxford has to ride again,' he said with steely confidence. 'From Singapore to London this time, finish the job the First Overlanders started all those years ago.'

I could hear fate knocking. I burbled that I made documentaries for a living and would kill to help in any way I could. He fixed his beady eyes on me, an expert gaze I soon learned was attuned to spotting bullshit.

'You'd better call Tim Slessor then,' he concluded after an uncomfortably long pause, a hint of scepticism still present.

I walked back to my dad's car in a daze, grasping a piece of paper with Tim's number. Dad was hard at work carving the outline of a Series I in the sand as I filled him in.

'Well, this is where big ideas start, son,' he said, standing back to admire his handiwork.

14 August 2018: London, England
376 Days BE

I approached the door of the little terraced house and, as instructed, rang the buzzer for the upstairs apartment. The door snapped open, almost as if he'd been waiting.

'Well, hello at last!' said Tim, ushering me over the doormat.

Even though we had exchanged a few short phone calls, little could have prepared me for the first meeting with the man himself. Only the night before, I had been rewatching footage of a wiry boy in his early twenties wading through rivers in India, hiking up sand dunes in Iraq, and joshing with gun-toting insurgents in Burma. That boy was undoubtedly stood in front of me now, his five-foot-five frame now slightly stooped, but proudly wearing all the battle scars and campaign medals of the sixty-plus years in between.

'Come in, come in,' he said, releasing my hand from a bone-crushing handshake.

I followed him upstairs in the wake of his rather stiff-hipped gait. He was dressed in a faded blue jumper – at least two sizes too big – well-worn, pale-blue jeans and clunky walking boots. I would soon come to realize this was the Slessor uniform: adaptable, hard-wearing and utterly no-nonsense, like the man himself.

'I hear from Adam that I may "fit" with some plans you have?' said Tim, parking me firmly in a squishy armchair in his cosy, book-lined living room. 'Or indeed,' he added, looking me square in the eye, clearly taking the measure of me, 'you may "fit" with some plans that *I* have …'

Feeling the sands beneath me shifting, I explained my growing kernel of an idea to recreate his historic overland journey for my latest documentary. As Tim was the man who had quite literally written *the* book on overlanding, his approval was essential. In an effort to win his blessing, I tried to set out my credentials as a filmmaker who had done his fair share of adventurous travel.

In turn, Tim began to fill me in on his own, much longer career as a documentary maker, TV presenter and author – a journey that began at the BBC almost immediately after returning from his epic overland voyage, and which had taken him from the Himalayas to the Arctic, from the Australian outback to the Sahara Desert.

He plucked dates, names and places spanning decades and continents from his memory with no effort at all, spinning his yarns with expert flair. I marvelled at how he recalled camping in Afghanistan as if it were only last week, and of crossing the Ganges as if it was simply another weekend away.

Still deep in conversation as dinner time approached, we moved to a Thai restaurant around the corner. The flavours and smells of Southeast Asia filled us both with nostalgia, and over steaming dishes of fried pork and rice washed down with crisp Thai beer, Tim grilled me on my time in Myanmar, a country that had cast a spell on us both. He still read its news voraciously, and as we shovelled wilted greens in thick oyster sauce, he pressed me for my thoughts on the country's tragic politics, all the while studiously avoiding talk of my plans to recreate the First Overland.

Only as the plates were cleared did I notice the time, a little shocked. It was 11 p.m. and the staff were waiting to lock up. We had been talking for five hours non-stop.

'It's getting late,' I said. 'I'll have to get home.'

'I'll drive you back,' he replied, waving for the bill.

Counting the beer bottles on the table and factoring in the age of the driver, I wondered if I should risk declining.

'Well,' he concluded, stepping out of the warm, scented fug of the restaurant and facing me square-on, 'if you and I are going to do this journey we'd better get started – before it's too late!'

I was stunned. Not merely by the idea of the drive to my house with Tim that awaited, but at the clearly ludicrous idea of an eighty-six-year-old man taking on the gruelling trek that had put men in their twenties through the wringer. I stumbled after him as we collected his battered old Ford from outside his house, my head full of questions and more-than-legitimate concerns.

I buckled up and tried to settle my racing pulse as Tim darted out of his parking spot. Perhaps this was why Adam had been initially reluctant to connect Tim and me, for fear of me encouraging Tim on a clearly reckless pursuit for a man of his age. Not for the first time in my life I felt the exhilarating rush of stepping into a story so much bigger than my own and from which I now had no escape.

As we sped through the city, I began to unwind as a perverse logic took hold – if I couldn't trust this eighty-six-year-old to drive me safely across London, I reasoned, how on Earth could I trust him to drive me across two continents?

29 September 2018: London, England

330 Days BE

We survived the hair-raising drive that followed that first encounter, and our friendship blossomed. Our meetings would become an increasingly regular fixture over the coming weeks; and today, as before, I was filled with butterflies of excitement as I turned onto that sleepy little street, where I found Tim waiting with the kettle on, ready to impart the next round of wisdom to his young disciple.

'We were overconfident, possibly to the point of arrogance,' Tim chuckled as he traced a finger across a black-and-white photograph he had taken down from his wall. Six bright, young faces looked out at us from his dining table, one of them his own. 'We weren't in any way qualified! But sometimes it doesn't pay to look too hard before one leaps.'

The idea, he recalled, had been conceived over late-night, gas-ring coffee in Adrian Cowell's room at St Catharine's College, Cambridge, in 1955. As final-year students, Tim, the geographer, and Adrian, the historian, shared a staircase, and to pass the cold winter nights they would pore over maps of the world dreaming of adventures in warmer climes. Adrian had his sights set on the furthest point from London on the Eurasian land mass – Singapore. Though it felt far-fetched, sitting in a student room in Cambridge, Adrian had found in Tim the perfect accomplice.

Before university, Tim had completed his National Service with the Royal Marine Commandos in Singapore and Malaysia (then called Malaya, and still under British rule). The nineteen-year-old Slessor was commissioned as a lieutenant in the fight to quell a growing Communist insurgency, and – Adrian had joked – had the distinct advantage of being able to recognize Singapore when he saw it.

The basic idea conceived, Tim and Adrian still had a mountain to climb. As Tim later wrote in *The First Overland*:

> The gestation from obscure idea to illogical fact is a
> long and complicated one. No money, no equipment,
> no cars, no political permission, and the failure of
> all previous attempts to complete the overland drive
> – these were some of the pre-natal problems.

Tim and Adrian would need a bigger team to take on this daunting challenge, and recruitment began immediately. Fellow Cambridge men Anthony Barrington Brown (known to all as BB) joined as cameraman, Henry Nott as mechanic and Pat Murphy as navigator. They were now five Cambridge men strong.

Adrian, however, with a keen eye for branding, was adamant they needed to recruit a man from Oxford – the 'Oxford & Cambridge Far Eastern Expedition' had a nice ring to it, he argued. A second-year economist, Nigel Newbery, put himself forward. The man who would be forever known by the rest as 'our young undergraduate friend' also happened to be a former paratrooper and a first-class mechanic. By early 1955, the team was complete.

Then began the 'wheedling and cajoling' (as Tim described it) to get the two cars, the equipment, the money and the press attention they would need to propel them 19,500 kilometres (12,000 miles) across the planet. First, the Rover Company – encouraged by BB's success in convincing the young Attenborough to give them film reels and a small advance – supplied two brand-new Series I Land Rovers at no cost. Then, after a flurry of letters banged out on an old typewriter, over eighty sponsors provided everything from fuel to tents, teabags and hard cash to help the team achieve their dream.

Tim told me all this in the same manner he always did – striding around his tiny flat, rarely sitting still. He was like a caged tiger, padding the perimeter of his comfortable little prison and furiously plotting his escape. He confessed to me that before I had first been in touch, his publisher had accepted an idea for a book titled *Before It's Too Late*. Grabbing a globe, he started to point out ten obscure points on it that he wanted to visit – or in five cases revisit – before he died.

'Number One: Foula!' His index finger came to rest on a tiny speck in the sea north of Scotland. 'The most remote inhabited island in the UK, I made a film there years ago.'

'Number Two …' spinning the globe with gusto, 'the Chatham Islands!' His finger landed on another dot of land about two finger-widths off New Zealand's North Island. 'That's a new one for me, but it's as far as you can possibly go from London before you start coming back on yourself. Always wanted to go.'

With an expert's touch, his fingers skipped to seven more points on the globe, each landing point as rich with story as it was remote.

'And, of course, the final chapter will be our adventure – Singapore to London.'

It was then that I felt the elephant in the room could no longer be avoided. In our meetings so far, we had talked an awful lot about adventures past, but surprisingly little about the joint venture we were really planning. As I had started slowly to tell those nearest and dearest to me what Tim, Adam and I had in mind, there was one immediate concern that kept being raised – surely Tim, at eighty-six, was suicidal to even consider such a gruelling journey?

I remember the moment distinctly. The light was fading on a warm autumn evening outside as I sat on the floor at Tim's feet, surrounded by maps. He was sitting in his favourite armchair, studying the gently dipping branches outside his window, while enlightening me as to the most space-efficient manner to pack the rear compartment of a 1955 Land Rover. When he had finished singing the praises of his neatly tessellated camp bed (which he still had tucked away in the attic, ready for action), I seized my moment.

'Tim – would you carry on if I dropped dead?' I asked, worrying he would spot the trap I was delicately laying for him.

He snapped out of his reverie. 'That's not a very happy conversation to have, Alex!'

It was one he was prepared to indulge, however, after some initial reluctance.

'Depending on the situation,' Tim mused, 'I'd most likely suggest we carry on at the earliest possible opportunity. The expedition is always bigger than the sum of its parts, Alex. No offence, of course,' he said, grinning.

'And what about if … *you* died?' I asked, my wince surely visible.

'Well …' he stopped to think. 'That is a more likely possibility, I suppose.' He paused again, deep in thought.

'By no means repatriate my body,' he announced. 'Either cremate me or pop me in the nearest convenient place. It'd be quite interesting to be buried in Kyrgyzstan,' he chuckled, before spotting my obvious discomfort.

'I mean you're dead, Alex!' he continued. 'There's not much point in repatriating my body to Putney, is there?'

'Have you spoken to your family about this?' I asked.

'My family? No problem,' he dismissed the idea, a little too quickly. 'They'd be jealous, most likely. I suspect my young grandson Nat would even want to come with me if he had the chance! I've spoken to my GP, and he said there's no major problems to stop me. Ultimately, it's my life, so it's my choice.' He studied the map at his feet, before offering: 'In some ways it would be better to be killed than get a bad injury in some of these places.'

'I suppose if you're going to do a job you should do it properly,' I agreed weakly, trying to wrap up this deeply uncomfortable but necessary chat.

'Look, Alex,' Tim started, fixing me with a grandfatherly stare, 'in 1955 people said we were geographically naive and politically inept, that we would never make it. If you say that to a twenty-three-year-old, all it does is encourage them to give it a bloody go. Now I'm eighty-six, and people have talked to me for years about redoing this journey, and somehow something's always got in the way.'

He went on, with a spark of frustration.

'I'll admit, this won't be like tootling up the M1, but it's only in overcoming problems in life that you gain a sense of achievement. Hell, I live in this little one-bedroom flat, I don't even have a garden! I do get very bored, you know. If I don't do it now, it'll be too bloody late. You're only here once.'

He waited a moment for his words to sink in.

'If for some reason I can't continue, then you've got to go on, for the old car's sake. If Adam hadn't found that car, we wouldn't be having this conversation. That's what this is really about – Oxford.

If I'm not there, Oxford has to get home to London.'

'You'd want me to go on without you?' I asked.

'Oh, shit, yes.' He stood up a little creakily, signalling the conversation was over.

He wandered over to a framed photo of Oxford and himself that Adam had arranged earlier this year. A bundled-up Tim was standing proudly next to a restored Oxford in the snow, after an emotional reunion with the Land Rover that had carried him across the planet.

'It'll be the Old Man taking the Old Girl home,' Tim joked, tapping the glass fondly.

As we brought our latest meeting to a close, Tim clearly noticed the reservations still etched on my face.

'I see I still need to convince you I'm up to the task!' he said, the grin returning.

I squirmed a non-committal reply as I said my goodbyes, trapped between my veneration for this grizzled adventurer and a chilling vision of my future self, scratching Tim's shallow grave from the frozen Kyrgyz tundra.

It was only a few hours after arriving home that I received an email from Tim, attaching his ticket receipt for a non-stop Qantas flight to Perth, the first step on his 20,000-kilometre (12,500-mile) journey to the Chatham Islands off New Zealand.

'I'll be turning eighty-seven on the flight,' he wrote. 'Consider this a test run. If I make it back, you're out of excuses.'

2

A Gamble on Wheels

3 November 2018: London, England
295 Days BE

'Not via Pakistan, please.'

The straight-to-the point subject title in the email was unmistakably Tim. He had not only survived his birthday sojourn across the globe but was also already hungry for the next big challenge. The audacious enormity of what Tim had just done to prove a point was still sinking in, but it proved we had an able octogenarian in the bag.

His email landed while I was on a bus heading to his flat for our first meeting since he had arrived back in the UK. Icy rain lashed the window, and I started imagining how warm Islamabad must be on a December morning.

> Baluchistan is the stamping ground of a fairly active Taliban. Quetta, the 'capital' of Baluchistan, is apparently the scene of almost as many bomb attacks as Kabul; they are just less reported. In short, I am very much against the 'west via Pakistan' idea. If pushed, I would vote for a route that goes via the Central Asian Stans and into Turkey, or via Georgia, or Baku. In short, the Silk Road.

We had agreed to meet today to decide the fine details of our route, but Tim evidently couldn't wait to get started and had spent the small hours poring over his maps. As I daydreamed about the sultry warmth of Pakistani spice markets, another email hit my phone:

> Totally agreed, Tim – Baluchistan best avoided. Just met my friend who is head of Pakistan desk at FCO. She almost had a heart attack when I even suggested possibility. Current proposed route is: Singapore–Malaysia–Thailand–Myanmar–India–Nepal–Tibet–Kyrgyzstan–Uzbekistan–Turkmenistan–Iran–Turkey – and on through Europe. We'll need at least three months on the road, four tops. Let's discuss!
> Marcus

Marcus and I had first met in Myanmar's crumbling capital, Yangon, back in 2013, when we were both in the early days of making it our adopted home. He had crossed the border after a stint in China to seek his fortune in Myanmar's blossoming travel and tourism market.

Carrying the battle scars of five years doing business in Myanmar's creaking kleptocracy, he was skilled at working around the knottiest problem. He was one of those rare creatures who still adored paper maps in the age of Google, had a voracious appetite for all things automotive, and – for some inexplicable reason, for a man who had spent so many years away from his birthplace in London – could plot out the fastest route between any two London Underground stations in his head. That kind of bizarre pedantry would, I suspected, make him the ideal expedition manager.

The three of us were soon sitting on the floor in Tim's living room, where our host had helpfully stretched gargantuan paper maps across every square inch of carpet. Tim skittered across the floor with age-defying ease, tracing a line from Myanmar westwards across northern India.

'You're fine up to here'. He stopped at India's border with Pakistan. 'But between there and Turkey, no chance. There's no question of tracing my old route through Syria and Iraq, and as for driving through Afghanistan today …' he inhaled through his teeth. 'No thanks!'

Tracing his finger back to the little lozenge of Nepal, sandwiched between the giants of India and China, Tim drew a line north into the vast emptiness of Tibet.

'This is our way home,' he concluded.

'You're right,' nodded Marcus, his face abnormally serious.

'It's not going to be easy – politically or physically – but it's possible. If the Chinese even let us overland into Tibet – which is a pretty rare ask that will require a *lot* of paperwork – and you survive weeks in the extreme altitude and cold in a car with no heating, you've still got to exit through Xinjiang, the most politically sensitive corner of China.'

I gulped.

China's westernmost province had dominated world headlines in recent weeks as the full jaw-dropping extent of a crackdown on the restive local Uyghur Muslim population was coming to light.

A BBC exposé from only last month had revealed newly built mass incarceration camps where hundreds of thousands of Uyghurs – men, women and children – were being corralled into camps for what the Chinese government called 're-education' and 'de-radicalization' programmes. These were old-school concentration camps with a chillingly modern twist – the Chinese state was throwing its full digital arsenal to monitor, imprison and brainwash Uyghurs on an industrial scale.

Tim was a BBC veteran, and I had been on BBC assignments in the past. After this latest report there was every chance we would be arrested for the simple crime of being in Xinjiang with a camera.

'Then the Pamir Highway through Kyrgyzstan, Tajikistan and Uzbekistan,' Marcus continued. 'We'll be forced to skirt along the border with Afghanistan for hundreds of kilometres with Taliban, ISIS, and drug traffickers for company.'

'We always found the Afghans to be very pleasant!' said Tim, tracing his finger across a country that had been an almost constant source of gruesome headlines for much of the last two decades. 'Apart from when we tried to camp in the Shah's orchard; then we were politely moved on by some nice men with rifles.' Marcus and I locked eyes over Tim's head – if we needed a reminder of how much the world had changed for the worse since Tim's original journey, there it was.

'Then there's Iran,' Marcus paused, chewing his lip. 'There's been massive demonstrations against the regime in the last year, and the government keep shooting the protestors. They've just banned teaching in English, and Trump's pulled out of the nuclear pact, which has ratcheted tensions to a whole new level. It's probably not the best time to be a Brit bumbling through Iran in a very old car.'

If Iran was out, Marcus observed, we could either go north through the central wastelands of Russia or hop across the Caspian Sea to Azerbaijan.

'Would that jeopardize our "overland" credentials?' I asked Tim.

Tim pondered for a moment, before replying: 'I've no desire to trek though Russia for weeks on end – far too dull – and I'm desperate to the see the Stans! So, if that means making the short hop from Turkmenistan to Azerbaijan by boat, I think it's excusable. The Caspian Sea is mostly freshwater, so in my books that's just a big river crossing.'

The guru had spoken. Regarding Iran, we decided to keep a watching brief, recognizing we were dependent on President Trump keeping things calm until we could hope to pass through. Given he had recently been described as having both the foreign-affairs knowledge and temperament of a ten-year-old by his own Defense Secretary, none of us were confident.

9 November 2018: Yorkshire, England

289 Days BE

Adam steered Oxford through a nondescript gate leading to a steep, rock-strewn path that would have caused a mountain goat to think twice.

'Rudland Rigg,' he announced. 'Just like Tibet, I'd reckon.'

Seeing how quickly our plans were progressing, Adam had invited Tim and me to his home in Yorkshire to get to grips with the car in which we were committing to spend a quarter of a year. While Tim was merely on a refresher course, I was about to have my first taste of driving in this iconic vehicle that had stubbornly bypassed sixty years of motoring innovation.

What hits you first in Oxford is the noise. Conversations need to be conducted at a shout to compete with the engine roaring and the wind whistling through countless cracks in the bodywork. Secondly, whatever the weather outside, you are sure to know inside. There is no insulation at all, only aluminium, glass and steel between you and the elements. A thin sleet was now whirling in Yorkshire, and small flakes of ice started settling on my coat. As I wriggled to fight the chill, Adam's mention of Tibet – where the temperature would plummet well below freezing – sent an additional shiver.

Additionally, thanks to Oxford's leaf-spring suspension (an innovation from the 1750s that Rover had thankfully embraced) every contour ripples neatly up your spine. Even here on the relatively smooth Yorkshire tarmac, it was almost as if Oxford was learning to read Braille. Finally, while you struggle to stay warm, in a straight line and in your seat, you get distinctively woozy on petrol fumes leaking from the twin fuel tanks beneath the front seats.

Adam yanked the handbrake upwards and slid out of the car, barely flinching as the biting wind whipped through the car.

'Your turn, Tim!'

'Here?' Tim exclaimed, looking at the forty-five-degree climb in front of us. 'You could've given me a warm-up!'

Tim's annoyance was only half sincere, and quickly gave way to excitement. He shimmied into position behind Oxford's expansive steering wheel, gave it an experimental wiggle, and did the same with the long, crooked gearstick. In a heartbeat, six decades fell away, his body easing into an apparently familiar position.

I climbed out of the back and into the passenger seat alongside Tim, Adam retreating to snap some shots of this historic moment.

'How does it feel?' I asked.

'Bloody marvellous!' Tim replied, beginning his pre-drive checks.

'Cold start in … into neutral … indicators off … lights on … ignition,' he mumbled, fumbling for a big yellow button by his knee. 'You press the button and … oh, SHI—'

Oxford leaped backwards, forcing Tim to slam on the brakes.

'It'd help to know she's in reverse!' he quipped, as I settled back into the seat I had just leaped from. Resetting himself after this inauspicious start, Tim found first gear and slowly pulled away to the foot of the hill before us.

Slowly, the 'Old Man' and the 'Old Girl' began to climb. Moorland stretched as far as the eye could see, a patchwork of dusky greens, browns and purples beneath the mottled grey and black of the winter sky.

The next few hours were a blur of thumping bumps and grinding gears as we took it in turns to charge Oxford across the moors. My first time behind the wheel began with a cautionary lecture from Tim.

'Now remember, there's no power steering, no synchromesh gearbox. You have to double-declutch – most people today wouldn't know what double-declutching is!'

In the interest of teammate transparency, I admitted I had no idea what double-declutching was.

Tutting his annoyance, Tim continued: 'No disk brakes, no air-conditioning, no heated seats and all that crap. This is motoring, like it used to be!'

My first foray behind the wheel went without a hitch, double-declutching and all. Though the steering was cumbersome, the pedals slack and the brakes spongey, I have never enjoyed driving a car more in my life. It was impossible not be fully in the present; I felt every mile under Oxford's tyres, lived every minute behind its wheel.

I started to understand why Tim used 'she', not 'it' when he talked about Oxford. The more time I spent in this old Land Rover, the more I realized this was no ordinary bundle of metal and wires. There was a ghost in this machine, and her name was Oxford. She could be kind and playful, or she could throw a wicked tantrum. She could also, as I would later discover, be borderline lethal.

Here on the moors, she was a playful old sheepdog who had been cooped up for years. She darted, rolled, spluttered and yapped, bringing childlike joy to us three lucky enough to drive her.

The winter light was fading fast and Adam eventually returned us to the station. Huddled inside Oxford, waiting for the London train, we hurriedly talked dates, times and plans of action. It was then that Adam dropped his bombshell.

'I won't be coming with you to Singapore, you know. I'll be staying right here.'

I looked at him, speechless. Was he really going to let Tim and I take his beloved car to the other side of the world without him?

'I don't like to fly. I'll be waiting at the finish line for you!'

While shocked, I was not entirely surprised. The better I had got to know Adam, the more I realized that his leaving Yorkshire would be like the ravens leaving the Tower of London. It would signal the end of the kingdom.

'Consider me the "home team" – the First Overlanders had one – I can post any parts you might need from here.'

'Will we need a lot of parts?' I asked, realizing with a chilling stab to the guts that I would now be responsible for getting Oxford across the globe with my less than rudimentary mechanical know-how.

'Oh, sure! The alternators are always failing, then there's the fuel pump – I'll pop in a spare – and you need to keep an eye on the battery … oh, and the jets on the carburettor will likely need adjusting when you're at altitude. Watch out for the bodywork – it's coming apart at the back already – and then there's that floating half-axle problem that gave the First Overlanders a lot of trouble. That can be a real showstopper.'

I nodded along to his list of maladies like a man processing a terminal diagnosis in a foreign language; but before I could respond, it was time to run for our train.

Tim and I said goodbye to Adam and boarded, exhausted. Tim soon began to doze. Too excited to sleep, I opened my copy of *First Overland*, flicking through Oxford's last great adventure with entirely new eyes. Before closing it, I reread the dedication, which Tim had amended for this fiftieth-anniversary edition:

> To all those who helped me
> with my spelling –
> for without that help the reading of this book
> would be almost impossible.
> T. S. May 1957

> And to my wife, Janet.
> We had not long met when I wrote
> the dedication above – she was one of my 'helpers'.
> Always supportive, now she is gone.
> T. S. August 2005

It had taken me some time to feel I knew Tim well enough to ask him how he came to live alone. He'd never raised it himself. When I finally plucked up the courage, he had in typical no-nonsense fashion told me the story of his long marriage to Janet. Where they had lived, where their two children – Jeremy and Kate – were born, their work together at the BBC (where they'd met).

Then how, in 2002, the doctors had missed the malignant mole heralding terminal skin cancer. Tim, never short on words, had ground to a halt at that point. Clearly, sixteen years on, her passing was still raw.

Now as I looked at Tim across the table, slumbering peacefully, the words of Dylan Thomas' 'Do Not Go Gentle Into That Good Night' about old age burning and raving at the close of day chuntered into my head, as if whispered by the clicking wheels below me.

Tim's old age was burning bright enough to be seen from space. I marvelled at him, almost enviously. This larger-than-life character was everything you could ask for in a grandfather. I had never known my dad's dad, and as for my mum's dad – well, that was tricky. His later years could not be more different from Tim's. As the expedition grew ever more real, I knew there was a meeting I could not delay for much longer.

As we pulled into London, I was woken from my daze by a text from Adam:

> Oxford booked on boat to
> Singapore next week.
> Arrives early January.
> Sort collection please.

My heart raced, and my exhaustion vanished. When a Yorkshireman says he is going to do something, you had better believe him. There was no turning back now.

19 July 2019: Manchester, England

37 Days BE

The expedition was gathering electrifying momentum. I had moved from Yangon back in with my parents in Manchester, establishing the official Expedition HQ in their garden shed alongside my dad's overly inquisitive chickens, too busy to care what the great explorers I'd grown up worshipping would have made of my ramshackle nerve centre.

My days were consumed with the hunt for the lifeblood of any expedition – money. The fact that I was cooped up in my parent's back garden at thirty-one years old reflected the state of my personal finances, so we would have to approach third parties to have any chance of funding this eye-wateringly expensive endeavour.

My copy of *First Overland* was always by my side during those days, like a second, much younger Tim that I could call on for advice. I still had butterflies realizing I could simply phone the author of this overlanding bible at any time to pick his brain.

In Appendix G, titled 'On Money', Adrian Cowell, the First Overland's instigator, told of the begging and borrowing the expedition resorted to for funds, rattling every cage for sponsors. Still, he admitted, the expedition was 'in fact, something of a gamble on wheels'. When they set off from London, they had enough to get them to Singapore, but no idea how to fund their journey home.

Fortunately, Tim's dream for one last great adventure was capturing hearts and minds across the world. First came the Singapore Tourism Board, seeing an opportunity to mark the two hundredth anniversary of Singapore's founding. Then companies from Opihr Gin to Bremont watches, and of course Land Rover themselves, joined in generously.

As our expedition funds began to grow, our team was expanding too.

We had briefly considered Pat Murphy and Nigel Newbery, the two other surviving First Overlanders. However, they would add 174 years to our team's combined age, increasing the medical risks dramatically. Thankfully both declined politely, citing health reasons, although both also made it clear they would be there in a heartbeat if their wives turned their backs long enough.

So, we needed an all-new team for this all-new adventure.

First to join was Larry Leong, who, after an inspirational meeting with Tim and the First Overland crew back in 2006, had become arguably Singapore's greatest overlander. He had completed the Singapore to London route twice before (once with his wife Simone and five-year-old daughter Lucy) in tribute to the First Overlanders, although never by the eccentric route that we were considering. Determined to help Tim achieve his dream, he offered himself, a support car, and his invaluable knowledge of the overlanding art.

Next were two old filmmaking friends also living in Yangon, Leopold (Leo) Belanger from Paris, and David Israeli from New York. Having worked with both of them on films in Burma, I knew they were made of the tough stuff this journey demanded, and David's Russian-language skills (as the son of Georgian emigrants) were sure to come in handy as we crossed Central Asia.

David's arrival in the team had the added benefit of resolving an outstanding and thorny problem – Iran. When I informed Marcus of David's inclusion, he replied: 'So let me get this clear: you want me to secure a visa through *Iran* for an *American* citizen called David *Israeli* ...?! I'm good, Alex, but I'm not a bloody miracle worker. I'm booking the Caspian ferry.'

Given one of our team was pushing ninety, having a skilled medical professional on board was key. When Dr Silverius Purba from Jakarta – aka 'The Doc' – emailed from the jungles of East Kalimantan in Borneo, he seemed too good to be true. Besides having been the resident doctor for all sorts of hair-raising motoring expeditions in Asia's remotest corners, he also owned an astonishing *nine* Land Rovers, and was a skilled mechanic. I realized he was a gift from above and signed him up after a single call.

Finally, there was our Belgian social-media wizard, Therese-Marie Becker. Tim and co had set off fully thirty-five years before Tim Berners-Lee invented the internet, and almost fifty before Mark Zuckerburg launched Facebook. Our journey was taking place in a very different age, and sharing our story with the world was expected and essential – not least for our sponsors, who were paying for the publicity. After a single call, 'Tibie' was in.

We were now a multinational, multilingual and multi-skilled team of eight, with three expedition cars to carry us across the planet – Oxford, Larry's Defender 90, and a Land Rover Defender 110 donated by Adam. In early May, Marcus, Tim and I announced that 25 August 2019 was Expedition D-Day.

Back in the chicken shed, my phone buzzed yet again. It wasn't Adam or Marcus, but a number I did not recognize.

'Alex, this is Kate – Tim's daughter. Dad's in hospital, in intensive care. It's not looking good.'

The bottom fell out of my world.

23 July 2019: Manchester, England

33 Days BE

For as long as I had known him, Tim had seemed in rugged good health, despite being in his late eighties. His excursion to the Chatham Islands, and the way he took our day on the Yorkshire moors in his stride, had eased my uncertainties about his fitness for the task ahead. It was the top question on the lips of potential sponsors, who asked it in various degrees of bluntness. 'But Tim will surely die, right?' asked one potential backer. To the contrary, I confidently replied, he seemed to be getting stronger as the big day approached. However, what had initially seemed like a bad bout of food poisoning turned out to be a blocked intestine. A severely weakened Tim urgently required surgery.

The sceptic's words came back to haunt me. What would I tell the team, the sponsors, the media, everyone waiting for the grand spectacle in only a few weeks' time? Tim and I had war-gamed him dropping out mid-drive, and felt the world would recognize an admirable effort. But we had no plan in place if he did not make the start line. He was the rock on which our expedition was built; the entire edifice was crumbling before my eyes.

Kate called again the next day. 'He's through the worst, but it's going to be a miracle if he's on the plane to Singapore, Alex. I spoke to him about the expedition this morning, and he had tears in his eyes.'

I didn't let on, but there were tears in mine, too.

'There's two things he's been really proud of in his life,' Kate continued. 'One was being in the Marines, and the other was the First Overland – "the Expedish", he called it. He never stopped talking about it when I was growing up; we were so bored of it!'

She chuckled weakly.

'He's always dreamed of doing it again. Even if he can't go with you, you've made an old man very happy. You gave him a project again, and he's a nightmare without one.'

I tried to remain composed, but the reality of Tim's illness had hit me harder than I could have imagined. After all those months of planning, I started babbling to Kate that the dream could be over, months and months of hard work lost.

Kate cut in to save me: 'You know, Alex, I might have a Plan B.'

Over the next few weeks, Tim's surgery – and subsequent recovery – went better than could have been expected.

Even then, while there was a growing likelihood he would be walking out of hospital, having him in Singapore for the all-important start was looking like complete fantasy. For weeks

Marcus and I had been sitting on our shameful secret, not letting word out to the team or our sponsors for fear of a scramble for the exit. The only way we could imagine letting this hulking cat out of the bag without causing the expedition's collapse was, reluctantly, to initiate Kate's Plan B.

Plan B was twenty-one years old, and still sobering up from his final weeks at Newcastle University when we first spoke via video call. Nat George – Tim's grandson via Kate – sounded as if I had just woken him up and, although he wasn't entirely happy about it, was willing to humour me. I soon came to realize that this was Nat's natural resting state.

'Have you travelled much?' I asked tentatively.

'Not much. To France to visit Grandpa's house, to Grenada every now and then to see my dad's parents. I'm off to Spain next week – to get pissed, mostly.'

'Well, perhaps I can show you some new horizons? How would you feel about standing in for your grandpa, just for the first month or so, until he's better?'

There was an uncomfortably long pause. He could smell my desperation, clearly.

'I'll have to think about it. I don't mean to sound ungrateful, but I've got some reservations.'

Only some? I thought.

'Grandpa told me about your route through the Stans, round Afghanistan. I'm not overly keen on jihadis, Alex. Also – four months in that old car … I've never even driven a modern Land Rover, never mind a sixty-four-year-old one.'

I tried to placate, to reassure, but I couldn't stomach telling him the whole fate of the expedition, of his grandpa's dream, rested on his decision.

'Can you give me time to think about it?' he asked.

'Of course,' I said, tension spiking through my faux calm. 'Do you think you'll be able to let me know tomorrow?'

'Okay.'

After yet another restless night, an email arrived: 'Despite still being very apprehensive about it all, I've decided that I can't let my grandpa down. I'll do it. Nat.'

I jumped from my shed-desk in ecstatic relief, startling a dozing chicken. All was not lost!

After a tense few days of emails and calls, having Tim's grandson carry the baton until Tim was better turned out to be *just* palatable enough for the sponsors not to pull the plug. Had it not risked making things a little awkward with the young stand-in, I would have kissed him.

7 August 2019: London, England

18 Days BE

I have never been a particularly religious man, but I would have given thanks to any god going for jump-starting the stubborn little motor that powered Tim's adventurous soul. A few weeks earlier I thought he wouldn't survive the night, but now, miraculously, he stood before more than a hundred well-wishers and TV journalists hanging on his every word.

Tim was reading aloud from his dog-eared expedition diary, bound in faded red cloth, gnarled fingers tracing letters written by that same hand sixty-four years earlier: 'September first, 1955. The Start. Seldom can such disorganization have been recorded on film.'

The crowd rippled with laughter. It was from here, the Grenadier pub, in this quiet cul-de-sac by London's bustling Hyde Park Corner, that the First Overland expedition set off for Singapore in the late summer of 1955. I had to pinch myself that it was really me beside my hero, back to full health, as we announced to the world his plan to do it all over again.

Turning towards Marcus, Adam and me, Tim said with a slight quaver, 'If someone had told me sixty-four years ago I'd be stood back at this pub to start another expedition, in the same old car, I would never have believed them.'

The crowd broke into rapturous applause. In among the sea of smiling faces I spotted Nat, beaming with relief that all the visa paperwork and preparations that Marcus and I had put into Plan B could be put back on ice.

Tim raised his glass.

'Next stop: Singapore!'

The time, it seemed, had finally come.

3

Harold

10 August 2019: Stockport, England

15 Days BE

All great journeys start somewhere. Not many, I'd guess, start in a nursing home on the outskirts of Manchester. Not many journeys in this world, at least.

Tomorrow I was boarding the plane to Singapore, where I would be putting the final preparations in place for our grand departure in two weeks' time. After saying goodbye to friends and family all across the UK, there was one more goodbye I had to say. I had left this one, the most difficult, until last.

I had come on a rare visit to see my grandad, Harold. The blocky, red-brick buildings of Brinnington Hall had been his home for two years as his dementia worsened, and now, aged eighty-eight, he had become entirely incapable of doing anything alone.

It was more than the busy schedule and geographical distance that had made my visits to him rare, I'll admit. Reluctantly, I followed my mum, Pam, through the doors that keep the residents locked away from a world in which they can no longer function – or, perhaps, a world that no longer wanted to face the discomfort of their existence.

I hadn't seen my grandad for over a year, having been forever abroad, or quick with excuses to avoid the ordeal. Now I was here with my mum as she visited her dad, a weekly pilgrimage she had kept up come hail or shine. The smell of disinfectant, turbocharged by sauna-like heaters, hit me like a wall. Mum greeted the drawn, tired but somehow still-smiling nurses by name as she bustled through. Each smile I saw made me feel more of a coward for staying away so long.

'Hello, Janice,' said Mum, waving to a lady in a floral dress who was parked in an armchair by the bay window.

'I'll be off out shortly, it's a lovely day!' Janice cooed back in sparkling soprano.

'She's sat there every time I come,' Mum whispered, 'her daughter can't handle her anymore.' Janice's expectant gaze returned to the window.

We turned the corner towards Grandad's room.

'I want to go HOME!' an angry voice boomed up ahead.

'Hello, Bob,' said Mum cheerily to a stooped old man shuffling down the corridor.

''Ello love!' Bob's angry face transformed to a delighted beam as he passed, eyes clearing for a moment before the thunder returned.

'I WANT TO GO *HOME!*' screamed Bob behind us, punctuating his anger by stabbing the thick carpet with his stick. *You and me both, Bob,* I thought selfishly.

As we turned the final corner, I spotted a verse painted in garish colours on the wall:

> This is the place,
> there is no place
> quite like this place
> anywhere near this place
> so this must be the place.

I bristled with anger. I couldn't think of a crueller ditty to confront someone who has lost all sense of place and reality. But perhaps it is the reassurance they need when all anchors are up and all that lies ahead is the fog of a pitiless purgatory.

I let Mum enter first, an act of chivalry driven by fear and shame.

Following into the little bedroom – my grandad's entire world – required all my courage. He was lying on his single bed, a tiny figure stretched out on his back, mouth open, completely motionless.

'Every time I walk in, I think he's dead,' Mum joked, weakly.

Though in his prime he had just snuck over five feet tall, he always had the presence of a much bigger man. In his youth he had been a champion boxer. Even in my teens, when I began to tower over him, I was under no illusion that he could flatten me in an instant as he taught me to spar in his living room.

Now the muscular, triangular form he had maintained well into his seventies had vanished, replaced by an emaciated wraith wearing grey children's pyjamas – the only set my mum could find to fit him. By cruel irony, his jet-black hair was still largely ungreyed, a reminder that the flesh was still willing even as the soul was clearly on its way elsewhere. I thought of Tim – almost identical in age – and his astonishing vitality. I winced.

Mum approached the bed, while I stood as far away as the space permitted, willing the wall behind to swallow me up. Mum gently touched his shoulder, and his eyes flashed open and he sputtered into life.

'Wha'? Why? What's happenin'?' he shouted, confusion and panic lacing every syllable. He struggled to form the words clearly in his Mancunian burr, as if his tongue was newly gifted.

'Who are ya?' he yelled at her, riddled with fear.

'It's me, Pam, your daughter. It's Pam,' my mum shouted over him in a firm loud voice, patting his chest and trying to calm him. Frail as he looked, he jerked violently to free himself from Mum's touch. Her continued calmness suggested this was a weekly ritual.

'Cup of tea, Dad?' she persisted, as he started to subside.

'Why? Why? Wha's wrong? Wha's wrong wi' meh?' he curdled, pitifully.

'Nothing, Dad, nothing's wrong,' Mum soothed.

I stood in awe of her toughness as she shuffled him, still protesting, into his armchair. She folded his hands around a cup of tea that a nurse had just delivered. The warmth settled him, and he flexed his fingers around the mug. Those hands had not just been bludgeons in the ring, I thought. For decades they had also been wands of creative magic. There was almost nothing my grandad couldn't build or fix.

He was born in north Manchester in 1929, the ninth of ten children. With so many siblings competing for attention, he preferred spending time alone. In solitude he indulged his bottomless curiosity for how the world fit together. His hopes of going to the local grammar school were dashed by school closures during the Second World War, but he kept his nimble fingers occupied by picking through the shrapnel of German bombing raids around his home. While the foundations of their little house rattled to the anti-aircraft guns thundering in neighbouring Broadhurst Park, he made a name for himself crafting trinkets and toys for friends and neighbours from what he had salvaged.

His bristling brain was saved by an apprenticeship at the nearby Avro aircraft factory, making the wings of Lancaster bombers (of *Dam Busters* fame). It sparked in the young Harold a lifelong passion for engineering. Signing up for night school aged fourteen, he went on to become a nuclear engineer, tinkering not with wartime detritus but the very stuff of matter. At home his hands never rested. Secluded in his cellar, he made jewellery for his three daughters, doll's houses for his five granddaughters, and – to Mum's horror – two fully operational crossbows for my brother Sam and me.

Now, that same brain that had pondered the origins of the universe, and those fingers that had set precious stones into delicate gold, struggled to agree on how to drink a cup of tea. Mum guided it to his mouth.

While he drank, Mum pottered around the room tidying, I suspected to fill in time. There was barely enough stuff to make a basic clutter. I stood quietly watching my now-becalmed grandad. I've been running away from this – from him – for years now, I thought, shamefully. What's worse is that I was about to do so again.

When in my late teens I began to understand dementia – the disease that had reduced my brilliant grandad to this delirious ghost – it struck a note of fear in me, a note that never stopped reverberating. What if this happens to me? There were two responses, I felt, to the idea that my future fate was sat here in the armchair in front of me.

Option One – end it all now in suitably dramatic fashion. What was the point of collecting a lifetime of memories and experience, falling in love and raising a family, if by the end you recognize and remember nothing, and are unable to treasure any of it?

Option Two – experience so much in the years I had left, saturate myself so entirely with life, love and indelible memories, that dementia, if it came, could never wring me dry.

After dismissing Option One due to lack of stomach, I had eventually settled on the latter.

I vowed to stave off the demons of dementia by pig-headed force of life. From small-town roots in suburban England, I would claim the world as my rubble pile, and I would hunt for shrapnel in its furthest, most exotic corners. It helped that since I was a kid I had always been obsessed with history. I had started by tracing my family tree looking for an inspiring ancestor on whose life I could model my own.

Unfortunately, mum's line had led me to the nobly illiterate stonecutters of Enniskillen, and my dad's – via a refuge for dissolute alcoholics in Regency-era Birmingham – to the hamlet of Bescaby in rural Leicestershire. I once jumped in the car to visit but was rather symbolically told to sod off by one of the residents.

Not to be deterred, in my dusty school library in south Manchester, I lived an alternative, imaginary life, immersed in the tales of great and glorious figures from the past in whose footsteps I could tread instead. Chief among them was, of course, my namesake, Alexander the Great, King of Macedon and all-round world-conquering, empire-building, overachieving badass (it's always healthy to set achievable goals). Later, reading politics and history in the ivory towers of Cambridge University, I drowned in the derring-do of the great adventurers like Burton and Lawrence, Younghusband and Hillary, Bower and Bell.

After devouring the exploits of these intrepid women and men, I burned to travel, to see the tapestry of humanity they had unfurled before me. In 2008, I was granted a scholarship to travel to Myanmar and Thailand for two months, to study their histories. That first visit to distant places, people and cultures unknown sparked a craving for perpetual motion, and I found ways to travel whenever and wherever I could.

My first jobs out of university saw me stationed in the insurgent-ridden southern Philippines, jetting into Lebanon one week and out of Kenya the next. Outside work I spent every spare penny and holiday I had going ever further afield, be it hiking in Honduras or bicycling in Bhutan. It was Myanmar, however – where I had first experienced the debilitating ecstasy of true culture shock – that stole my heart.

Over the years, on my increasingly rare visits home to the Sunday dinner table, I would chatter excitedly at my grandad, wanting him somehow to share in adventures he could only have dreamed of as he worked long hours to provide for his wife and daughters here in England.

I tried to tell him where to stand to see the glint of first light on Yangon's gold-covered Shwedagon Pagoda, and how it filled your soul with wonder. I wanted to take his arm and lead him down the backstreets of Mandalay, hunting for the most delicious *ohn no khao swe*. I longed to have him hike by my side in the Chin Hills, listening to the Baptists mull the Bible with rifles in the pews.

But the words washed over him. The man I had known – so solid and sure – was crumbling before me as the dementia began to devour him. In time, Grandad's lunch visits stopped, and eight decades of life were slowly reduced to three square metres in

Brinnington Hall. It was a painful truth that Mum had tried her best to shield me from, until today.

Above Grandad's head was a clutter of frames containing fragments of his former life. Boxing gloves, playing cards, grinning gap-toothed grandchildren, and a certificate for fifty years of membership of the Institution of Mechanical Engineering. I knew that none, if prompted, would mean anything to him now.

In a childish way, I resented him for it. I had just started to live the adventurous life I had so long dreamed about, but he was too far gone to notice. When travels had brought me to Tim, my childish resentment only grew stronger. Tim was a man who embodied everything I dared to think old age could be, a man who was going into the final furlong at a frenzied sprint, not this cruel, crumbling second childhood that I found my own grandad in.

Stood in that little room, I was confronted by a shameful secret. The reason I was so drawn to Tim was that he seemed to be everything a grandad should be, and that – due to his dementia – my own grandad was not.

I noticed one photo was missing from my last visit.

'Where's Grandma's photo gone?' I asked Mum, quietly.

'He asked me to put that away,' she said, matter-of-factly.

The missing photo showed my grandma, Joyce, as an elven seventeen-year-old, mid-pirouette. Even in the faded black-and-white, you could see her grace and feel her poise as she balanced on pointed toes. Her eyes were cast down in quiet concentration, a look I had seen dance on the face of my mum and her sisters. Before Harold and her daughters, ballet had been Joyce's world, her most treasured possession being an autograph from Rudolf Nureyev.

That photo was one of only two I had ever seen of my grandma, but from them I had built a full-scale moving model in my mind. Sometimes in my younger years I had talked to her quietly in moments of pain, and in moments of joy, seeing her conjure up a warm smile, watching the corners of her eyes crinkle when she laughed, like my mum's.

Joyce was not a subject we talked about much. We were a family that would much rather avoid a difficult topic. Painfully British in that regard. It wasn't until my late teens that I asked my mum for the full story of Joyce's untimely death.

In April 1981, my grandad had been on holiday in Majorca with Joyce and my mum's youngest sister, Anne – then just nineteen. Harold had been attempting a tricky right-hand turn when a car collided at full speed into the passenger side.

While Harold walked away with a blow to the head, Joyce, who had been in the front passenger seat, and Anne in the rear, were both severely injured and taken to intensive care in Palma. Weeks later, Anne was finally flown home to recuperate. Joyce, however, never woke up.

I grappled with these facts as I grew older, and one question kept repeating – what must it have been like to carry that burden for half your life? The knowledge that if you had waited a few seconds more, the love of your life would still be with you?

Only after falling madly in love, then feeling the debilitating loss of my first heartbreak, could I have been qualified to broach that question with my grandad. Even then I'd have to overcome the barriers that age, deference and gruff masculinity all throw up to a conversation like that. But when I was finally ready, he was too far gone to ask.

Looking back there were clues, though, if you knew where to look. In his older age, before the dementia took root and blended his neurons, he turned to writing poems about his life. Some he had typed up and shared with the family, a highly unusual act in a man I'd only known as intensely private and sparse with words.

He had confided in a poem titled 'Me':

I feel I am getting old at last,
My youthful days so long have passed …
It's not the end so much I fear,
But the loss of those I hold most dear.

While packing his things before his final move to Brinnington Hall, however, my mum had found another poem simply titled 'Joyce'. This one was different from the others, hidden away, and written by hand in a dense copperplate:

My wife Joyce was my only one true love,
But she was taken from me by the one above.
The reason for this I know not w h y
I do not understand how hard I try.

You could see the words and letters on which he laboured with his pencil. He had stalled on the *i* of *wife*, scored a little harder on the *l* of *love*, spaced out the letters of *why* as if they were delivered in a silent bellow.

My grandad had stopped working shortly after the crash, recognizing something was not right with his head. Mum told me she thought the blow he had sustained could have brought on the dementia. Perhaps, she thought, it could have been the final ripple of that seismic day. I'll admit it helped to have a reason, a cause, something to blame for what can feel like the most random, vicious cruelty.

I had my own theory, one that explained why he had wanted the photo of Joyce stowed away so late in the day. Perhaps my grandad had carried the consequences of that fateful day on his small, stocky frame until he could carry it no more. Maybe, I thought, this was a mind trying to un-remember, to unburden forty years of pain.

'Who's that lad?' Grandad suddenly said, his voice trembling, gesturing towards me.

'That's your grandson, Alex. You remember Alex. Remember,

I told you – he's going away for a while?' my mum explained softly, soothingly.

'Who? Who? He's scaring me.' His eyes fixed on mine, then looked down sheepishly. I realized I had been staring at him these last few minutes, lost in thought.

I looked away, distraught. Hot tears burned at the corners of my eyes. I backed out of the room. It was not the reunion I had imagined, but perhaps it was the one I deserved for avoiding this meeting so long.

As I leaned on the wall of the corridor outside, I heard Mum shuffling Grandad back onto his bed. Angry Bob trundled past me on his endless commute, still trying to irrigate the carpet. Closing my eyes I saw a very different corridor, one that wound through a canopy of English oaks and was littered with autumn leaves. Aged six or seven, I was trotting behind my grandad in the woods near his home. Trying too hard with my little legs to match his confident stride, I fell into a ditch. He turned back to haul me out with an easy strength, wiping mud from my trousers as I sobbed with shock and the shame of letting him down.

He had hugged me tight, one of the few times I remembered this most reserved of men doing so. I had nuzzled my face into his favourite old jacket until the tears stopped running and my chest stopped heaving. I could still smell the leather in my nostrils. Wordlessly, he had broken a nearby branch in two in his powerful hands, handing me the smaller half to steady myself. He had walked by my side all the way home, matching my little stride now, walking steady as a rock.

An arm took mine, breaking the spell.

'Time to go,' said Mum.

PART 1

SINGAPORE TO NEPAL

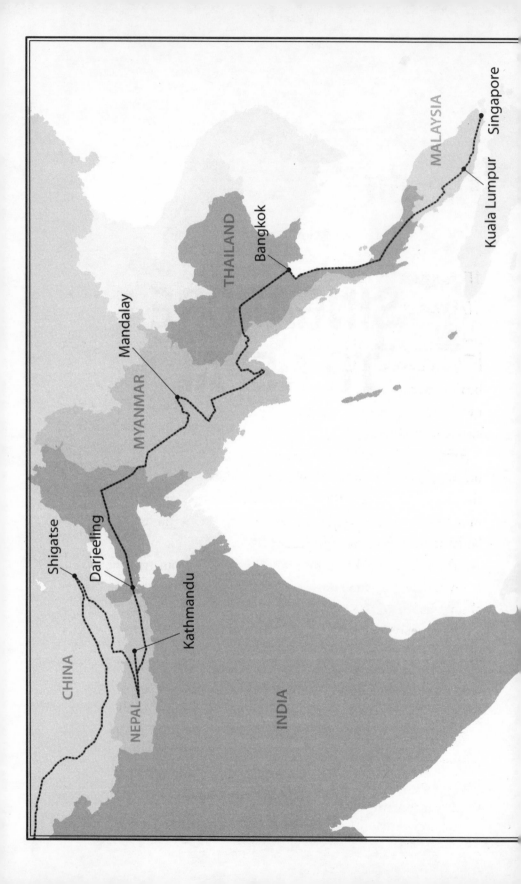

4

Flag Off

15 August 2019: Sentosa, Singapore

10 Days BE

From the pool of the plush Outpost Hotel in which the Singapore Tourism Board had installed us, I looked out onto one of the busiest ports in the world, state-of-the-art fighter jets patrolling overhead. Singapore's founder – Sir Stamford Raffles – would have swooned with delight.

After fifteen years' marauding the seas around Southeast Asia on behalf of the British East India Company, Raffles identified the sleepy island of 'Singapura' as an ideal trading post, positioned in a chokepoint of growing global trade. In January 1819, he laid the foundations of an ordered, law-abiding and – given his swashbuckling background – surprisingly puritan trading haven.

Over the following two centuries, this underpopulated backwater, almost identical in size to Anglesey, had become a phenomenally wealthy, peaceful, multicultural city state, close to topping most global rankings on quality of life.

Marcus's huge feet plunged into the pool by my head.

'It's time to collect Oxford!' he announced, like an oversized kid at Christmas.

A few months earlier, Oxford had sat in a container aboard a tanker like those below, awaiting collection from our friends at Jaguar Land Rover. Ever since, she had been stored under wraps in the Wearnes Automotive dealership.

The dealership was a palace of glass and polished metal, a pristine temple to the twenty-first-century automobile. The latest Land Rover models – the Evoque, the Velar, the Range Rover Sport – sat proudly in enormous display windows, alongside sleek offerings from Ferrari, Lotus and Lamborghini. It was enough to make any petrolhead hot under the collar, and the air-conditioned calm of the showroom was a badly needed cold shower. I had been in less-sanitized hospitals; every surface glistened and gleamed, the air thick with the scent of polish.

Oxford, I knew, was somewhere inside; the dark spirit that refused to be exorcized, a stark reminder to all the carbon-fibre newcomers around her of their humbler, grittier roots. We were directed to a lumpy shape in a distant corner, covered with steel-grey cloth. No slick Jaguar lines, or soft Bugatti curves; Oxford could have been mistaken for a pile of discarded furniture.

We each grabbed a corner of cloth, peeling it back giddily, and Oxford slowly emerged. First her tyres, then her GIN and TONIC jerry cans, next her windscreen. Though the cloth repeatedly snagged on jagged corners, and she reeked of fuel and leaking fluids, to us she was the most beautiful car in Singapore.

The ordeal of getting her here by ship had added a few grey hairs to Marcus's thick black mop, so I let him take the wheel. Oxford roared as he brought her to life; tyres screeched on slick, polished floor, Marcus puffing and panting as he battled the unpowered steering.

In Yorkshire, the challenge was keeping frostbite at bay as icy winds whipped through Oxford's numerous cracks and gaps. In Singapore – where temperatures never drop below the mid -twenties at night and rise well into the thirties by day – the problem was the exact opposite. In the tropical sun, Oxford became a furnace on wheels.

On the move, opening every window and the air flaps beneath the windscreen provided partial relief. Stopping in traffic, however, was slow torture. Singaporeans looked on in baffled amusement as two dripping Englishmen coughed and spluttered their way through an immaculate city in which, by law, few cars are more than ten years old.

Half a century had passed since Oxford last drove the streets of Singapore. Although the city through which she now chuntered was almost unrecognizable, and even if it was on Oxford's behalf, it felt damn good to be back.

Marcus and I had arrived first to establish the beachhead. The rest of the team were due to arrive from tomorrow, giving us an evening with our veteran overlander, Larry. Although we had been phoning and emailing for months, we had never met in person.

We spotted him at a table in the middle of a hawker centre, one of Singapore's iconic temples to food: a bulky, middle-aged man with close-cropped dark hair, sporting a faded-green Land Rover T-shirt, waving calmly among the bustle.

Larry was a mine of sound advice and cynical experience. Military discipline (gleaned from two formative years in the Singaporean Defence Forces) was clearly central to his overlanding art.

'We rise early, eat early, depart early, arrive early,' he said, punctuating each command with a pair of chopsticks. 'No driving in the dark, and there must be a co-pilot in the car beside the driver at all times. No sleeping on the job!'

Marcus and I scribbled notes.

'We have to hydrate – dehydration is the overlander's secret enemy, particularly at altitude in Tibet. Dead people are extra weight,' he grinned.

Between ordering sharing plates of Singapore's finest street food, Larry told story after story from his time on the road. Despite so much to worry about before we even set off, I felt a little more reassured with Larry's experienced head on the team.

From the next day, our odd little family began to assemble. Tibie arrived first, diving into the whirlwind of meetings and phone calls with the energy and irrepressible positivity she would soon be famous for. While full of charm, as the daughter of a professional soldier she had a steely toughness at her core.

David was next. I had last seen him in Yangon, an emaciated wreck following a brutal battle with typhoid. Luckily, he was back in rude health, filled with the wicked wisecracks expected of this proud New Yorker with a sideline in stand-up comedy.

Next, Doctor Silverius Purba arrived from Jakarta wearing a medical-kit satchel, black fingerless driving gloves, and a broad, toothy smile I soon realized was a delightfully permanent fixture. 'My hobby is doctor, my profession is Land Rover driver!' he joked, unleashing a belly cackle that caused me first to jump, then to chuckle along. If laughter was the best medicine, the Doc was well stocked.

Then came Leo. My old filmmaker friend sauntered in looking irritatingly relaxed. It took a lot to ruffle Leo (and believe me, I'd tried). No matter the situation, he could tackle anything, so long as he had his morning *petit café*.

Only Tim was missing. We had scheduled him to arrive as late as possible – two days before our departure – accompanied at Kate's insistence by Nat, to ensure he arrived safely. The whole team erupted into spontaneous applause when Nat and Tim finally joined the fray. For Leo and the Doc it was the first meeting with the man whose dream we had all pledged to make real, and they set about introducing themselves.

Walking through the hotel lobby, Tim looked at our gilded surroundings, smirking. 'Some *expedition* ...' he quipped. It was a fair jibe – the First Overlanders had set off in 1955 prepared to spend most nights under canvas. He had pushed for us to do the same but, given his advanced age and the arduous journey ahead, Marcus and I had quietly planned to have Tim sleep under a proper roof (although nowhere near this plush) wherever we could.

To our pleasant surprise, Tim was joined by two fellow First Overlanders, Pat and Nigel. They had not obtained wifely permission to join us on the road, but clearly nobody could stop them seeing Tim off on his next great adventure.

After giving Tim a full day's rest, we regrouped on 24 August. Tomorrow, we would begin. Marcus and I convened a team meeting to explain the plan.

'There's no way we're leaving Singapore quietly,' I announced. 'We're aiming to break a record for the greatest number of Land Rovers ever assembled here.'

'And at one of the country's most famous venues,' Marcus added. 'The Singapore Formula One Grand Prix starting line.'

That was a real coup. The chief exec of one of our sponsors, AKE, happened to be married to the owner of Singapore Formula 1, who had gifted us the pit lane.

Rallied, the team set to packing the cars. Oxford was kept light to protect her wheel bearings and to allow her to keep up with the newer cars, so most of the kit went into the five-year-old Land Rover Defender that Adam had sent out as a support vehicle.

Marcus claimed this shiny black workhorse – quickly dubbed 'PAC' after the first three letters of its number plate – as his own. Leo and David carefully stacked bags of camera equipment into the rear, turning PAC into a mobile filmmaking studio over which the First Overlanders' cameraman, BB, would have no doubt drooled.

Alongside PAC was Larry's mottled red-and-black Defender, veteran of two overland campaigns. Larry had lovingly dubbed it 'Enterprise', and it was packed like an accountant's sock drawer. The team marvelled at the meticulous positioning of every item, prodding neatly stacked boxes containing all manner of gadgetry and supplies. Larry was apparently prepared not only for an overland but a nuclear apocalypse too.

While BB was sadly no longer with us to pass on tips to his successors, Pat and Nigel were on hand to compensate with gusto. As Tibie and I heaved spare tyres onto the top of PAC, I overheard Pat saying to Marcus in his cheerful tenor: 'Best advice I can give you is to lay out all your stuff, then chuck half of it!'

Meanwhile, Nigel was coaching the Doc – who would double as lead auto as well as human mechanic – on how best to care for our iconic vehicle: 'Make sure you drive *very* fast over any corrugated roads, otherwise she'll rattle into pieces.'

Nat watched the whole scene with bemusement, perhaps still counting his lucky stars that he had avoided being roped into this madness. I noticed that despite being six-feet-three he had a habit of stepping into the background and avoiding the limelight.

His famous grandfather, meanwhile, was fielding a steady queue of journalists from the world over. Despite the buzz that filled the air, I couldn't help noticing how tired he looked. For months I had imagined Tim during these final moments, prowling like a proud sergeant major, tightening a strap here, admonishing a novice there. Instead, he looked drained, bristling at the endless questions from journalists from around the world.

I stopped to help him, just as an unfortunate cub reporter put the question we had been asked endlessly over the last few months: 'Why do it? Why drive from Singapore to London?'

We'd tested numerous philosophical replies: 'To celebrate the enduring spirit of adventure ... to see how the world has changed in sixty-four years ... to prove the world is a kinder place than we think ...'

But Tim's exhaustion got the better of him.

'Why do we need a reason?' he snapped, the pugnacious twenty-three-year-old shining through. 'What did Mallory say about why he wanted to climb Everest? Because it's bloody there!'

I nodded in agreement. Ultimately, we were doing this because we were fortunate enough to be able to. Meeting Tim had only strengthened my belief that mad adventures like this were the very point of life, and didn't need explaining. Now I stood on the brink of putting that philosophy into practice alongside a master of the art.

25 August 2019: The Outpost Hotel, Singapore

My alarm buzzed: 6 a.m. – Flag Off Day.

I had been preparing for this for over a year. After a brief battle of intellects with the hotel's over-intelligent robotic toilet, I was ready in minutes. I jogged to the car park to check the cars had not been stolen – implausible in crime-free Singapore, but my nerves were jangling. I headed for breakfast, the team already there in various states of excitement. Tim, I noticed, was yet to arrive, no doubt savouring a few final moments of peace.

We were due to meet at 7.45 a.m. to head to the start line at the Singapore F1 pit building. With thirty minutes to go, I looked to Nat, buried in a trough of eggs Benedict.

'Sad not to be joining?' I asked.

Nat – mouth full of eggs – raised his eyebrows, then nodded his head towards the tottering breakfast buffet on the one side and the expansive swimming pool on the other. He swallowed.

'Well, Mum insisted I pack a bag, just in case, but looks like I won't be needing it! You can take on the jihadis; I'll stay here with the eggs Benny and the singing toilet.'

I laughed but could no longer contain my nerves regarding Tim's absence.

'Want to check on your grandpa?' I asked, feigning calmness.

'Sure. We'll meet you in the lobby,' he replied, pocketing a couple of pastries on his way out.

My heartbeat was accelerating. Tim and I were due on BBC News in forty minutes, and it was a good twenty-minutes' drive to the start line.

The elevator pinged and Nat emerged, ashen-faced. 'Something's wrong. He's not answering the door.'

Grabbing a receptionist who could override the high-tech keypad, Nat and I scrambled to Tim's room, where Nat carefully opened the door.

'Grandpa? Are you okay?'

'Nat ...? Oh, Nat ...' replied Tim from within, his voice barely above a whisper.

We ventured inside to find Tim on the floor. If he had not already spoken, I could have sworn he was dead. His face was so swollen he was almost unrecognizable.

Mute with panic, we grabbed him under his arms and levered him onto his bed. Whatever strange magic had been powering him to this point had clearly run out. He muttered weakly that he had been lying there for hours.

'Get the Doc! Quickly!' I shouted to the receptionist.

'What on Earth do we do?' I asked Nat, pleadingly. His eyes and mouth widened, wordlessly. He was as lost as I was.

'You bloody go,' rasped Tim, looking at Nat and I in turn. 'You have to.'

Looking at the man whose dream had inspired all this, I felt callous. Had I done this? Had I pushed Tim too far, simply to fulfil my own dreams of adventure?

'Go, Alex!' Tim croaked, with all the energy he could muster.

'I'll wait for the Doc,' Nat said faintly, rediscovering his voice, 'I'll catch you up when I know what's wrong.'

With one last desperate look I ran from the room, crossing paths with the Doc sprinting the other way. I slowed to turn around, but the Doc pushed me onwards.

'Go, Alex, this is my job. I'll call with news.'

I sprinted into the car park, careering into a baffled Marcus.

'We have to go, now!' I barked, jumping into Oxford. David and Leo leaped into the back, cameras perched on their shoulders, as I pulled away. The madness had begun, and we hadn't left the car park.

As our convoy thundered through Singapore, I explained the situation by radio to the rest of the team. Meanwhile, what looked like all of Singapore's Land Rovers – of every shape, age and colour – emerged all around, making their own way to the start line.

What on Earth would I tell them? I still had no answer by the time we arrived. As 11 a.m. approached, the pit lane filled with cars and over a thousand people.

'Ninety-five Land Rovers, can you believe it!' shouted Marcus as we stepped out into the crowd, struggling to take it all in.

Despite the warmth of the crowd, the only people in the world I wanted to see were Tim, Nat and the Doc. With fifteen minutes to go, I still hoped that Tim would rise again as he had done weeks before. He could not miss this. If he could only be here to say goodbye, I thought, then he could feel like he had achieved his dream.

But we were not to have our fairy tale. My phone buzzed, it was Nat: Tim been admitted to hospital with a severe lung infection, there was no way he could join us. Without having to say it, it was clear we both knew then what that news meant.

With ten minutes left before we were due to set off, finally admitting to myself that the cavalry was not coming, I mounted the stage. Silence descended. I stared mutely across a sea of Land Rovers and expectant faces. I had been going to say it had all been about Tim, for Tim, because of Tim. Now, however, I was standing on stage without him.

I started speaking. My words felt hollow, heavy in the mid-morning heat. At the point I had been due to hand over to Tim, a ripple formed at the back of the crowd. It was another Land Rover making its way through the spectators towards the stage. The back door opened and out jumped Nat, immediately mobbed by reporters. Even from afar I could see his panicked expression, but his arrival confirmed there was no turning back.

As Nat worked himself away from the gaggle, I explained to the crowd what had happened, how Tim had fallen ill at the last moment, and was now in hospital. 'But like any good adventurer,' I said, finding my stride as Nat reached the foot of the stairs, 'Tim had a Plan B.'

Plan B scrambled up to join us, more panic-stricken now than he had been beside his grandpa's bed.

'Nat is about the age Tim was in 1955, and he'll carry the torch for his grandfather,' I announced, surrendering to the tide of the story writing itself around me.

I passed Nat the microphone, and he shot me a desperate look as a thousand pairs of eyes turned to him. I knew it was cruel, but there was nothing else I could do. We were riding the tsunami together now.

'Well,' he cleared his throat, the crowd hanging on his every word, 'the fact that he was willing to do it aged eighty-seven means I'd be silly not to aged twenty-one.'

The crowd roared agreement. Their applause ringing in our ears, we headed for the cars. The heat and noise would have rivalled any F1 start as Oxford bolted over the line with me at the wheel, a dumbstruck Nat by my side.

Nothing had gone to script, but our expedition – the oddest, hardest and most wonderful 111 days of my life – was underway.

5

Land Rover Heaven

25 August 2019: Singapore to Malaysia
Expedition Day 1

Oxford powered into downtown Singapore like the fiery head of a comet, scores of Land Rovers forming a roaring tail in our wake. There was no need to navigate; a police motorcycle had been assigned to escort us to the Malaysian border, its blue-and-red flashing lights our lodestar across Singapore.

People lined the streets, waving and clapping our convoy through, as if the crowds that had welcomed the First Overlanders sixty-four years earlier had simply been on an extended tea break. Oxford, meanwhile, looked magnificent. A Union Jack fluttered on her left front wing, placed there by the British High Commissioner herself, and the red-and-white of the Singaporean flag fluttered on the opposite wing.

While all was smiles outside, inside we were reeling from the morning's drama. I turned to Nat, who was watching the blur of downtown Singapore in stunned silence. Finding Tim on his hotel room floor just hours ago was unsettling enough for the rest of us, but for his young grandson it must have been deeply distressing.

'You okay, mate?' I shouted over the roar of Oxford's engine.

He nodded, clearly putting on a brave face.

'What was the last thing your grandpa said to you before you left?' I asked.

'Have a good trip,' he replied with a chuckle, some of the colour returning to his cheeks.

I smiled back, trying to look calmer than I felt.

Time for further reflection was, for now at least, over. The momentum of our journey was already sweeping all before it. Larry had kitted out our vehicles with shortwave radios, and via them we now debated frantically how to collect the Doc, who had stayed with Tim as he was admitted to hospital. Tim was now in the hands of Singapore's best doctors, but the expedition could not continue without its own. There was no way Oxford could divert without causing bedlam, so Larry and David in Enterprise nobly volunteered to peel away.

Marcus, driving PAC alongside Tibie, soon lost his way in the downtown traffic. Before we had crossed half of the mere 30-kilometre (20-mile) drive across Singapore, the expedition was scattered to the winds. It was not the most auspicious of starts. Oxford, however – containing myself, Nat and Leo, with his camera rolling – did not seem to care. This was her moment, and she began to find her stride as the roads widened towards the expressway to Malaysia.

In the blink of an eye, the madness was over. Several dozen Land Rovers who had survived the melee through Singapore's congested core began to flash and beep goodbye, turning home. Oxford waited for the silhouette of PAC's carefully stacked roof to appear, and after a further thirty minutes the blocky outline of Enterprise hoved into view, bristling with antennae and the ever-smiling Doc.

Shock, relief and joy across all our faces, we clambered out to assemble our passports for the border check. After the last two weeks of frenetic preparations, and the months of work before that, I realized it was the first time the expedition had been entirely alone with our three cars. The brief moment of peace was quickly shattered when we pulled across the border into Malaysia, to be greeted by a bank of flashing lights atop three police cars.

At first, I thought we were being pulled over for some unknown infraction, until one of the policemen explained they had been tasked by the local government of Johor to guide us safely through. It was our first taste of the ripples our story had already made beyond Singapore, and it was only going to get stranger as we drove north towards our first stop: Malaysia's capital, Kuala Lumpur.

We had only been on the road for an hour but already into our second country, such was the miniscule size of Singapore. As we powered north-west on the AH2 through Johor and the growing heat of the day filled the cab with a musty, damp heat, I glanced at the seat where Tim would have been. Instead, my co-pilot for Malaysia – and possibly longer now, given news of Tim's hospitalization – was his young grandson, Nat.

While I had spent a year getting to know Tim, I realized I knew very little about my new travelling companion. He was dressed, sensibly, in loose black shorts and a baggy black T-shirt. Arguably, he had been intending to go back to bed after we left, but the outfit suited Oxford's sauna-like environment perfectly. Meanwhile, I had opted for a ridiculous 'explorer' get-up evoking a young Indiana Jones – complete with the iconic brown leather bushman's hat – and was now sweating uncontrollably into my thick denim jeans. *We must look quite the mismatched pair*, I thought.

As Nat stared wide-eyed with wonder – and not a little fear – at the brave new world unfolding around him, I started to feel the guilt return at the way I had dragged him off his sofa and halfway round the world to keep Tim's – and my – dream alive.

'This is mad,' was all Nat could bring himself to say.

I nodded in agreement. The enormity of Tim's absence from the expedition he had inspired was beginning to hit me. I had dreamed so many times of this moment when Tim and I would cast out on the open road alone, role-playing the conversation we would be having as we retraced his tyre tracks here in Malaysia after more than sixty years. I had imagined him telling me stories of his first visit to Malaysia, five years before he drove through here in Oxford and in far less welcoming circumstances.

For more than 130 years, Malaya (as it had been known) had been under some form of British control, but from 1948 Communist-aligned forces had run a deadly insurgency against the British. In 1950, aged nineteen, Tim was deployed with the Royal Marines to help quell the rebellion, one of many in the region as Cold War divisions crystallized. Malaya was gripped by a bitter conflict largely fought in impenetrable jungle. Insurgents attacked mines and plantations in a bid to cripple the economy, and in 1951 even assassinated the British High Commissioner.

In response to the 'Emergency[1]', Britain sought to crush the bloody revolt using evermore brutal tactics. Mass resettlement, search-and-destroy techniques and the first use of the highly toxic herbicide Agent Orange would all be copied as the operating manual for America's much longer, bloodier fight in Vietnam. Unlike the Americans, the British emerged as victors in their battle – albeit pyrrhic ones. Independence for Malaya was an unstoppable political movement, and the country negotiated its breakaway from Britain in mid-1957.

When Tim drove back into Malaya in Oxford in early 1956, he had been away only four years, but had returned to a far more tranquil world. A short amnesty had been declared in September 1955 while peace talks continued, and when he visited his old stomping grounds he found British troops mainly confined to barracks. Only the gravestones of his fallen comrades reminded him of the conflict-torn world he had known.

At checkpoints across the country, they had been greeted by British police officers wearing Sten guns, a sign of the old colonial system's seemingly reinstated authority in the country. He noted in his diaries that 'it gave me quite a kick to be driving down that road once more, to see half remembered places along the way suddenly

---

1   In a canny PR exercise, and to stifle the damage to the economy, the British labelled the conflict the 'Malayan Emergency'. Anything close to 'civil war' would have voided the insurance policies of British companies underwritten in faraway London.

swing back into clear reality'. His joy at being back was mixed with more than a little distaste at how the colonial hierarchy – with its genteel whites-only clubs and local staff referred to as 'boys' – had reasserted itself like a persistent weed. Even then, it was clear Tim could sense the beginning of the end for Britain's long rule in Malaya.

Now in 2019, I could see how the country – known as Malaysia since gaining full independence in 1963 – had gone to great efforts to exorcize the ghosts of those years under British control. We had left behind the neat privet hedges of Regent Street and Duchess Road in Singapore and now zipped past towns with deliciously exotic syllables like Simpang Renggam and Yong Peng. The thick green plantations, the backbone of the colonial economy that Tim had noted passing by in the 1950s, were still there, stretching out for miles into the low rolling hills either side of the road, but today they were more likely to be oil palms than the rubber trees of old.

Around us, shoals of young men on motorcycles weaved through the convoy at terrifying speed. Despite the police presence, they wore no helmets, and casually stretched themselves flat out in Superman-like poses at full speed. Even though I had been here a matter of hours, Malaysia's youthful, reckless energy was as intoxicating as the tropical smells streaming through Oxford's badly fitting bodywork. While trying not to mangle these suicidal motorcyclists under Oxford's wheels, I took a moment to recognize that I was finally on the adventure I had dreamed of for so long.

Our police escort suddenly dived off at an exit around 95 kilometres (60 miles) short of Kuala Lumpur. It felt like an eternity since we had eaten, but our escort ignored the tempting KFC sign, carrying on instead into the car park of a large sports stadium. Dozens of Land Rovers greeted us in formation, surrounded by marquees with tables set to feed a small army. My mind instantly cast back to that weekend with the Series One Club in Anglesey. So much was familiar here as the crowds decked in Land Rover caps and T-shirts of every colour and size swarmed out, a testament to the truly global Land Rover religion I had heard so much about from my dad. Only the sticky heat, darker complexions and heavenly smells of simmering *nasi goreng* curry marked us out as being on the other side of the planet entirely.

A huge inflatable arch (prodded intermittently by a small man with a large stick to keep it upright) billowed loosely over a stage, behind which footage of myself and Tim driving through Yorkshire played on loop. It was utterly surreal, and as we dined with our host – a minor relative of the Sultan of Johor, it turned out – we were presented with commemorative plaques and T-shirts. I was asked to make a speech to a puzzled crowd, all of whom had been expecting somebody half a century older. The disappointment was tangible, and I began to wish I could fold away into the brim of my stupid hat.

After countless pleasantries and seemingly endless photos with Oxford, the police signalled it was time to move on. One more surprise awaited, however. A loud, perfectly bald man – Napoleonic in stature and ego – introduced himself as Vicky, head of the Rovernuts (Malaysia's foremost Land Rover fan club, I was assured). Vicky informed us that he and the assembled squad of more than forty Land Rovers would escort us through his country. I nodded mute acceptance, surrendering the expedition to be a baton in this bizarre Southeast Asian relay race.

Arriving to the crowded chaos of Kuala Lumpur that night, all of us were exhausted. While the Rovernuts clambered over Oxford late into the night, examining her every bolt and rivet with absorbed fascination, we snuck away to sleep. The weight of the last few weeks hit me hard as I collapsed into bed.

It was only day one and yet all was confusion and chaos. For the last few months Marcus and I had fixated on getting this cavalcade to Singapore, and for the last few days all our focus had been on how to leave it. Now here we were on the road at last, but without Tim by my side I felt woefully unprepared for what was to come.

I hadn't realized how much I had been relying on Tim's reassuring presence and experienced head. But Tim was now hooked up to beeping machines in a Singaporean hospital room and all I had was a copy of his book and his diaries, which would become my constant companion from now on. I turned to the last few lines of Tim's diary from his own first day on the road back in 1955:

> It was too early for relief and too late for any more last-minute arrangements. For the moment, we had nothing more to do than drive.

Just like Tim all those years ago, I realized that all I could do now was surrender – to events, to the road, and, right now, to sleep.

26 August 2019: Cameron Highlands, Malaysia
Expedition Day 2

Next morning, we found ourselves back in Kuala Lumpur's choking traffic, sandwiched between our police escort in front and Vicky and his Rovernuts behind. It was not quite the freewheeling road trip I had been envisaging from my countless re-reads of Tim's book, and I found myself coughing and spluttering in time with Oxford as her fumes mixed with those streaming in through the open windows. After more than an hour of slow crawling, my knee was already aching from Oxford's stiff clutch pedal, and even the poor, sun-baked street urchins begging for money seemed to be avoiding our sweat-drenched palms.

At last, the traffic cleared, the police bid us goodbye and Vicky stormed to the front of the convoy. His bright-orange Land Rover Defender would now be our lodestar guiding us 240 kilometres (150 miles) northwards to our next night stop. Fitted with a huge black snorkel and four dazzling spotlights atop the windscreen that beamed day and night, Vicky's car was impossible to miss.

Over breakfast, Vicky had delivered an impassioned lecture about our next destination. 'Once we reach the town of Tanah Rata,' he boomed, enjoying every syllable, 'you will be starting your ascent into Land Rover Heaven!'

Having visited 'Land Rover Mecca' in Wales only last year, I felt my spiritual promotion was going a little fast for my liking, but Vicky's zeal was intoxicating.

As we headed north through Putrajaya and Perak, the road gradually began to climb. The temperature dropped in tandem, bringing instant relief to Nat and myself in Oxford. We had barely started our long journey, but I could already feel the effects of driving this old car on my body. Callouses were forming on my hands and a knot of muscle burned between my shoulders from the lack of power steering. My feet were plastered in black dirt after I had resorted to operating the pedals barefoot in a vain effort to cool down. Even as the temperature dropped, I struggled to keep rivulets of sweat from my eyes.

Nat was relishing my suffering far too much for my liking, so as the roads started to empty of traffic, I decided it was time for him to step properly into his grandpa's shoes.

Nat had seen Oxford for the first time in Singapore only a few days ago. He had a habit of looking mildly unimpressed most of the time, but I had noticed his distaste sharpen when he saw the old car in which his grandpa had crossed the world. Despite Nat's distinguished overlanding heritage, he confessed he'd never even been inside a Land Rover. Given the choice, he admitted, there was a long list of cars he would choose to drive (with the humble Ferrari 458 at the top.) I handed over the wheel with a dose of schadenfreude to the Young Pretender.

Back when the Series I was designed, the average height of a British male was five feet seven inches. The First Overlanders had all hovered around that height, and thankfully I was about the same. I was lucky, I now realized, as neither the seat nor the steering wheel were adjustable. Nat, almost a foot taller than his grandpa at six feet three inches, had to curve his back into a deep 'C' to see out of the windscreen, and stick his elbows out to the side chicken-style. It was a chiropractor's nightmare.

'It'd be easier to cut a hole in the roof and stick my head out,' he joked, with a serious edge.

Wiggling the gearstick and flexing his neck like a prize fighter, he started Oxford up.

'No pressure,' I quipped, forty Land Rovers honking and revving excitedly behind us, all of them acutely aware of the heady symbolism of this moment.

Nat's face clouded in a scowl of concentration – what I later came to recognize was his 'driving face' – as he crunched into first gear and gently let out the clutch. I had kindly stopped at the foot of a steep, winding hill, to make sure his first drive wasn't too easy.

It must have been in the Slessor genes, however, as Nat slowly climbed the hill and Oxford's gears along the same road Tim had driven back in 1956. He was sweating furiously with the stiff wheel and the barely existent brakes; but, like Marcus and I before him, he soon learned it was impossible to drive Oxford without a masochistic enjoyment. Within minutes he was pumping the pedals and grinding the gears like a seasoned pro. My heart filled with joy as Rovernuts zoomed ahead to take photos; I knew Tim's would have too.

As Nat settled in, I was free to enjoy my first time as a passenger on the journey. I stood on the seat with my upper body through the roof hatch, feeling the cooling breeze whip through my hair, thankfully taking the sweat with it. We were climbing upward into thick forest that marked the Cameron Highlands, the highest point accessible by car in the country.

The Highland region, named after a British geologist who had mapped it for the colonial government back in 1885, was a literal breath of fresh air after the sweltering lowland climate we had endured since arriving in Singapore. The temperature here rarely exceeds 25° C, and the British had identified its potential both as the perfect place to pretend they were not in Malaysia for a few precious weeks each year, and as a promising spot to grow tea – one of the mainstays of Britain's colonial economy in this corner of the Empire.

While the British overlords were long gone, the plantations prospered as if nothing had changed. Either side of our convoy stretched mile after mile of neatly ordered vegetation, dumpy green shrubs scored with winding passageways carved by generations of pickers, as if we were driving through Mother Earth's very own brain tissue.

The plantations were not the only legacy the Brits had left. As we climbed further into the Highlands, I noticed that as well as our small fleet, almost every other car we passed was a Land Rover of varying age. Many were unrecognizable at first, given their shabby state. A considerable number were parked randomly in ditches or patches of grass, missing wheels, doors and roofs, slowly being reclaimed by the forest. Their paintwork was even more mottled and decrepit than Oxford's, and I wanted to cover her headlamps to shield her from the distressing sight.

To my surprise, we started passing Land Rovers in similar condition to these abandoned ghosts actually moving – albeit roaring and sputtering at snail pace – up and down the steep hill roads. Their drivers whooped and waved to us as they passed, carrying anything from bundles of shrubbery to what looked like the population of entire villages.

Vicky's Defender came belching alongside us. 'Welcome to the Land of the Land Rovers!' he bellowed.

It was as if the dead had risen. The British, it turned out, had flooded the Highlands with English-built Land Rovers after the Second World War. Post-independence, they had been lovingly maintained, still forming the backbone of the plantation economy now. Maurice Wilks had dreamed of building a car that could be used by anyone, for anything, and in every corner of the world. He would have swelled with pride if he had been in the Cameron Highlands today.

Vicky's arm signalled out of the window, urging us to pull into a side road. Climbing out and gratefully stretching our legs and backs, we were ushered quickly through the gates of a tumbledown workshop. Excitably – his default state – Vicky led the team through a series of metal gates.

'Behold – where Land Rovers go to die ...' he announced with dramatic flair, hopping onto the wrecked bonnet of an ancient Defender.

We climbed up alongside him, and the resulting view left me speechless. The sun was dipping, leaving a rich orange halo that framed the crumbling carcasses of what Vicky told me were more than 600 Land Rovers.

'Why are there so many Land Rovers still, so long after the Brits left?' I asked.

'The British were very smart,' he began, smirking. 'When they agreed to Malaysia's independence, they put a clause in the agreement to say that for fifty years after independence, all government departments must use Land Rovers, and replace them every seven years!'

'Just think,' Vicky whispered reverently, 'every single one has a story.'

David, Leo, Nat and Tibie began to leap from rusting bonnet to dented roof, testing their new-found knack for recognizing different Land Rover models. I watched them disappear into the distance as Vicky began to explain his obsession with this car designed and built on the other side of the planet.

'It all started with my father, you see ...'

Vicky's earliest memories were of sitting on his father's lap back in the 1970s as his father drove an old Series II around these hills, where he worked as a hydrological engineer. They were his happiest recollections of a father he had sadly lost young, and as soon as Vicky was able to earn enough to afford one, he bought his own Series II to keep his father's memory alive. It started a lifelong obsession, and he joked that he hoped that one day he would take his last breath tinkering under the bonnet of his beloved Land Rover.

'You've got have something to *love* in life!' Vicky concluded, clearly overcome with emotion. 'That's what makes us *human*!'

I nodded in agreement, watching as the sea of wreckage in front of me transformed into a graveyard of individual cars, with individual lives, each like a grizzled old workhorse put out to pasture. While I was amazed at the way complete strangers were opening up to me because of the adventure I had found myself on, I felt a sharp twinge of sadness at the thought of Tim sleeping in his hospital bed, the fire of purpose drained from him as we motored off on his dream expedition without him. He should have been here talking to Vicky, not me.

That night in the hilltop town of Tanah Rata we ate and drank long into the night, while Vicky and the Rovernuts shared their 'come to Rover' moments. As they showed off their cars, they talked of fathers and grandfathers, uncles and brothers, and I began to see how the Land Rovers they so lovingly maintained were so much more than a means of transport – just like for my dad back in England, they were epitaphs to lost loves and happier times.

And Oxford? Well, to Vicky and the gang she was a symbol, the first to complete that greatest of all pilgrimages they longed to make one day – overland to England, the birthplace of Land Rover.

'You weren't joking about the Land Rover religion,' said Nat as we headed for bed. For a man who clearly hated being in the limelight, he was still reeling from all the attention that had been turned on him in Tim's absence by countless reporters and Land Rover fans in the last forty-eight hours.

While I was more comfortable around cameras and journalists, given the last twelve months of plugging the expedition, in the face of these true believers I was struggling as much as Nat not to feel wholly inadequate to be the one taking Oxford across the planet. I confessed I now understood it was not only Tim's dream we'd been entrusted with, but the dreams of so many Land Rover fans around the world.

'No pressure then,' said Nat as we turned into bed, blissfully able to sleep without air-con for the first time since our arrival on the far side of the Earth.

6
Turn Left at the King

29 August 2019: Malay–Thai Border
Expedition Day 5

Marcus's paperwork skills were to be put to their first real test as we crossed into our third country. A crucial letter for our cars was missing, and the border guards – armchair-and-doughnut physiques stuffed into painfully tight uniforms – refused to budge. Unable to produce it, Marcus resorted to a rather shameful but ultimately effective tactic of showcasing coverage of our journey on Malaysian and Singaporean news channels.

Meanwhile, the rest of us said emotional goodbyes to Vicky and the Rovernuts. Their pilgrimage over, these faithful disciples of the Land Rover creed were returning home. When we crossed into southern Thailand, however, religion would no longer be a matter of crankshafts and wheel arches, but of life and death.

The border between Thailand and Malaysia was settled in 1909 by a treaty between the King of (what was then) Siam and Britain to mark the northern extent of British control. Like many such lines drawn by European powers during this period, this border spelled trouble for the future by placing the majority Muslim Pattani region inside strongly Buddhist Thailand.

Following efforts in the mid-twentieth century by the Thai government to 'Thai-ify' the area, local separatists took up arms, sparking bouts of violence that continued to the present day. The conflict has been sustained by a complex web of ethnic rivalries, militant Islam, drugs, crime and tit-for-tat killings.

Taking no chances, we skirted west of the region, speeding north without stops to avoid a night stay. In what was becoming normal procedure, a convoy of Thai Land Rover fans who had been following Tibie's social-media updates met us near the border. As we arrived in safer regions, the biggest remaining danger I could see was the leader of this new fleet of Oxford's fans, who appropriately introduced himself as 'Beer'.

Stocky, bearded, good-humoured and tattooed, Beer was – even before 10 a.m. – clearly pissed. As he greeted me with a bone-breaking roadside hug, I could smell the alcohol both on his breath and in the pint glass I subsequently spotted in his hand. Jumping into his own immaculate Series II Land Rover, Beer became our enthusiastic, if dangerously unsteady convoy lead as we continued north; one hand on the wheel, the other on his pint, Beer slowed down only when he needed to reach for a fresh can. With about 950 kilometres (600 miles) and several days' drive to Bangkok, I wondered whether we would run out of Beer before Beer ran out of beer.

Luckily, it seemed Beer was escorting us only for the first day, and soon the expedition hit its stride on the firm tarmac of Thailand's Route 4. Before long, Larry suggested we make our first stop in Thailand at a favourite landmark from his last two journeys along this road – the Pho Ta Hin Chang Shrine.

I had spent much of the last decade visiting pagodas, stupas and shrines in this corner of the world. I'd become more at home with the arcane rules of a Buddhist temple than I had ever been in an Anglican church but watching Nat's baffled reaction stripped back the years.

'Shoes off,' I warned, as we approached the gold-roofed shrine, set only a few feet back from the road. Both Nat and I leaped as a lorry blared its deafening horn behind us.

Larry chuckled. 'It's for good luck!' he explained, and I realized that every vehicle sounded their horn in passing.

Besides the orchestra of beeps, what was unusual about this shrine was the number of stone elephants covering every available space. Some were as tall as a man, others only scraped knee-height; some were draped in garlands of flowers, others painted with rainbow patterns. All their trunks were raised to the heavens, mid-trumpet.

'The shrine was built in the 1950s to honour the Hindu god Ganesh,' Larry explained. 'The Thai government was building the first road south to Malaysia, but the construction workers couldn't get beyond here due to a huge rock in the way. The locals told them to pray to Ganesh and sure enough the rock gave way. This shrine was their way of saying thank you.'

Ganesh – revered by Hindus worldwide for his ability to move obstacles for the faithful – had been tapped up a few months too late for the First Overlanders. The journey south from Bangkok presented their final obstacle: there was not yet any motorable route to Malaya. A 160-kilometre (100-mile) stretch of jungle with only the faintest track lay between them and their final destination. They rumbled down it for hour after gruelling hour, smashing the cars almost to pieces, until finally emerging onto a road that would take them south to Singapore. Given our own bumpy start, I felt we had better give this deity any dues necessary.

The best way to thank Ganesh, it turned out, was to purchase a chain of Chinese firecrackers from the rumpled, orange-robed monk tending the shrine. These were hung inside a concrete tube and set alight, adding deafening staccato explosions to the already thundering traffic noise. Nat, clearly enjoying his new-found piety, purchased more.

Deity appeased – or at least deafened – the journey resumed. Our rate of progress would have shocked Tim, as would the range of services available. Pulling into a Tesco supermarket, I imagined the First Overlanders gawping over their mess tins of watery porridge as we gorged on international cuisine and Starbucks coffee.

When Oxford was last here, her team were hardened professionals.

On the road more than five months, they had survived every trial the world could throw at them. They followed a finely tuned routine, each person knowing his part intimately. During our own preparations, Tim had repeatedly stressed the importance of each team member having a clear role.

Even in the chaos of those early days, it was deeply satisfying to see each of the team settling into their job. Tibie broadcast updates across Facebook, Instagram and Twitter to a growing army of social media followers. Marcus set our daily rhythm, signalling stops and calling for driver rotations to prevent exhaustion, while confirming accommodation in upcoming countries. Larry, the wise old head, ironed out the kinks in our routine, provided the steadiest of backstops to our little convoy, and fixed any tech problem the team encountered.

Meanwhile, Leo and David hung from windows capturing the stunning scenery around us, then worked late into the night logging their visual trophies; and the Doc fixed upset stomachs, scratches and sniffles, and was first up in the mornings to check the vital fluids in his most valued patient – Oxford.

My time was spent keeping sponsors and journalists happy, ensuring funds kept flowing and maintaining team harmony. I discovered that bottomless supplies of chocolate in each car were invaluable.

Nat, who as 'Tim's grandson' was still being very reluctantly mobbed by adoring fans, interviewed on live TV, and feted as a minor celebrity by the Land Rover faithful, was very much still finding his place. Even though he dearly hated the limelight, from the long hours we spent driving together in Oxford I could sense a quiet desire to be more than his grandpa's stand-in.

To cheer him up, I suggested he check in with the man whose fame he was currently caretaking. We pulled over and phoned Tim back in Singapore, who since falling ill had been under the watchful eye of Larry's wife, Simone. She had texted me that morning to say he was, at last, strong enough to talk.

'How are you feeling, Grandpa?' asked Nat. I realized it was the first time they had spoken since Singapore.

'Not too bad,' Tim responded, his weary voice telling a very different story. 'It could be better. I'm looking forward to getting out of hospital tomorrow. How are you getting on with Oxford, Nat?'

'Not so easy to drive, is it?' Nat replied. 'I don't know how you did it! Everywhere we go Oxford's being mobbed. People keep asking me to sign things on your behalf, Grandpa, it's very strange.'

'Oh, well that's why you're there, Nat! Thank you very much for flying the flag. I'm very lucky to have a grandson like you,' choked Tim, now clearly quite emotional.

'When do you think you'll be able to swap back in, Grandpa?' Nat asked, dodging the praise.

'Let's worry about that later, shall we?' Tim concluded, exhausted by the effort of talking.

Nat said goodbye and hung up. I could see he needed space, far from home in a strange country with a bunch of people he had just met. We were all rooting for Tim to return to us as soon as he was able; but, with that date currently anyone's guess, Nat was now facing weeks of driving through increasingly risky terrain. I was sure the enormity of his accidental adventure was now sinking in. I couldn't help but feel responsible and, no better ideas forthcoming, I bought him some chocolate.

As we gobbled up the isthmus taking us towards the main bulk of Thailand, Nat's head switched repeatedly between Google Maps and my copy of *First Overland*, clearly working on a puzzle. He had admitted earlier that he'd never read the book – no need, he had joked, as his grandpa always talked about it. Since their chat on the phone earlier, however, his attitude had changed, and it had become his bible during the long hours on the road.

'Fancy a swim?' he asked breezily, pulling his nose out of his grandpa's story.

Sweaty from head to toe after another sauna session in Oxford, we radioed the convoy that we were taking a detour. Nat, it turned out, had been quietly triangulating the exact beach where in February 1955 the First Overlanders had stopped for a swim. We wound downwards towards the ocean, salt-laced air whipping through Oxford's vents.

We drove right to the waterline, the sea almost lapping Oxford's tyres. Slamming the door, I could feel Tim and the boys marvelling at this same idyllic spot sixty-three years earlier. 'Naked swimming,' Tim had written in his diary.

In the present, Nat and I were feeling a little more conservative, particularly as a group of children were playing nearby. The water lapped up to our knees, soothing ankles tired from the brutal workout of Oxford's pedals. It felt like a good time to check in with Nat.

'How do you like being famous?' I asked.

He smirked. 'Everywhere we go they say: "Where's Tim? Where's Tim?" Are we not good enough?'

The response so far to Oxford's journey home had shocked all of us. We were only beginning to understand what Tim's original adventure had meant to people all around the world. Likewise, we both felt the strain of covering for his absence, and I remembered the image of Tim on the floor, his dream in ruins. I confessed as much to Nat.

'I don't see how he could've done this,' said Nat, reassuringly. 'I'm tired and I'm only twenty-one!'

Crunching the sand between his toes, he stared out to the horizon.

'It's strange to think, he was our age once.'

I agreed. Watching and rewatching the *First Overland* film reels, and poring through photos from all those years ago, it was still hard to square Tim the wiry twenty-something with the Tim I'd only come to know in his late eighties.

'I rate his ambition, though, to still want to do it at eighty-seven,' Nat said. 'You won't catch me doing anything like that at eighty-seven; I'll just be sat in front of the TV!'

An image of my grandad, also in his late eighties, laid out on his care-home bed flashed through my mind.

'Well, here's hoping we all get to eighty-seven like your grandpa, hey?' I said, trying to shake the thought.

'Some of us will get there sooner than others,' Nat said, grinning.

'Git,' I replied.

Realizing this was the first time in all the chaos I'd had a chance to do so, I thanked him for standing in.

'It's a pleasure, mate,' he said, 'and I guess it's only for a few weeks until Grandpa gets better.'

'And until then you're happy to stick around with a bunch of people you've just met?' I asked.

He thought for a moment, almost too long for comfort.

'You're all mad, but it'd be very boring if you weren't.'

Dusting off the sand, we rejoined the gang at a beach-side guesthouse, where we were being treated to dinner by Land Rover fans from all over southern Thailand. The swim had loosened muscles that had not relaxed since we set off from Singapore, and for the first time in a week on the road I began truly to relax.

Larry was already deep in conversation by the barbecue with an old overlanding friend, Aleena. A successful businesswoman, she had travelled the world scratching her itch for automotive adventure. She'd been to the UK ('Home of Land Rover!') and had carved a path through the Amazon rainforest. She talked about her first Land Rover as if it was her first child.

Between his transglobal journeys, Larry had spent years shuttling the Malay peninsula with Aleena and her gang. Larry was clearly delighted to be back with the woman he described as his guru, and I listened as they swapped war stories of past adventures together. I couldn't resist putting the question to the expert that had been bugging me.

'Why all the fuss about Oxford, about this journey?'

'You're a symbol of freedom,' she responds grandly, handing me a chicken kebab straight off the grill. 'Overlanding is all about freedom. You just pack your car and you can go anywhere, escape everyday life. That's why Tim did it, it's why we do it, and it's why you're doing it. You're here to inspire others!' She slapped me hard on the back, causing me to choke.

I felt humbled, even more so than I had done with the Rovernuts in Malaysia. I realized the journey was not ours anymore, and that was okay. We had become a mirror for the dreams of complete strangers who travelled hundreds of miles to come find us, feed us, home us and share their fantasies of one day doing exactly what we were doing now. As wonderful as that was, I confessed to Aleena that it didn't lessen all the worries I had about getting to the end.

'Just enjoy it, Alex, and enjoy doing it in Oxford. The fact that she is going to break down all the time gives you something to do along the way!'

Bangkok had been a fairly regular haunt for me in the last decade. The bustling Thai capital of more than 8 million people was my preferred transit hub from London to Yangon, and my sanctuary of choice when Myanmar became too hot to handle.

As I drove Oxford into the outskirts of the city, Marcus and Nat were busy doing what they usually did during any downtime together – bickering about Premiership football. As supporters of bitter rival football teams Arsenal (Nat) and Tottenham Hotspur (Marcus), they always seemed to have an endless supply of criticism to throw at each other. Thankfully, their most recent match had ended in a 2–2 draw, and I quietly thanked the football gods for helping to keep our little overlanding family together.

'You haven't won the Premier League once!' snapped Nat, rolling out the most damning barb he could find.

'Well, at least even the thickest Tottenham player gives better TV interviews than you do.'

'That's low,' replied Nat.

'He's got a point,' I chuckled. 'Maybe while you're filling Tim's shoes you could take some inspiration from your footballing heroes? See how many footballing cliches you can squeeze in?'

'Well, I suppose it is an expedition of two halves,' Nat said drily.

'Perfect,' said Marcus, nodding encouragement.

Nat's impromptu interview-technique practice session was cut short by David's voice on the radio, channelling his best American airline pilot.

'Convoy, this is PAC. We are now approaching Bangkok, and passengers should be aware it has the world's longest city name!' He paused, audibly inhaling a deep breath: 'City of angels, great city of immortals, magnificent city of the nine gems, seat of the king, city of royal palaces, home of gods incarnate, erected by Vishvakarman at Indra's behest ... '

Before we could reply, an almighty crack split the sky, as if Indra, God of Thunder, had answered David's invocation. Within seconds the king of the Vedic gods unleashed his full wrath on our little convoy.

My view blurred completely. The motorized wipers – pathetic at the best of times – had gone down with their ship. Within seconds Oxford's roof was breached, drenching Nat in lukewarm rainwater. My much-ridiculed hat acted briefly as a water break, but soon overflowed, dumping water into my lap.

Marcus launched himself out of the worst of the internal waterfall and from a foetal position signalled our distress via the radio: 'MAYDAY! MAYDAY! Oxford is *sinking*!'

With traffic rushing from all sides, the situation was truly dangerous, and as soon as feasible I pulled into a layby, where PAC and Enterprise joined us. Nat and I were soaked through, Marcus only slightly less. The team sat waiting for the worst of the rain to pass in a roadside café, but as I was already drenched, I stood in the open and took in Bangkok's skyline, remembering the first time I had felt rain like this.

I had arrived in the summer of 2008 to spend two months studying the history and culture of the Thailand–Myanmar border. While other British students on my flight landed in Bangkok for sunshine, drinking and debauchery, weeks of intensive language courses and history lectures lay ahead for me. Then as now, I had marvelled at the feel of warm monsoon rain coursing across my body – try this in northern England and you would soon die of exposure.

Attempting to ram Thai and Burmese into my brain (try cramming Elvish and Klingon simultaneously and you'll understand), I was immersed in the bitter rivalry of these two ancient civilizations – similar to the potted history of England and France, only with more elephants and possibly even more utter bastards.

I had arrived during a chaotic moment in Thailand's history. A bitter power struggle between popularly elected strongman Thaksin Shinawatra and the establishment forces centred around the army and the palace had exploded onto the streets of Bangkok. Protestors in red (pro-Thaksin) and yellow (pro-monarchy) T-shirts battled in the streets and occupied government buildings. Amid the chaos, ageing paedophile rocker Gary Glitter had barricaded himself into an airport hotel, refusing extradition to the UK on child sex charges. It was an odd time for my first visit, but it certainly left its mark.

The rain subsiding to a drizzle, Nat and the Doc volunteered to pilot Oxford the last few kilometres wearing plastic shower caps borrowed from a previous guesthouse. These became compulsory wet-weather uniform for anyone riding in Oxford in the rain, the sort of pragmatic ingenuity I knew would have made Tim proud.

While in the course of Tim's long life he had witnessed the British Empire go from top dog to a distant memory in Malaysia, here in Thailand a seismic change had taken place within the few years since my last visit. It was evident in the face looking down at us from endless, identical roadside billboards in gaudy golden frames. Since 1946, one man had ruled over this country with overwhelming public support – Rama IX. When he died in 2016, he had ruled longer than any head of state in history. For twelve months after his death, his supporters wore only black and white, and newspapers and television broadcast in monochrome.

Now his son – Rama X – peered nervously from those same billboards. He had good reason to be timid. Rama IX had been a saintly, paternal figure. His son, the new king, was an infamous philanderer plagued with scandal, who in a move worthy of Caligula had recently promoted his pet poodle Fufu to Air Chief Marshal. His accession to the throne had prompted exceptional unease in a country already riven with political tension, and which expressed itself in abstract ways due to the country's strict *lèse-majesté* laws that made criticism of the monarchy an imprisonable crime.

Despite this sense of background unease, I knew Bangkok would be a well-earned chance to let our hair down. There was a precedent: Tim's stay in Bangkok back in 1956 had been such fun that it was the first time in five months he had stopped keeping a daily diary. (Perhaps something to do with the burlesque show he mentioned in the margins, but I hadn't shared that with Nat.) The First Overlanders, nearing their epic adventure's end, were greeted like heroes, feted by journalists and royalty alike. 'The expedition's head became vastly enlarged,' Tim surmised.

Even though we were only 10 per cent of the way into our journey, we had our own official lunches with sponsors, drinks with diplomats and appointments with the press. We spent three happy days in the city, cleaning clothes, tuning up the cars and trying without success to get Nat to expand his diet to locust, crocodile and the local speciality durian (a fruit with the consistency and smell – we both agreed – of sweet sewage.)

On 3 September, it was time to leave. As the team reassembled around the cars, I noticed how in the last few days Nat had begun to stand taller, to laugh louder. Without being asked, he had started joining the Doc on his morning check-ups of Oxford, and spending hours logging footage and charging batteries with our filmmakers

David and Leo. There was no doubt, I thought to myself, between Nat or Thailand's new king, which one would carry their enormous mantle better in the coming weeks and months.

As we headed out in familiar convoy joined yet again by local Land Rover enthusiasts, Marcus's voice crackled on the radio from PAC: 'Exit Bangkok at the next junction, then turn left at the King.'

Once our convoy had recovered from turning left at three of the many hundred royal portraits all situated a few yards from each other, the expedition struck out north-west for the Myanmar border. England was far away, but part of me was nearing home.

7

The Road to Mandalay

4 September 2019: Thai–Myanmar Border
Expedition Day 11

> 'No one is ever in a hurry in Burma, and though this
> can be most aggravating, one is forced to acknowledge
> that it is probably doing one's soul no end of good.'
> Tim Slessor, *First Overland*

I sympathized with Tim, having been kept for hours at the Mae Sot border crossing, waiting impatiently to enter the country that since 1989 has been known as Myanmar. Still, it was with excited eyes that I looked across the Thai–Myanmar Friendship Bridge into the country that had been my happy home for much of the last ten years.

This dilapidated bridge, the first built between Thailand and Myanmar, with its wreaths of razor wire, neatly symbolized a relationship that had always been prickly at best. For centuries, marauding armies from both sides had ransacked, plundered and subjugated the other across the thick jungle separating the two nations. Today these hills still simmered with smuggling, conflict and lawlessness. I had first trekked along the Thai–Myanmar border in 2008, meeting with only a few of the tens of thousands of refugees who had fled the Myanmar military and now lived in ramshackle camps in Thailand's western hills. Some contained generations of families with little hope of ever going home.

I had first entered Myanmar over this same bridge in July 2008. I was forced to take a minder and, despite my twenty-four-hour 'tourist visa', I felt most unwelcome. The people of Myawaddy – the only town I was allowed to visit – were noticeably poorer than the Thais across the river. No one carried a mobile phone and there were no internet cafés. People there lived in info-darkness.

In contrast, in Thailand I had been glued to coverage of Cyclone Nargis, which had just hit southern Myanmar. The world recoiled as the estimated death toll hit hundreds of thousands, and Myanmar's paranoid, xenophobic military junta refused any offers of outside help for fear of meddling foreign influence.

As we finally crossed the border, my heart leapt as I saw telltale signs that I was heading home: curling Myanmar script, distinct from jagged Thai; men in cotton *longyis*, and smudges of yellow *thanaka* on the cheeks of the women who queued on foot alongside us; the flash of the border guard's stained teeth as he spat red juice from the betel nut in his cheek. Even after all these years, the crumbling romance of this country was as intoxicating as ever.

My time in Myanmar had given me a taste of the life of adventure and derring-do that I had dreamed of back in my school library, and enough wild stories to bore a score of grandchildren. Here I had jittered with joy walking in the footsteps of my literary heroes such as George Orwell and Norman Lewis. Today, however, it was a tired old Kipling quote[2] that sprang to mind:

> This is Burma, and it will be quite
> unlike any land you know about.

---

2   Rudyard Kipling is always famously linked to Burma because of his poem 'Mandalay' and has done much to shape the romantic views held towards Burma ever since. However, it is often overlooked that Kipling spent only three days in the country, during which time he went nowhere near Mandalay. Orwell, on the other hand, spent years living and working in Burma, and came to love and loathe it passionately in equal measure.

Back in 1956, crossing what was then still Burma had been a defining milestone for the First Overland expedition. Success would set them apart from all those who had tried, and failed, before. For the first time on our journey, however, we were deviating from the First Overland route. Following their trail across northern Myanmar today was impossible due to separatist conflicts in Myanmar's northern Shan and Kachin ethnic-minority regions. The early shots were being fired in those conflicts as the First Overlanders drove through back in early 1956, and it was exhausting to consider that the armed violence had continued ever since.

Instead, we were crossing into southern Myanmar to make our way to Yangon, the country's largest city and former capital. There we expected a hero's welcome, as it was a city still filled with family and old friends. To get there would mean crossing through the Karen hills, where the Karen minority (many of whom were Christians) held the dubious accolade of maintaining the world's longest-running civil war against Myanmar's central (and mostly Buddhist) government. It had kicked off in 1949, only months after the country's independence from Britain, and it was the Karens who now made up the majority of the refugees I had met mouldering in the camps in Thailand.

I had spent many years picking my way through this part of Myanmar, trekking through the rich green jungles collecting stories and the odd dose of bone-cracking dengue fever. Navigating the baffling patchwork of armed groups who controlled the hills, I had made some very happy memories and lifelong friends, even being invited to the wedding of one – a minor warlord's daughter – complete with elephant ushers. (Mary still runs the best guesthouse in Loikaw.)

Now Oxford was galloping through the deep brown puddles in the mud-road that wound down towards the capital. For the first time it was just the three expedition cars (plus one lead car containing an obligatory 'tour guide'), and we were enjoying our new-found solitude. We might not be on the First Overland route for a little while, but I felt that on these roads we were getting the authentic 1950s experience after more than 2,000 kilometres (1,250 miles) on smooth highway. Gone were the spotless service stations of Thailand and Malaysia; your best bet for a roadside snack in the Karen hills would be negotiating a live chicken strung upside down from a passing motorcyclist.

While in PAC or Enterprise it was possible to catch up on email admin, reading or even take a bumpy nap, inside Oxford it was all hands on deck at all times. In these hard conditions, we rapidly learned that driving Oxford was a team sport. The driver had to have every brain cell and muscle engaged on keeping the car in a straight line, while the co-pilot worked the wipers, mopped fog from the windscreen, and kept the driver topped up with water. Larry's insistence on the co-pilot being awake and alert now made complete sense. You had to keep talking; a tired driver's closing eyes would be fatal. Marcus's favoured approach was to reveal outrageous personal secrets to shock the driver into alertness.[3]

On the toughest stretches, when light was low, a crew of three was needed: one would work the wheel and pedals, one would change the gears on the driver's cue, and another would operate the single spotlight that alerted others to our erratic presence on the road (Oxford's main headlamps gave about as much light as a scented candle). For fifteen long hours we battled 400 kilometres (250 miles) through eastern Myanmar, until finally the hulking skyline of Yangon hove into view.

Formerly known as Rangoon, Yangon's crumbling, mould-streaked, colonial-era buildings loomed overhead, glistening like giant, blackened toads. Oxford looked futuristic by comparison. She had last chugged through in April 1956, on her way back from Singapore.

---

3 It worked a treat, and one day I'll publish the lot.

Tim's diaries do not show much fondness for my second home. I had sympathy – he was desperate to escape the damp, choking heat of the city and head to the cool of the Shan Hills. He didn't know it, but he was visiting this place during a brief heyday of stability.

For the eight years prior to his arrival, the country had been under a democratically elected government after more than a century of British rule. While the hated colonial masters might have been replaced by home-grown leaders, the situation was far from placid. Even in 1956, it was clear to Tim that the Rangoon government faced serious challenges from insurgents of all stripes – ethnic minorities, Communists, Chinese nationalists. A few years after the First Overland's visit, the democrats would sadly fail the many tests against them. To calm the chaos across the country, the nations' military under the magnetic yet ultimately malevolent General Ne Win were invited to 'restore order' temporarily in 1960. When I first arrived, forty-eight years later, in the country the military government had renamed Myanmar, they were still in power, and restoring order was still very much a work in progress.

The military's imprisonment in 1990 of Daw Aung San Suu Kyi, leader of the country's democratic opposition, had become a global cause célébre. She had been under house arrest since then, when her election landslide in the wake of a national uprising against military rule had panicked the ruling generals. The country I encountered in 2008 seemed a place of angels and demons, a morality play in stark black and white.

It took years of living and working across Myanmar to unpick that first impression. Here, 'goodies' and 'baddies' switch clothes so often it becomes impossible to follow. The country beat out my youthful naivete and optimism, substituting in a pragmatic affection for the ordinary people, who were simply trying to get by amid battles between the venal and powerful (often both).

After ever-lengthening stints in the country, Yangon became my second home from 2013. Like Tim, I experienced another brief window of light. Daw Aung San Suu Kyi had been released and was now an opposition MP, a new constitution allowed competitive elections, scheduled for 2015, and the country was undergoing an intoxicating boom in tourism and overseas investment.

Draconian censorship laws were lifted, internet and mobile phones spread across the country, and Myanmar was feted as a shining example of how democracy and hope could triumph over tyranny and fear. The 2015 elections were electrifying, and I danced in the streets until the small hours as Myanmar returned to democracy for the first time since Oxford's last visit. Daw Aung San Suu Kyi – long-time nemesis of the military junta – took over government alongside them. Myanmar's fairy tale, it seemed, had come true.

As I trekked up and down cutting my teeth as a documentary filmmaker, however, reality soon bit. Change could not come quickly enough for Myanmar's long-suffering people, and democratic euphoria soon turned to gloom. Talks to end Myanmar's internal wars collapsed; fighting intensified, and badly needed foreign investors scarpered. Myanmar went from destination of choice for Bono and the Obamas back to the pariah of old, as the horrific plight of the Rohingya Muslims haunted TV screens around the world.

In the autumn of 2019, Yangon was more subdued than it had been two or three years before. Gone were the bright-eyed idealists, the carpetbaggers, the faint-of-heart. Instead, expats too stubborn, too invested or too jaded to leave (in other words, my dearest friends) got on with getting on, continually outflanked by the Burmese, Indians and Chinese who have always really run the place.

Luckily it still paid to know people in this town, and Marcus had pulled some strings to have the expedition housed at the Savoy Hotel. Collapsing into the palatial bed, I could hear my inner-Tim tutting at the opulence while he pitched a ghostly camp bed on the floor.

Our stay in Yangon was joyous but brief. After a few days of catching up with old friends and relishing being stationary enough to do laundry (fellow overlanders will understand the critical importance of the latter), we headed north to the new capital of Burma – Nay Pyi Taw. This preposterous vanity project commissioned by Myanmar's last dictator, Senior General Than Shwe, and opened in 2006, was to be our next overnight stop. I had visited many times before for permits or other official duties; usually reluctantly, as it exemplified everything offensive about the military's long rule here.

Traffic in Nay Pyi Taw was never a problem. Than Shwe designed his new city the same way my mum approached school uniforms – that is, buy big and hope they grow into it. Roughly four times the area of London, the population is nine times smaller. In the centre, outside the colossal new *hluttaw*, or parliament, is a preposterous twenty-lane highway devoid of a single vehicle and rumoured to be ready to double as a major military runway in the case of invasion by the Americans, which Than Shwe was always said to fear. At what would have been rush hour, the expedition fanned out across the empty expanse, enjoying the opportunity to drive alongside each other while leaving seventeen lanes spare.

'I might move out here, get a bit of peace and quiet,' said Nat, sat beside me in Oxford. He leaned his head out of the window to escape the sticky morning heat that Oxford's cab only served to amplify.

'Any idea of the speed limit?' he asked, after pulling his head back in. We both looked at Oxford's speedometer, the needle quivering at 65 km/h (40 mph). During our drive in Yorkshire, Adam had proudly told me how Oxford was capable of 100 km/h (62 mph) (so long as she was pointed downhill) – the same top speed Tim had marked down in the 1950s.

'No idea,' I confessed.

'Well, I don't suppose we're ever in danger of breaking it,' Nat mused.

Marcus had come up trumps again; we pulled into the Hilton Nay Pyi Taw for the night. The Hilton was staggering in scale and opulence. We were each given our own plush suite, only reachable from the lobby via a fleet of golf buggies. As I settled into a giant sofa in what I had deduced was my backup drawing room, my phone pinged.

It was Marcus. 'We need to talk right now. Big trouble. Come to Suite 47.'

After navigating five corridors, three courtyards and a short golf-buggy ride, I arrived at Marcus's door. He sat on his own enormous sofa, chewing his fingers ferociously.

'The Chinese border is closing. We're stuck.'

'For how long?' I asked.

'At least a fortnight, but it could be longer. It's the seventieth anniversary of the foundation of the Communist Party, and the Chinese government is having a last-minute panic about foreigners entering Tibet.'

'Crap. Can we go another way?'

'Yes, but only if you want to (a) risk kidnap and death through Pakistan, or (b) add around six weeks to our journey by going back to Bangkok and then into China through Laos. And the Chinese letting us in that way is not a given either.'

I sat on the sofa opposite, still comically far from Marcus, weighing up the options. Much to Marcus's annoyance, I had made much in the build-up of 'getting to London in 100 days' simply because it sounded cool. Marcus had calculated it was *just* doable, but a two-week delay would push us over, risking bruised egos at the very least. A six-week delay would have us arriving back home in 2020, which for those on the team with partners and families would cause mutiny. That said, kidnap and/or death did not sound like great options either.

Marcus had reached out frantically to our network of British diplomats in Yangon, Nepal and Beijing, but none could help. How times had changed. In the First Overland's day, parts of the map of Asia still remained that trademark pink of the British Empire, and a letter from the Foreign and Commonwealth Office moved mountains. Earlier still, British adventurers had entered Tibet with an army at their back. Now, with Britain's government immobilized by Brexit, and with insufficient funds (and, I should stress, willingness) to hire a private army, we were at the Chinese government's mercy.

'We have to risk it, and hope they'll reopen the border after two weeks,' I ventured, gauging my old accomplice's reaction. 'I mean, how long can the party last? Communists are frugal types, right?'

Marcus frowned, but agreed our alternatives were unviable. We had no Plan B for this problem.

Leaving Marcus sending more desperate pleas for help, I returned to my palatial apartments for an early night. I had an appointment to keep with an old friend, and I did not want to be late.

9 September 2019: Nay Pyi Taw, Myanmar
Expedition Day 16

The next morning we were leaving the Hilton's opulence behind and joining the northbound 'Road to Mandalay', whose romance was famous in the West thanks to Kipling and Sinatra (neither of whom ever visited the city).

Rudyard and Frank have a lot to answer for. There is absolutely nothing romantic about the Yangon–Mandalay Expressway. Glimpsing 'China across the bay' is geographically impossible, and seeing 'flying fishes play' would indicate only that one of the road's depressingly regular deadly collisions had involved a fishmonger. They can be forgiven, perhaps, as they were referring not to an actual road, but to the Irrawaddy River, which until this road's construction was the best route to Myanmar's old royal capital, Mandalay.

In 1885, the British used the river to launch their third and final invasion of the Kingdom of Burma, which they had been gobbling up since the First Anglo–Burmese War of 1824. While it was a tragically one-sided affair sanctioned by Randolph Churchill (father of Winston), which few in Britain today know anything about, for many in Myanmar it remains a painfully humiliating episode in their national memory.

Embarrassed by my own ignorance when I arrived, I had spent three years making a documentary about Myanmar's royal family who still lived in the country, hidden among the people their ancestors ruled as demigods. Over lunch in a roadside café, I gave the team one of my non-consensual historical lectures, recounting Britain's ruthless dismantling of a millennium-old monarchy, and the exile of the last king – Thibaw Min – and his family to British-controlled India.

The British turned the sacred palace of the 'Lord of the Rising Run' into an army base, before flattening it with incendiary bombs during the Second World War. Myanmar never forgot this insult to its national pride, and the military strongmen who later ran the country evoked the grandeur of their lost royal past wherever possible. Indeed, the name of the city we were leaving behind – Nay Pyi Taw – was a prime example, translating to 'Abode of Kings'.

Tibie and Nat were piloting Oxford capably ahead, while I was alongside Larry in Enterprise enjoying the late-afternoon sun and the ever-decreasing humidity as we headed north. Larry's car had become the expedition's 'health and wellness retreat' for any overlander burned out by the frontier life in Oxford. Enterprise was the Tardis of Land Rovers, replete with high-speed internet, countless screens, dials, and surround sound speakers connected to Larry's voice-controlled smartwatch. Soothed by a Chinese folk cover of 'Jingle Bells', I watched the sun start to sink over flooded paddy fields stretching either side of the expressway.

Water buffalo stood stomach-deep in water, staring lazily into nothing. Ox-drawn carts trundled across, drivers in their conical bamboo hats oblivious to traffic. This was the old Myanmar, a scene that had endured the tumult of the last sixty-three years and beyond. The expressway seemed like a temporary inconvenience that would one day return to paddy.

I confided our China-border secret to Larry, as we would need our most experienced head and only native Chinese speaker's help. He had crossed Tibet in 2007 and knew how sensitive the central government were about this historically restive area. As the years had passed, Larry remarked, overlanding had if anything become *more* difficult, despite the advances in technology.

'We're more *safe* than the First Overlanders, but much less *free*,' he mused philosophically. It was an observation I would come to ponder repeatedly in the weeks to come.

While the First Overland had set off with an address book and some vague offers of help, much of what lay ahead was a mystery. For some sections of their journey they were relying on maps years or even decades out of date. They would have to chance it – and if anything went wrong, it might take weeks for anyone to find out. While this posed serious risks, it gave them a freedom to freewheel that we would never have in a world where news spreads at the speed of light, and our cars could be tracked to the nearest centimetre by the smartphones in each of our pockets.

The China border was only one example of the rigidity we faced. Without the right piece of paper from the (now closed) embassy, we were doomed. Marcus had spent months agonizing over countless other potential stumbling blocks. One misplaced *carnet de passage* and a car would be impounded. One minor traffic violation and Adam would be sent letters in York, demanding redress. We could hardly bribe border guards with bottles of whisky and packets of cigarettes, as the First Overland had at times been able.

Even our nationalities impacted our ease of travel, I noted. The Doc, an Indonesian citizen, required reams of paperwork and assurances that he would leave each country and not claim asylum. The Brits faced restrictions in Central Asia that the French and Belgians did not, while the futility of trying to get an Iranian visa for an American called David Israeli had caused Marcus to change our route entirely. Conversely, Larry's Singaporean passport was like a free pass almost anywhere besides China, where there was residual bitterness over a travel ban Singapore had imposed during the Cold War.

While I could video call my family from Larry's car, Tibie could upload countless videos of our antics, and our security team knew where we were at all times, it came at a price. Today's overlanders were more traceable and thus thwartable than ever before.

Safer indeed, but much less free.

Evening approached and Mandalay was growing close. My phone disturbed the sleepy peace of Enterprise. 'Are you almost here, bro?' asked an excitable and familiar voice I hadn't heard in months.

'Yes, mate, we'll be with you in time for sunset!' I replied.

Larry, calm and collected, whispered, 'Play Celine Dion, "Only One Road",' into his watch.

Most first-time visitors to Mandalay are disappointed. Steeped in the ill-informed romance pedalled by tour operators, outsiders turn their nose up at a city that was mostly rebuilt in the 1950s. The old heart of the Kingdom of Burma today forms the crossroads of overland trade between her gigantic neighbours – India and China – and is choked with HGVs.

In the centre, however, lies a clue to its grander past – the towering Mandalay Palace, and its huge moat (some 70 metres/230 feet wide). A perfect square formed by 3-kilometre (2-mile) long, redbrick walls, each with three imposing gates topped with red-and-gold, five-tiered *pyatthat*. The occasional seven-tiered *pyatthat* denote gates reserved for royalty, now long defunct.

Waiting in the lobby of our nearby guesthouse was a delightfully familiar face.

'A-*lex*!' it boomed, crushing me in a hug. 'Welcome home!'

My old friend Aung Sithu is one of many reasons I will love

Myanmar until my dying day. Together we had explored it top to bottom, presenting the country's first-ever adventure-travel TV show. Almost overnight, Sithu had become Myanmar's first homegrown 'explorer', and this naturally boisterous, gregarious character rather enjoyed his celebrity.

In many ways Sithu was the typical Myanmar man, but six years working in Brunei had taught him an ease with outsiders that many of his fellow citizens never get the chance to learn. More than anyone, he had become my window into the soul of this country.

'We'll have to go now; the sun is getting low. Drop the bags and get back in the cars!'

The rich orange of early evening blanketed the city, outlining the bulk of Mandalay Hill and, atop it, the twinkling lights of Sut Aung Pyei Pagoda. Sithu – sitting in Oxford's front seat between Nat and me – directed us to a back road winding right up to the summit. Residents of Mandalay on their evening walks leaped in surprise as an ancient Land Rover roared past, Sithu bellowing warnings through the roof hatch.

Reaching the summit, Sithu led us to the pagoda platform. At midday it can burn naked soles, but in the evening the soothing warmth of the floor enhances the pervasive aura of quiet calm. Bells and gongs chimed gently. Sithu guided us around the pagoda, the sun's orange disc kissing the horizon.

'What are these?' Nat asked, pointing to a cluster of smaller golden figures covered in offerings of flowers and flashing lights.

They were, Sithu explained, the thirty-seven 'nats' – guardian spirits unique to Myanmar, a legacy of pre-Buddhist beliefs that had permeated the national religion. Each had met a gory death and stood as a warning for some vice or another. If not properly propitiated, they could cause all sorts of mischief.

'Nat worship is big in Myanmar,' I added.

'As it should be,' said Nat.

Sithu brought us to the southern side of the pagoda complex, looking out over the perfect square of the palace walls distinguishable far below, filled with dense green foliage broken only by the golden tips of wooden buildings. The team gathered either side of him to take in the exquisite view.

'This was the home of the last king of Burma, Thibaw,' said Sithu, gesturing to the dense green square. 'Thibaw was my great, great, great grandfather.'

Beside me, Nat's eyebrows raised. He and the team took in Sithu with new eyes. My old friend did not enjoy telling this unhappy story, but as a favour to me, he had agreed.

'So you should be living there?' asked Nat, pointing to the golden buildings.

'Exactly!' Sithu replied.

Piecing together the history I had forced on him earlier, Nat asked, 'So it's because of the British that you're not in line to the throne?'

'Yes,' replied Sithu, more solemnly.

'Then I'd like to apologize, on behalf of our nation,' offered Nat after a moment's pause, putting an arm around Sithu's shoulders.

Sithu chuckled, leaning into the embrace. 'It's okay,' he said, 'it's the past, bro, you can't bring it back.'

My old friend was right, in more ways than one, as we were about to discover the very next day.

8

A Man a Mile Road

14 September 2019: Mandalay, Myanmar
Expedition Day 21

Next morning, we pushed aside empty dishes of my favourite noodle salad, *nan gyi thote*, to make way for Marcus's beloved, dog-eared map of Myanmar. I traced the route the First Overlanders had taken. They had entered from India about 900 kilometres (550 miles) due north of Mandalay at the town of Ledo and headed south-east through Kachin and Shan states before entering Thailand via Kengtung. Little did they know it then, but they would be one of the last recorded commuters[4] on the famous 'Stilwell Road', a transport route hacked through the hostile terrain of northern Myanmar during the height of the Second World War.

The brainchild of General 'Vinegar Joe' Stilwell, the road was pitched as a crucial strategic lifeline to connect Allied railheads in India to Yunnan in China, to enable supplies to be sent to Chiang Kai-shek's Chinese nationalist forces – the 'Koumintang' – and keeping them in the brutal battle with the Japanese. This one-time

---

4   Another of the last recorded users of the road, at least in Western eyes, was Group Captain Peter Townsend, who decided to drive around the world in a Land Rover after famously having his heart broken by Princess Margaret. He followed in the First Overland's tyre tracks after soliciting their advice on the crossing of Burma. His travelogue – *Earth, My Friend* – makes for an interesting, if at times pretty melancholy take on how to stick one to your ex.

US–China alliance was another glaring example of how much the world had changed since Tim's journey through here. Now the US and Communist China (Mao's Communists having defeated the Koumintang in China's 1949 civil war) were the world's two great economic superpowers, locked in a bruising trade war, which masked a greater existential struggle for global supremacy.

Churchill had presciently described the road as 'an immense, laborious task, unlikely to be finished until the need for it has passed'. He was right on both counts. Due to the disease and climate, the 1,600-kilometre (1,000-mile) project earned the grisly nickname of 'A Man a Mile Road', claiming the lives of more than 1,000 US servicemen (the majority African American) and many more local labourers whose deaths were not deemed worth recording. By the time the first cargo convoy set out in early 1945, the war with Japan was almost over. Stripped of its purpose at the end of the war, the jungle quickly reclaimed both it and the makeshift headstones of those who had given their lives to build it.

Back in early 1956, as Tim and co had approached the India–Burma border town of Ledo, where the Stilwell Road began, despite best efforts they had managed to glean very little intelligence on the present condition of the road:

> … most of our collected information was negative …
> under the encroaching jungle the abandoned roads
> would not have lasted long; their embankments
> washed away by ten years of monsoon rainfall; the
> latest maps of the region were made in 1944, and told
> us there had been bridges – once. Furthermore, the
> recent earthquakes in Assam might have disrupted
> what little there was left. But all our informants were
> speaking from supposition and not from actual facts.
> We at least should be able to go and see for ourselves.

The intimidating physical barriers ahead were matched only by the onerous mountains of paperwork needed for their crossing, which had taken weeks of pleading letters to the British, Burmese and Indian governments at various levels. As their intended route passed through an area of rumbling separatist fighting by the Naga hill tribes agitating for independence,[5] none of the various mandarins in their way were keen to be held responsible for the possible deaths of six Oxbridge men in the wilds of Burma, while the wounds of decolonization were still so raw.

As they left Ledo on the crisp morning of 15 January 1956, the date chosen to be in the driest window in a notoriously rain-drenched region, they were truly stepping out into the unknown. They had calculated there were just over 400 kilometres (250 miles) of Stilwell's road between them and their next destination of Myitkyina, in Burma's Kachin State, but the condition of that road was a mystery.

'It might take three days,' Tim wrote, 'it could take three weeks; we hoped for the former, but were prepared for the latter.'

Prepared they were. The groundwork for what Tim and co referred to as 'the assault on Burma' had begun almost 2,000 kilometres (1,250 miles) prior to Ledo in Calcutta, and Tim likened it to being 'disturbingly reminiscent of a small-scale military operation'. While the cars were taken to the local Rover garage for a thorough overhaul, the men set about disposing of anything deemed superfluous. Each of them would have to part with precious belongings, be it socks, sardines or their university tie: 'Better take one – never know about these rebels; probably Balliol or Trinity men, and sure to ask us to dinner.' In their

---

5   Tim still gleefully retells the story of the expedition's 'subtle blackmailing' of the newly independent Indian government to get their permission to exit to Burma. As he wrote at the time: 'Independence is a world-wide fashion these days, and Mr Nehru, India's premier, is its international champion. Naturally, then, he is anxious that any such claims for independence as exist within India's own frontiers should not receive undue publicity. It could be awkward for him ... '

place would be gallons of extra fuel, sledgehammers, crowbars, axes and machetes.

One of my favourite photographs from the First Overland's collection shows the team posing in multicoloured waterproofs – 'like six of the seven dwarves' – beside their Land Rovers, and the full gamut of their kit spread out in front of them.

Meticulous preparation aside, it was a gruelling grind. The First Overlanders would have to overcome crumbling bridges, knee-deep mud, raging rivers and the knottiest jungle as they battled their way along the last remaining whispers of Stilwell's great dream. All around them lay the litter of the war, which had ended only eleven years before – pieces of aircraft, the rusting chassis of American transport trucks, and even the odd blown-out tank. They were the last poignant reminders of the bitter conflict fought in this inhospitable land by combatants from all over the world. Brits, Americans, Indians, West Africans, Chinese and representatives of an array of the local hill peoples would meet their end in this brutal terrain.

In the end, they covered the 400 kilometres (250 miles) in three punishing days, which was still impressively quick going. As they cracked open their precious stock of beer and salted peanuts for a celebratory party in Myitkyina, Tim recalled a feeling of anti-climax perfectly captured by Nigel: 'All those blasted crowbars and shovels – we've hardly used them. Y'know, this isn't going to look a bit good in the book.'

However, it was only the beginning of their Burmese odyssey. Ahead lay some of the most treacherous miles through ratcheting conflict between the central government's army and ethnic minority rebels, which they were incredibly lucky to pass through unscathed.

The more I read about it in Tim's book and his expedition diaries, the Stilwell Road section of the journey had become for me the most extraordinary – and given my deep affection for Myanmar, the most romantic – section of the First Overland's already remarkable journey. For days now I had been dripping honey into the ear of the habitually cautious Marcus, hoping to bring our expedition manager round to my madcap plan. Now we were so close to it, he was prepared to listen. As I traced where I thought we might be able drive on a section of the old Stilwell Road that had been reported intact, Sithu's expression grew severe as he followed my finger.

'Absolutely no chance,' he said, shaking his head.

Marcus had long said the same, but I still held a glimmer of hope that we might rejoin Tim's old route.

Sithu continued, 'If you'd tried a few months ago, perhaps, but not now. Last month the fighting started again in Kachin and northern Shan. Bridges have been destroyed and thousands of people have had to leave their homes. You're crazy to drive anywhere in that old car, but you'd be crazy and dead if you tried the road to Ledo.'

Sithu's words cut through the last of my bravado. My dreams of driving on the Stilwell Road – or whatever was now left of it – would have to wait. We would be crossing into India much further south, at the town of Tamu in Sagaing Region. We would have to pick up the First Overland's road once we had made safe passage into India, country number five on our long journey home.

15 September 2019: Tamu, India–Myanmar Border
Expedition Day 22

While Marcus shuffled papers with a Myanmar border guard he had just stirred from a mid-morning nap, Sithu and I said our goodbyes. It felt strange to be crossing new frontiers without him, and seeing his stocky frame retreating in the rear-view mirror only heightened my nerves about the unfamiliar territory ahead. Myanmar, as radically different as it was in so many ways to my home in England, after almost a decade had become a place where I felt intensely at ease. After much practice,

I could read the subtle body language and spoke enough Burmese to keep myself out of the worst kinds of trouble. What lay ahead was to me a truly alien land.

On the Indian side of the border, the authorities were not snoozing. Great metal fences thirty feet high and topped with razor-wire greeted us, while concrete watchtowers with armed guards loomed overhead. From among them the neat, bespectacled figure of Rajan Dowerah jogged towards us, a broad grin on his face and a pale blue hardback book held aloft. I had made contact with Rajan through an old friend, who assured me there was no better guide to this remote corner of the world.

'It's *Oxford*!' he shouted over the engine noise, patting her excitedly.

'Nat, Nat!' he yelled. 'You have to sign this, please!' He jogged to Nat's window and pushed the book through the window. It turned out to be a pristine first-edition copy of *First Overland*.

'I'm a *huge* fan of your grandfather's,' Rajan explained breathlessly. 'I had dearly hoped to meet him – I hope he's okay?'

We had met many a superfan on our journey, but Rajan was quickly shooting to the top of the table. Though he was a professional guide, he had refused to take a penny from us – he merely wanted to be part of a story he had fallen in love with since first stumbling across Tim's book in a second-hand bookshop on a visit to England.

For the whole of human history, north-east India has been one of those 'places in between'. There were few excuses for non-residents to come to these north-eastern states – the 'Seven Sisters' as they are commonly called. On the map, they don't appear to be part of India at all. Attached by the tiniest sliver of land (only 22 kilometres/ 14 miles across at its narrowest point), they look as if they are being nudged aside by Bangladesh. Politically and culturally, the citizens of Manipur, Nagaland, and Rajan's native Assam differ as much from each other as they do from Delhiites or Mumbaikars.

These days only 1,000 people crossed this border each month,

Rajan told me, almost all locals from Manipur or Sagaing on cross-border business. A senior official had travelled overnight especially to process these eight foreigners from six different countries – it was clearly a once-in-a-career moment that his glacial pace suggested he was intent on savouring. Finally, we were released from the holding pen, and into what Rajan declared as India's 'Wild West' frontier.

We passed through Manipur without incident – bar deciding to celebrate my thirty-second birthday in a depressingly alcohol-free Imphal – and crossed into the neighbouring state of Nagaland. The roads began to disintegrate into dark red mud and flooded gravel, mere statements of intent, which the ever-steepening hills seemed determined to shrug off. What had been a drizzle became a full-throated downpour. For the first time on our journey, Oxford was beginning to struggle, lurching and gurgling as if she were choking.

Opening the bonnet, the Doc's expert fingers danced across the engine before quickly dismantling the carburettor. It was thick with a red paste made from the dust of Myanmar and the rains of India. The spark plugs too were filthy, probably from the questionable fuel we had been forced to buy in remote Myanmar villages. We would have to limp on until we could find a proper workshop, he concluded.

Oxford's faltering pace, the horrific roads and the abysmal weather were balanced out by the fanatical enthusiasm that descended on Rajan now we were on the move. Since reading Tim's book, he had dreamed of his own great overland journey. Short overland trips to Yangon or Bangkok had whetted his appetite, but never, he admitted, did he imagine that he would one day be inside the car that inspired him.

'The Oxford,' he kept exclaiming, patting her dashboard.

While Rajan was captivated by Oxford's interior, I was far more bewitched by the view unfolding out of her window. As we crawled ever higher into Nagaland's forbidding hills, below us an endless sea of jungle-strewn hills in darkest greens, framed by the smouldering orange of the setting sun. It was a view that can't have changed in millennia. For the forests below, Oxford's last visit to this place was a mere Sylvanian heartbeat ago.

'Welcome to Nagaland,' said Rajan, following my gaze. 'The view is *very* pleasant – the people, sometimes not so.' The Nagas, he explained, were infamous for being some of the most proudly antisocial people on the Indian subcontinent. Back in the day, they had raided and killed almost for sport Rajan's native Assamese, who lived on the plains below their hills.

When the British arrived in the 1800s, the Nagas had continually stormed British positions until the Raj sent such force of arms that the Nagas decided to call it a draw, so long as they were left alone. During the Second World War, they had chosen to fight with the British against the invading Japanese, mainly thanks to a fearless, Sten-gun wielding anthropologist called Ursula Graham Bower.

'She sounds excellent,' said Tibie, parked in the back of Oxford. Engrossed in Rajan's history lesson, I had momentarily forgotten she was there, which was a difficult task given her current outfit. Since this morning, she had been decked out in a shocking-pink and gold sari, complete with matching bejewelled headscarf that rattled when she moved.

Much to my shame, Tibie had pulled me aside in Imphal to remind me that in India there was a worrying prevalence for female tourists to be targeted for sexual harassment, or worse. While we men could dress in the morning without thought, she pointed out, she would have to be more careful. She had disappeared with Rajan to a nearby tailors, and this morning had unveiled her new look to the team. True to form, I thought: if Tibie was going to be forced to blend in, she was going to do it in style.

After the war, Rajan continued, the Nagas – fiercely protective of their freedom – had raised the middle finger by declaring independence from Britain the day before the rest of India. This had precipitated the fighting that loomed over the First Overlander's journey as they approached the Indian border from the west.

'The Nagas aren't much kinder to each other. Until very recently they were famous headhunters,' Rajan declared.

'Like … the recruiting kind?' Tibie asked, hopefully.

'No. Like the head-chopping and stealing kind.'

I saw her hand rise protectively to her throat.

While the fierce animosity of Naga sub-tribes, each with their own languages and customs, had been softened by the spread of Christianity and the English language, violent conflict between different Naga groups was still common, Rajan warned.

A few kilometres on, he was proved right. Stretched across the road were a dozen diminutive Naga women, squatting on their haunches and furiously brandishing sticks twice as tall as they were. At Rajan's insistence, I brought Oxford to a halt and killed the engine.

'When there's a problem, Nagas often send the women out first, as they're less likely to ramp up the conflict,' Rajan explained in a low voice. Behind me, Tibie tutted.

As Rajan tried to establish the problem, a wiry young man approached from behind the women.

'Who are you?' he shouted, in perfect if irritated English.

'I'm Alex,' I said, holding out a hand. He took it cautiously before visibly relaxing slightly.

'I'm Alex too,' he replied, before shouting to the women to move the roadblock.

'You've come at a bad time,' he said, as we walked side by side down the hill away from the convoy.

'This morning men came and burned our houses,' Alex explained, seething with anger. 'We're having a land dispute with our neighbours, but they have gone too far – they poured kerosene on our houses and chained the doors shut. They were trying to kill us!'

Sure enough, tendrils of thick black smoke rose as we neared Alex's village. I could not hide the shock from my face.

'We've closed the road until the local authorities come and fix this,' Alex continued. 'You had better wait outside the town hall. Our elders are meeting the police. You will have to stay here until they have come to a decision.'

'How long will that take?' I asked, trying to not sound impatient.

'I don't know. Maybe a few hours, maybe a few days. You will have to wait.'

We crossed through a second roadblock guarded by men armed with machetes and rifles. We could not go forward and nor did it appear we'd be allowed to go back. We were stuck.

For several hours we sat in the searing heat as the discussions in the hall went on. The atmosphere outside where we were marooned was increasingly hard to read. Locals, mostly men, seemed to flip between scowls at our unwelcome presence, and intense curiosity around Oxford. Nat, who seemed to be taking the situation in with enviable calm, came to stand beside me with a sly grin on his face:

'Have you noticed that even in the middle of a land dispute people are still having their pictures taken with Oxford?'

'Maybe she can simmer things down a bit,' I replied.

'We come here to bring peace,' said Nat, bowing his head with mock solemnity.

Sadly, the distraction proved only fleeting. Traffic built up either side of the roadblock, and increasingly irate drivers began to shout at the villagers to unblock the road. A scuffle broke out and tensions rose markedly. Larry, usually stoic, looked uncharacteristically worried, only accelerating the sinking feeling in my gut.

'My friends in India warned me: "Stay out of it, these things can get very ugly." All the rifles they're carrying,' he said, nodding to the assorted weaponry on show, 'all live rounds.'

I beckoned to the others to board their cars and climbed into the now noticeably lightly-armoured Oxford.

As tensions ratcheted further, a shouting match started at the roadblock in front and men appeared from nowhere carrying sticks and rocks. My mind began to race. At worst we would have to barge our way out under fire. Oxford's copious gaps and cracks seemed gaping. In that moment I felt a terrible wave of guilt cross over me for landing my companions in this mess. My mind flashed to Tim still recuperating in Singapore, and imagined the look on the faces of my companions' families receiving the news they had been butchered in a shootout in Nagaland.

Suddenly, truckloads of uniformed, heavily armed men entered the village, increasing the weaponry on show dramatically. One man, clearly in charge, marched straight to Oxford.

'Where are you going?' he asked, clearly annoyed that he had three carloads of potential foreign casualties to complicate his day.

'Kohima,' I said, naming the town we were hoping to reach before night fell.

'Well, you'd better go then,' he snapped. He waved for his men to escort us through the homemade barriers, parting the angry crowd of drivers who had been waiting for more than three hours to pass. PAC and Enterprise pulled away. Oxford, however, had other ideas. She refused to start at first – and once she did, she rabbit-hopped up the hill through the armed crowd. Luckily, after a few tense yards, she sputtered into a cruise and a wave of relief crashed over me.

When Adam had trained me to hill-start Oxford in Yorkshire, I hadn't considered that I might have to do it at gunpoint. I should have listened more closely.

9

Ghosts

18 September 2019: Kohima, India

Expedition Day 25

'Once we listened to the news, and this corner of the world had been important. Today … it is forgotten.'

I closed *First Overland* and looked out from our guesthouse deep in the Naga Hills. Tim recalled how, during their passage through to Burma, the wreckage of ferocious battles between Japanese and Allied forces had littered this corner of India. To illustrate his point, he had even shown me a photo of the First Overlanders posing in a burned-out Japanese tank.

If in 1956 Tim thought this place was forgotten in Britain's national memory, in 2019 it might as well never have existed. The battle for Burma between 1942 and 1945 was one of the most brutal chapters of the war, as Japan tried to neutralize Britain by seizing its entire Asian empire. If they had succeeded, the Second World War could have ended very differently. Unlike the heroes of Dunkirk and D-Day, Britain largely forgot the sacrifice made by thousands of her sons – and many more from across the Commonwealth – in north-east India.

Kohima, the capital of Nagaland, had long been on my bucket list. Back in 2017, I had filmed a documentary about the Second World War in Southeast Asia, interviewing the handful of surviving veterans who had fought here against the Japanese. In the centre of Kohima stands the Commonwealth War Cemetery. Once through the gates, a hush fell over the team. In front of us stood the small headstones of more than 2,000 British and Commonwealth soldiers, arranged in neat lines.

Walking between them, we spotted men from all over the UK – Durham, the Highlands, Manchester – as well as Nepalis, Indians, and West Africans. A tiny cross-section of Britain's Fourteenth Army, one of the largest and most multinational forces ever assembled. Whether Christian, Hindu, Sikh, Muslim or Jew, all were buried here strictly according to the burial rules of their faith.

I stopped to read one headstone for Private L. B. Lewis of the Worcestershire Regiment, who died on 19 June 1944, aged just twenty-five. The inscription read:

> Leslie, as long as life and memory last,
> I will always remember you. Dad.

I thought of Leslie's father, writing those words in war-ruined England. He must have received a letter telling him his son had died at Kohima. He might as well have been told Leslie had died fighting on the moon, so distant and foreign was this place. These words were the only part of him that would touch a resting place he must have known he would never be able to visit. After the drama at the roadblock, I thought of my own dad getting a similar message today. I felt very far from home.

After some downtime in Kohima, on the morning of 21 September we set off early on the westward road to Rajan's native Assam. Outside of the cars was a blur of colour and chaos as we passed through the crowded and deliciously polysyllabic towns of Bokakhat and Jakhalabandha, teeming with bustling markets spilling into the streets. Around us Hindu temples, Muslim mosques and Christian churches battled for real estate and souls, while across the street, banners proclaiming the superior wisdom of Marx and Lenin loomed with a sneer. Rajan gamely tried to help me make sense of it all. He pointed out that in Assam alone there were more than one hundred recognized ethnic groups, and at least thirteen recognized languages.

Today Assam was gripped by an identity crisis, Rajan explained, one quickly engulfing the whole of India under its nationalist leader Narendra Modi, questioning who was and who was not 'Indian'. Assam had only weeks earlier updated the National Register of its more than 30 million citizens, declaring almost 2 million of them 'foreigners'. For many it was surprising and distressing news, and although many outside observers saw it as a cynical ploy to disenfranchise Assam's large Muslim minority, many Hindus and tribal peoples had suddenly been declared 'foreign' in the process.

Assam's dodgy census was causing outrage across the country, and the world, but India's national government was still considering it a pilot for the rest of the country. If Assam's experience was anything to go by, India could soon have a full-blown civil war on its hands.

While still battling a headache from all the detail that Rajan was throwing at me, I realized at the town of Guwahati that we were crossing the Brahmaputra River, the waterway that tumbled out of the Himalayas, via Assam and out through Bangladesh to the Bay of Bengal. The bridge itself was unremarkable, but it signalled something far more profound. We were back on the First Overland route at last. Our crossing lacked the drama of the First Overlander's back in late 1955; there was no bridge at all back then, and the team had a hair-raising crossing on a rickety ferry.

'I have a little surprise for you!' Rajan announced, as we motored westwards at breakneck speed through his home state – Oxford clearly spurred by the subtle ripple of her tyre tracks from sixty-four years earlier. Rajan was even more excited than usual.

'Tomorrow when I tell you to, you'll have to let me drive.'

The next day was both hot and wet, which – in addition to the suicidal behaviour of Assamese drivers, pedestrians and India's famed holy cows – was to be my abiding memory of our time driving through Assam. As I drove in Oxford through the latest deluge, I had finally relented to wearing one of Nat's trusty shower caps – there really was no better way to cope with Oxford's involuntary waterworks. Style be damned.

Meanwhile Rajan was clearly looking for something, concentrating on every passing road sign and muttering to himself in the seat beside me. Without warning, he signalled me to pull over, before taking the wheel and pulling Oxford down a nondescript side road.

'Welcome to the Deka Julia Tea Estate …!' Rajan crowed, almost as if we had reached London, before adding, 'I think.'

Either side of us stretched the neat rows of waist-high bushes we had last seen sprawling across the Cameron Highlands. We were back in the ordered world of the tea plantation. Tim and co had stayed at a bungalow on this very estate before making their great assault on Burma. It was one of Tim's most treasured memories, but none of us had thought the bungalow might still be standing.

Nat, crouched in the back of Oxford, leafed quickly through his copy of *First Overland*.

'No expedition can ever have had such an enjoyable or luxurious base camp,' he shouted over the engine noise, reading Tim's summary of their time as guests of the plantation's British managers.

'Mr and Mrs Hannay came down the steps of their bungalow and across the lawn to meet us …' he continued, as Rajan pulled through the tattered gates.

Its wooden frame was splintered and cracked with large patches of mould on the panelling, but the Hannays' bungalow was still very much there, and barely modified from its original condition.

It was not the Hannays who came out to greet us – they must have long since passed away – but a portly Indian man, who introduced himself as Dr Sharma. The bungalow was now his medical centre, where he provided care to the 19,000 workers and their families who lived and worked on the 5,000-acre estate.

'We cannot survive without our pickers – no machine has yet been built that can pick tea better than the nimble human finger!' he explained.

I watched Nat grip the banister, even quieter than usual, as he scaled the same stairs his grandpa had done more than sixty years earlier. We had driven thousands of kilometres in Tim's tyre tracks, but there was something visceral about walking in his actual footsteps.

Rajan began to read:

'Hey, Tim,' called Nigel from the adjoining bathroom, 'there's hot water coming out of the tap marked "Hot".' I ran to inspect this wonder, and, as it was only the second time on our journey that we had seen hot water running from a tap merely for the turning, both of us nearly scalded ourselves.

We skittered excitedly through bedrooms and bathrooms, trying to figure out who slept where.

'Grandpa would know?' suggested Nat.

I dialled the number given to us by Larry's wife Simone and huddled around the speaker. As the dial tone purred, I realized that although Tim felt ever-present with us on this journey, the hectic pace we were setting meant we had not checked in on him since arriving in India.

'Hello?' answered Tim.

'Hello, Grandpa.'

Nat had to explain several times to Tim – now discharged from hospital and gradually recovering his strength in a Singapore hotel – where we were sitting, such was Tim's incredulity that the house was still upright.

'Amazing, amazing, amazing! You've made my day, made my week!' he purred, deeply moved.

'Can you remember where you slept?' asked Nat.

'Gosh, yes! I could take you to it if I were there. Downstairs on the left.'

From memory, Tim guided us through the house, still barely believing what was happening.

'Thank your hosts for me, will you? I imagine it's not the Hannays anymore?' Tim chuckled before saying goodbye and hanging up the phone. I watched Nat, who was clearly deep in thought.

'That was a bit surreal, wasn't it?' I ventured.

Nat smiled. 'Not as surreal as us turning up at this geezer's house and him just welcoming us with a cup of tea. Can you imagine if an Indian turned up at a house in England and said, "Sixty-five years ago we stayed here"? I bet he'd get told to jog on!'

I smiled. I had quickly learned Nat gave little away when it came to his state of mind, often leaving me to worry on his behalf about how he was handling the fallout from his grandpa's dramatic exit from our story. The better I got to know him, however, the more I could see my worries about the weight of the mantle he had shouldered were unfounded. Tim's no-nonsense pragmatism was firmly written in his grandson's genes.

Before we said our final goodbyes, I stood on the shaded veranda where Tim had no doubt stood all those years ago. Looking down at the lawn, I could see the ghosts of six young men unpacking and repacking. There was BB dusting off his lenses, Tim tip-tapping away on the expedition's typewriter, composing what might be his last letter home. It was here they had put their affairs in order before entering Burma, preparing to go further than any overlander had ever been.

Since its inception, our journey's whole purpose had been to bring Tim's history back to life. But here in this garden of ghosts, I finally understood that, with Tim or without him, this was something we could never really do. Here more than anywhere, we were so tantalizingly close to them, yet still so painfully distant – separated by the relentless passage of time. For a few brief minutes

Above: Tim and I plan our upcoming adventure at Tim's house in London, while Nat (the unsuspecting Plan B) looks on.

Below: Surviving First Overlanders Nigel, Pat and Tim – joined by Oxford's restorer, Adam (second from left), Marcus and I – outside the Grenadier pub where they set off from in 1955. The Land Rover is a replica of Oxford's missing companion, Cambridge.

Above: Flag Off at the Singapore Formula 1, 25 August 2019. The Last Overland team (R-L David, Leo, Nat, Tibie, Larry, Marcus and I) are joined by First Overlanders Nigel and Pat, and supporters from across Singapore.

Below: Nat and I in Oxford on the road to Malaysia just after Flag Off, after Tim's sudden departure from the trip.

Above: Me cooling down on top of Oxford on the road to the Cameron Highlands, Malaysia.

Below: The Land Rover Club of Southern Thailand welcome the Last Overland. Our enthusiastic guide – the aptly named Beer – readies himself (right).

Above: A less-than-happy face after a long late-night drive through Myanmar's monsoon rains, aided (or not) by Oxford's 1950s wipers.

Below: Nat and I at the legendary Pat's Garage Land Rover workshop in Ratchaburi, Thailand. The first, but certainly not the last, workshop Oxford visited on our journey ...

Above: The Last Overland team take in the sunset over the temples of Bagan, Myanmar, atop Enterprise, Oxford and PAC.

Below: Filmmaker Leo multitasks at the dazzling Hsinbyume Pagoda, Mandalay, built to mimic the shape of the Buddhist heavens.

Above: Nat, Tibie and I warm up over delicious home-cooked food at the top of Tonglu hill, near Darjeeling, West Bengal, India.

Below: Trapped in a roadblock caused by a turf war between two rival clans, I attempt to dissolve the tension with an introduction to the First Overland.

Above: Nat learning on his descent from Tonglu hill that when the weather outside Oxford is frightful, you're sure to know inside shortly after.

Below: David and I take in some of the Nagaland State Government's innovative public service announcements on our passage through north-east India.

Above: Gorkhland guide Mr Bunty (L) and Larry (R) help the Doc (C) guide a struggling Oxford towards yet another workshop in West Bengal, India.

Below: Nat, Oxford and I get up close and personal with the elephants of Kaziranga National Park, Assam, India. The elephants patrol the park to protect their fellow (endangered) resident, the Indian rhinoceros.

we had brought Tim's voice back into this building, but nothing could bring back the four days he had spent here, filled with dreams of a future now long in the past.

I realized that from here on out, having abandoned hope of going west via Pakistan, we would soon be departing their route for thousands of kilometres until we rejoined it in Turkey. While they were near the final stage of their journey during their visit here, we were still only beginning ours – in the coming weeks, we would write a new story entirely.

History doesn't repeat itself, but it does rhyme, Mark Twain once wrote. Below me I watched a new generation of overlanders go about their business. Marcus and Larry huddled over a map discussing our onward journey. Leo, David and Tibie disassembled cameras and tripods before stacking them carefully in PAC. The Doc and Nat had Oxford's bonnet propped open, no doubt checking on that dodgy carburettor.

I knew then that this was the right time to say goodbye – for now – to the First Overlanders. Rather than trying and repeatedly failing to relive the past, it was time to embrace the diversions that lay ahead and make some history of our own.

On 23 September, in a simple guesthouse outside the small town of Jaldapara, my mum called. It was a conversation I had anticipated for years, but the blow was not any softer for that.

'It's Grandad. He's developed a bad lung infection. The doctor said he probably won't last the night.' She sounded calm and practical, as ever.

'Are you okay?' I asked, suddenly overcome with grief.

Silence. I thought the call had dropped, until a single sob crackled down the line. I hadn't heard my mum cry in twenty years.

'He shouldn't be here,' she managed through the tears. 'If he was an animal they'd have put him down years ago. I'm sorry, I have to go, the doctor is here. I love you.'

The tears came unbeckoned. That night I didn't sleep. Moments before dawn the power went out, except a single bulb that flicked on by itself and woke me.

I checked my phone – a message from Mum.

'Can you call?'

He had passed in the night, shortly after all three of his daughters had been to his bedside. In the final moments, how much he had suffered no one could know, he had long lost the ability to say.

I breathed in Indian air deeply, trying to banish the haunting image. Instantly the smell of rain on earth transported me back twenty-five years, tramping behind my grandad in the woods. Ahead I saw the stocky figure in the black leather jacket retreating out of sight, and I knew now that no wail or cry from me would stop him. At first, as his outline blended with the trees, a wave of relief washed over me. Relief for Mum, and for him – the years of pain, confusion and suffering were finally over.

Then came a bolt of red-hot grief again, mixed with overwhelming loss. The realization dawned that even if I did make it home to England in one piece, I would never set eyes on him again. I couldn't help but dwell on that last terrible meeting with him, and how I had wished he were something he was not.

'I have to go; I need to call your brother,' said Mum. 'And don't even think about coming home for the funeral. Say goodbye to him on the road – he'd have liked that.'

As she put down the phone, the ripples of shock began to spread. For a while I could do little more than sit in mute silence. As the sun rose higher in Jaldapara, I watched the night's dew rise from the tea-bushes, filling the air with slow dancing wraiths. For weeks we had been driving with ghosts. For years, I had been living with one. It was time to say goodbye to them all, whether I liked it or not.

10

Hello Darjeeling!

24 September 2019: West Bengal, India

Expedition Day 31

'I think I've got *Oxforditis*,' Marcus shouted to me above the now familiar roar of Oxford's engine at cruising speed.

'What's that?' I asked, snapping out of a daze – a difficult feat in Oxford.

'Well, how does your back feel?' he replied.

'Like there's a ball of hot lead in it,' I confessed.

'And your throat?'

'Hoarse.'

'Do you have any of the following: gritty eyes, a persistent cough, a sore left knee, chronic rising *and* falling damp?'

'Yes, yes, yes and … yes,' I answered.

'Then my friend, I can confidently diagnose you with Oxforditis. Let's hope it's not terminal.'

I was grateful my old friend had pulled me out of my thoughts. When I had shared the news of my grandad's passing, Marcus and the team had quietly closed ranks around me. As the days passed, I could see an unspoken rota had formed to gently coax me out of my shell.

All morning I had been dwelling on my grandad after a message from my mum. She'd sent a picture of him as a much younger man, slim and dapper in an immaculate greatcoat, gloves and cravat, smiling confidently into the camera.

'He looks just like you,' she wrote.

His hair went left to right across his forehead, exactly as mine did, and in his eyes and smile I could clearly see my own staring back. It was face full of light, of hope, of endless possibility. Nat's words from Thailand about the younger Tim came back unbidden: 'It was strange to think they were our age, once.'

I was shocked. I had never seen him like this, never noticed the uncanny likeness. Since seeing it, I couldn't shake the feeling that even before the dementia had started to take hold, I'd known so little about this man who was – in part – responsible for my existence. I'd been focused so much on the disease that had consumed him, and on my efforts to stick two fingers up to it, that I had started to forget the man himself.

I was starting to see the impression I had of who he was – or indeed wasn't – was so incomplete. It had been woven from a few threads of my unreliable memory, embellished with my own prejudice, and hardened by whatever meaning I chose to find in the scraps he had left behind. It had led me to compare him, so unfairly, with Tim, and to find him wanting. I knew now he deserved better than that.

In a strange twist of fate, I had come to know Nat's grandfather better than I would ever know my own. By undertaking this journey on his grandfather's behalf, and literally driving in his grandfather's tyre tracks, I saw now that Nat would have a chance to truly know his grandfather in a way I had never, and now could not. As I studied my grandad's young face, it was something I'll admit I envied Nat for.

Today we were marking the one-month milestone on our journey, and outside the window it felt like a visual page was turning. Gone were the sticky, congested towns and flooded rice paddies of the Brahmaputra plains; around us rose rolling hills, thick with green forests patrolled by troops of curious monkeys.

My mind flicked to a line in Tim's book from when he had passed through this very point: 'That day, for the first time on the journey, we smelt the tropics.'

Almost sixty-four years later, Oxford was powering across that same pungent frontier, but this time in the opposite direction. Now, with Tim's grandson on board, Oxford was leaving behind the smells, sights and sounds that had been the norm since departing Singapore one month ago. As the chaotic first stage of our journey came to an end, it had been replaced by determined calm across the team. Now functioning like a finely tuned machine under Marcus and Larry's instruction, we would happily spend hours driving in silence, listening to music (Fleetwood Mac being a consensus choice). Conversation was saved for when an issue of great philosophical importance arose.

'You never see monkey-shaped roadkill,' mused Leo, his camera pointed out of Oxford's windscreen. 'Too intelligent.'

'No cats either,' added David, thoughtfully, with his camera pointed out of the rear window.

Fortunately, neither had been filming when a stray dog, to my eternal regret, had run under Oxford's wheels that morning – luckily the first and only such casualty on our journey.[6]

The uniquely terrifying experience of driving India's roads had hardened us all, and there was a new seriousness to any member of the team who stepped behind a wheel. 'Be careful driving in a country where people believe in reincarnation,' Rajan had warned me. 'They've one foot on the gas, and one in the afterlife.'

Little surprised us anymore; whether it be whole families walking in dead of night in the middle of the road, carrying an entire dining table and chairs set; or thundering juggernauts driving on the wrong side of the road honking furiously for *you* to move out of their way. Add in the steady tide of cows – suicidal in their sanctity – and you soon learned that a moment's lapse in attentiveness could be fatal.

The rapid drop in temperature and a steady drizzle aided

---

6   In my defence, I'm almost certain it was hit by a lorry first and mercifully I finished it off.

concentration. That morning the team had unpacked our cold-weather gear from on top of PAC. Marcus had warned that, given the time of year we were travelling, it would likely be cold and wet all the way to London. It was a sobering thought.

Nat was hunched behind Marcus and me in a raincoat, thick trousers and his now obligatory shower cap.

'You did say you couldn't wait to be out of the stifling heat?' I kindly reminded him.

From the look he gave me, it didn't help.

As I squinted through Oxford's rain-spattered windscreen, I knew that ahead of us somewhere lay the greatest mountain range on Earth – the Himalayas – and the gateway (if the Chinese would deign to open it for us) to Tibet. The mountains were a formidable natural barrier, which this old car would soon have to cross for the first time in her long life. Travelling in the far north of Myanmar, I had peeked at the very edge of those mighty mountains through binoculars. Soon, I would be driving through their heart.

Between them and us, however, lay hundreds of kilometres of steep, twisting roads through north-east India and Nepal. It was a very different world to the one Rajan had guided us through, and it was time for us to part ways. We did so at Coronation Bridge, a swooping white arch of reinforced concrete spanning the broiling Teesta River. Built in 1937, ten years before the dismantling of the Raj, to mark the ascension of Emperor George VI of India, it seemed an almost comical symbol of imperial hubris.

I was sad to see Rajan go: his infectious enthusiasm for our journey had buoyed me these last few difficult days, and his constant stream of helpful background context had made our immersion into this strange new world smoother than it should have been.

Now we were guideless deep within West Bengal, an Indian state containing more than 90 million people, stretching from the sprawling megacity of Kolkata all the way to the Himalayas. Merely one state within the behemoth of India, a country of mind-boggling size and scale. The only thing more incomprehensible was how Britain had ever presumed to rule it.

Suddenly a battered old Mahindra Bolero screeched to a halt on the bridge, beeping its horn excitably. Out jumped the guide who would take us all the way to the border with Nepal – a man we had communicated with only via email, signing off as 'Mr Bunty'. He had quickly become Marcus's favourite among the guides we'd yet to meet, the sheer enthusiasm for our arrival fizzing through his correspondence. Now here he was in the flesh – all five feet three inches of his portly frame wrapped in a bright-red England football jersey and crowned by a woolly hat with flapping ear protectors. He jogged towards the car (Mr Bunty only ever jogged, I was soon to discover), bearing a handful of white, silk-like scarves, which streamed behind him in the stiff breeze.

'Welcome to Gorkhaland!' he beamed, laying a scarf (or *khata*) around each of our necks.

I didn't want to spoil the moment by confessing I'd never heard of such a place. While I knew of Gurkhas, those famous warriors from neighbouring Nepal, a 'Gorkhaland' within India was new to me.

Mr Bunty climbed into Oxford between Nat and me and filled us in on this maybe-nation. The Gorkhaland movement campaigned to separate the north of West Bengal, whose majority share a language and culture closer to Nepal than the Bengali-speakers down south. Since the early 1900s, many had struggled and died for the cause. While some autonomy had been granted in recent years, the issue still simmered.

Attempts in 2017 to make the Bengali language compulsory in schools across West Bengal sparked violent protests and demands for a new state. In recent weeks, the Indian government's decision to carve up the state of Jammu and Kashmir had returned the issue to the fore, and tensions were high. Mr Bunty pointed to cindered signposts and battered bus stops.

'Do you think you'll have your own state soon?' asked Nat.

'It's hard to say. I'm not a Gorkha!' he replied. 'I'm Lepcha. We're indigenous to these hills, here *long* before the Gorkhas came.'

Absorbing Mr Bunty's news, I realized I was now adding yet another subgroup to the tapestry of Asia's peoples and cultures I'd been weaving in my head. Since leaving Singapore, we'd passed through community after community who wanted to redraw that neat map of nations I'd learned at school, unhappy with whom the cartographers had lumped them in with.

The only thing that united these disparate peoples – the Karens, Kachins, Manipuris, Nagas and now the Gorkhas – was that they were all fighting and dying to live within lines on a map of their own choosing. What was more, it was becoming clearer by the day how many of those lines had been drawn by starch-collared men from my own country, thousands of kilometres away, who had sometimes never even set foot in the land that they were demarcating. They had a lot to answer for.

Hoping to move to more positive aspects of Gorkhaland, Mr Bunty pointed out the fluttering, multicoloured prayer flags, marking the hinterlands of the regions where the Buddha's teachings dominated, and then to the sprawling tea estates that made these hills famous around the world.

'And, of course, there are Land Rovers! So many Land Rovers! Wherever you Brits went in Asia, you left them behind.'

Alongside lines on maps few agreed with, I thought.

'Not much further now, Kalimpong is just around the corner,' said Mr Bunty, bouncing in his seat. After our first full day driving Oxford in this newly cold and wet environment, I was heartened by the idea of a hot cup of India's finest tea and a shower.

My daydream was brought to a swift halt by the arrival of complete and utter chaos.

Oxford had pulled into Kalimpong's town centre to be immediately swamped in a tide of people and noise. What looked like the entire population was packed into the central square, squeezed onto balconies and rooftops as far as I could see, cheering, yelling and lighting fireworks. I could only imagine that India had won the Cricket World Cup, such was the fever pitch of the scene. Quickly, however, I realized that all excited eyes were turned on Oxford.

'Is this for us?!' I found myself shouting to Mr Bunty, barely audible over the cacophonous noise.

'Of course!'

Even though we had only just discovered Gorkhaland, it was clear that Gorkhaland already knew plenty about us.

Nat and I were dragged gently but firmly out of Oxford, where our foreheads were applied with splodges of rice in a deep-pink paste. Then, before the paste had time to dry, scarf after scarf was placed around our necks, overlaid with thick garlands of bright-orange marigolds.

Then the crowds parted to reveal two-dozen drummers and bagpipers, each dressed in dark-green uniforms, sparkling white puttees, black berets and dashing tartan capes. We heard them before we saw them – it was impossible not to. The drum roll signalled the pipers to start, and as one the band began to march on the spot in perfect unison, blasting a version of 'Scotland the Brave' so fast it sounded like a tape player gone rogue.

Seconds later, the band started marching forward, and Nat and I were swept along in its wake. A quick-thinking Tibie rescued the idling Oxford and began to lead the convoy following us. It was the most surreal experience on our journey so far, made even more so by the mobs of reporters thrusting microphones and cameras in our face. Oxford's return to these lush hills was clearly big news, and for now, all we could do was surrender to the madness and ride along on her venerable mudflaps.

The next morning, I stood on my balcony wrapped in blankets, bathing my face in the steam of a crisp Kalimpong tea and staring out at the mighty Kanchenjunga, the third-highest mountain in the world. Or at least that's what I was assured was behind the thick bank of grey-black clouds encircling our lodge. This little moment of solitary peace had become a morning routine since my grandad's death. The rest of the team, sensing instinctively I needed space, kindly protected it.

In these morning moments, words Tim had written looking at this very same mountain sixty-four years earlier lingered in my mind: 'It was one of those days when one looks and looks, afraid to miss anything. Clenching one's mind, one thinks, I *must* remember this.'

While the sharp pain of grief had begun to ease, the deep unnerving fear I had about the disease that claimed him had only intensified. I had embarked on this adventure to make memories that would last a lifetime, as the First Overland had done for Tim. The idea – however irrational it might be – of them being taken from me while I was still alive was weighing heavily, filling me with a despondency I'd rarely experienced. So, each morning I'd resolved to sit and stare intently at every new horizon, stubbornly clenching my mind as Tim had done, trying to force my brain not to forget.

With so much ground to cover each day, these moments rarely lasted long. That day we were on the road to Darjeeling by 8 a.m. The rain was so relentless now it felt like we were driving underwater.

'The rain falls here almost year-round!' explained Mr Bunty with a perverse pride.

Even for me, used to the weather in Manchester, that was too much. It was a miracle the people here didn't have gills. The only thing brightening up the otherwise slate-coloured view were the periodic archways of colour and light crossing the road.

'They're *pandals*,' explained Mr Bunty, wedged between the Doc and me inside Oxford's cold, clammy cab.

'They're being built for Dashain, a Hindu festival honouring the goddess Durga. She's not one to upset.' Mr Bunty illustrated his point with pictures of Durga on his phone, her many arms laden with a variety of cruel and deadly weapons used in her role as goddess of creative destruction.

Meanwhile, the Doc was battling our own four-wheeled goddess. Oxford was in particularly cantankerous form, the steep hills and rain causing havoc with an old car weary from weeks of continuous hard driving. She groaned like a wounded buffalo if pushed above 25 km/h (15 mph), making our progress that day painfully slow. It was only due to the Doc's decades of experience with his own Series Is that she was still moving forward.

'We must go to a workshop, before she stops completely,' warned the Doc.

'Never fear!' exclaimed Mr Bunty. 'Darjeeling has the best Land Rover mechanics in India.'

Glimpsing Darjeeling from above was like removing the top off an anthill. A complex one-way system by some miracle kept this madly congested hill town moving; and as Oxford limped into its outskirts, it was if she knew she was at the hospital gates. She conked out and refused to restart, blocking the main road and causing a similar commotion to our arrival in Kalimpong, albeit with a much angrier edge.

Nat, David and Leo leaped from PAC to push her clear of the road, just as the town's famed miniature railway came chuffing through in a cloud of steam and angry whistles on its slow pilgrimage to India's highest railway station. It was the same steady plod the train had been making since the British installed it here in the 1880s, at the height of the town's imperial pomp. The fact that Oxford had danced with her back in 1955 was long forgotten by this antique engine, chugging ever onwards as earthly empires rose and fell.

As we wrestled a limping Oxford towards our guesthouse for the evening, I took a look at the team. They were not faring much better than Oxford. Grubby, damp and tired, we were all in desperate need of a wash and a warm bed. Sadly, Mr Bunty had different ideas, detouring the convoy from the haven of the guesthouse gates down into the nearby central square, where another huge crowd was waiting. Feeling that strange mix of resentment that only ageing, jaded rock-stars must experience, I bristled at the thought of yet another adoring crowd, when all I wanted was to sleep. As the rain pelted down, we were escorted onto the stage to yet more fanfare and applause that I felt we didn't deserve at all.

The spotlights beamed down on our dishevelled group, who looked more like a police line-up than the band of intrepid travellers that the master of ceremonies was currently lauding. As he whipped the crowd into a frenzy, I steeled myself to say a few words. Much to my surprise, and relief, the MC turned and said: 'And now ... please welcome Nat George, the grandson of the famous Tim Slessor, to the stage!'

The spotlights fell on Nat, who was instantly overcome with a look of blind, debilitating panic that I hadn't seen since that fateful morning in Singapore. He looked at me, I looked at him, and then I nodded my head to encourage him forward. But it wasn't the same shy boy who stepped forward now, I noticed. Swallowing hard, Nat grabbed the microphone. Alone, he stood on the stage with thousands of cheering townsfolk at his feet.

'Hello, Darjeeling!' he practically boomed, as the crowd whooped and hollered their reply. My heart swelled as he thanked the town for their incredible welcome. Nat from one month ago would have rather died than been standing there, but you could barely see the tremor in his knees now. Being forced into his grandpa's enormous shoes was not something he had ever asked for, but seeing him now, I knew Tim would be as delighted as I was at the way his grandson was growing in the light of his accidental fame.

With the celebrations finally at an end, it was time for bed at last. Luckily for us and for Oxford, we had planned to take a few days of badly needed rest here. It allowed us to deposit our talisman in the capable hands of Ratan Gurung, Darjeeling's foremost Land Rover mechanic. This tiny, oil-stained genius wordlessly set to dismantling Oxford's engine into its constituent parts, spending two full days polishing and cleaning every bolt and nut before reassembling the whole apparatus as new. If he was deeply moved by the experience of working on such a famous Land Rover, his hangdog expression didn't betray it.

Just like the British colonists who built it, we soon discovered that Darjeeling was a good place to put our feet up. While each of us caught up on our respective jobs, Marcus continued to work away the hours on the problem of our entry into China, still an unsolved secret between him, Larry and me. We held whispered conferences late into the night, wargaming what to do if our agreed gamble of 'turning up at the border and hoping for the best' did not pay off. The answer was depressingly elusive, and sooner or later we would have to share with the rest of the team that the fate of our entire journey hung perilously in the balance of an anonymous bureaucrat in distant Beijing.

11

Ayo Gorkhali!

1 October 2019: West Bengal, India
Expedition Day 38

'It's Grandpa's birthday today,' said Nat, heaving kitbags into PAC with unusual speed. The reason for his haste was understandable – after leaving Darjeeling we had made the short journey south-west to the town of Mirik, where we overnighted in preparation for crossing the Nepali border. Mirik, for reasons of perpetual rain and insect-ridden beds, would rank at the top of places to which none of us was keen to return. Given the ubiquitous chill and damp, I mused silently on how it had ever got its name, which in Lepcha means 'place burned by fire'.

As we pulled back onto the road, I had a flashback to January, when Tim had been interviewed by the *Financial Times* about his upcoming adventure. He had joked about having a shot of whisky in Tibet to mark his eighty-eighth year. I looked at Nat – tired, grubby and unshaven – driving Oxford beside me, and pondered how Tim might have been faring had he not been taken ill. Nat had been right back in Thailand, I thought – his grandpa could not have handled the pace we'd kept up this past month. I started to wonder if we could either.

I'd had my first email from Tim that morning since his safe return to London, where he was still recuperating from his hospital ordeal:

It was a great disappointment having to pull out of something that I'd long dreamed of … But it's largely assuaged by my enormous pride in the fact that Nat has taken my place … Wonderful. He phoned me the other day; he's having the time of his life. I know from my own experience of sixty-three years ago that the journey and companionship will be with him for the rest of that life.

Tim was still being non-committal on when, or even if, he would be joining the journey; and, given the gruelling pace we were setting, I had mentally parked any thoughts of return until we'd resolved our passage through China. For now, at least, Nat was staying put. As my mood improved the further we drove from Mirik, I began to see how undertaking this journey with Nat had profoundly changed its nature, and perhaps for the better. Rather than driving down the grizzled adventurer's memory lane, through Nat's perspective I could now see the world with fresh eyes. With the ordeals that I knew lay ahead, fresh eyes were the least we would need.

At the border town of Kakarbhitta, we bid Mr Bunty and Gorkhaland goodbye and crossed into Nepal – the sixth country on our long journey home. Nepal would be the last country for some time where we could still feel the echoes of Tim's original journey. The expedition cars had made a rare split back in late 1955, with Tim, BB and Nigel heading north to Nepal in Oxford, while Adrian, Pat and Henry in Cambridge headed east through India, until they were all reunited in Calcutta.

Oxford, Tim later discovered, was only the third civilian car to use the newly built road heading up to Nepal's capital, Kathmandu. Before then the British ambassador faced a three-day hike to take up residency, while his official limousine was carried behind on the shoulders of eighty coolies. Even by the time of Oxford's arrival, the road was very much still under construction, with Mother Nature doing her best to hold up the road builders wherever she could.

Since 1955, the political wheels in this little mountain nation, sandwiched between the giants of India and China, had revolved in a manner as fiery as the famous curries it exported. The country had tried parliamentary democracy, civil war, and absolutist Hindu monarchy, until the latter was fatally wounded by Nepal's Crown Prince shooting most of his family (and then himself) dead in 2001. Today, this multilingual, multi-ethnic and multi-faith country was a federal republic governed by a fittingly chaotic coalition of Marxists, Leninists and Maoists.

As we were still waiting for the Chinese embassy in Kathmandu to open and pass judgement on our fate, we had replotted a circuitous route via Pokhara, Nepal's second-largest city. For most foreign visitors, Pokhara offers a chance to trek Nepal's stunning Annapurna massif, but we would spend our time here getting to know Nepal's other famous export – the fearsome Gurkha soldiers.

The Gurkhas take their name from the ancient Gorkha kingdom, which from the 1760s conquered much of modern-day Nepal before colliding with the expansionist British East India Company (EIC). In early 1815, while Napoleon and Wellington were squaring up at Waterloo, on the other side of the world the EIC's redcoats were locked in a vicious struggle in the Himalayan foothills.

The ferocity and fearlessness of the Gorkhas left a lasting impression on the Brits. Embracing the age-old adage of 'If you can't beat 'em, join 'em', at the war's close in 1816, a new Gurkha regiment was formed under EIC control. Today, thanks to that deal, which has survived more than two centuries, the Brigade of Gurkhas still forms a vital part of the British Army. We had been invited by Major Sandy Nightingale, who ran the famously brutal selection process, to see what it took to become a Gurkha.

Pulling into the British Army headquarters in Pokhara was like turning suddenly into a corner of Surrey. Only the Annapurna range in the backdrop, looming like icebergs suspended in the sky, gave away that we were in the heart of Nepal. Major Sandy, stocky and earnest, greeted us in camo and shirtsleeves before showing us to our barrack rooms.

That evening, over a spicy Gurkha soup cooked in a great drum over an open fire, Sandy's team of senior Nepali officers told stories of their deployments around the world for another queen and country, with Sandy teasing and joking with the fluent Nepali he'd had to acquire to become an officer in the regiment.

'Ascension Island!' exclaimed Binod, Sandy's second-in-command, as we shared Oxford's incredible resurrection story. 'I went there once, on my way to South Georgia.'

'The European Georgia, or the American one?' David asked, confused as we all were.

'Neither! It's a microscopic little rock in the South Atlantic, 1,500 kilometres south-west of the Falklands, part of the great British Empire!' teased Binod. 'The Argies invaded it back in 1982, and that kicked off the whole Falklands War. Now they send we Gurkhas to keep an eye on it, just in case they try again.'

I had read much of the Gurkhas' legendary bravery in Britain's numerous twentieth-century wars. Indeed, just down the road there were Second World War veterans who had served in Italy, Libya, and the Middle East still being cared for today in Pokhara by a British charity called the Gurkha Welfare Trust. The words of one senior British commander had once summed up their reputation: 'If a man says he is not afraid of dying, he is either lying or he is a Gurkha.' It was hard to square with the kind, gentle men currently cooking me dinner, but Gurkhas continued to serve all around the world, and Britain's foes would no doubt still tremble at the sound of 'Ayo Gorkhali!', the Gurkha's spine-chilling war cry.

I couldn't help but marvel as I listened to their war stories over the fire's fading embers, and it prompted a question I had been chewing over. We'd been driving through the detritus of the British

Empire since setting off from Singapore. How had this 200-year-old bargain survived in a post-imperial world?

'It does feel like the last relic of Empire,' Sandy nodded self-consciously. 'But it seems to work for everyone. The British Army depends on them, and becoming a Gurkha is a golden ticket for young men here. Every year, more than 12,000 of Nepal's toughest and brightest try to pass selection, though only 400 will make the cut.'

'How hard can it be?' I joked.

The major wasn't a joking man. The 6 a.m. mountain sunrise saw me standing alongside Marcus in shorts and a T-shirt, both sporting a traditional Nepali wicker basket, or *doko*, on our backs containing fifteen kilos of sand.

A suspicious wave of 'food poisoning' had struck all but Marcus and me, leaving only the two of us to tackle the final, toughest test of Gurkha selection – the infamous 'Doko Run'. Ahead of us, a gruelling five-kilometre (three-mile) uphill climb through gravel and winding mountain tracks. Aspiring Gurkhas train for years before attempting it. As Sandy blew his whistle, our strict expedition regimen of sitting on our backsides digesting lager and curry was exposed.

The rough basket needled my spine and kidneys, spreading pain to my neck and forehead. I couldn't believe that until recently the official basket had weighed twice as much. Sweat seared my eyes, mixing with sand and grit kicked up by Marcus, who stormed ahead. I had hoped that my more Gurkha-like frame would give me the edge over my lanky comrade, but soon his loping strides gave him a lead of 50 metres (165 feet) and growing. Sandy trotted alongside me, trying not to enjoy my suffering too openly. Up ahead Santosh, the Gurkha's lead trainer, did the same for Marcus. Spine poker-straight and barely breaking a sweat, it was only later I learned with amazement that Santosh was nursing a badly broken toe.

The beauty of the brilliant blue sky and crystal-clear mountain streams that rippled around were sadly lost on me that morning. All I could see was the few metres of gravel in front, and – when I could bear to look up – the sight of Marcus getting ever smaller up ahead. The altitude, well over 2,000 metres (6,500 feet), compressed my lungs. It was an excruciating experience that, to me, justified the Gurkhas' fearsome reputation all by itself.

After a seeming eternity of misery, Sandy gestured to the finish line that was marked by a Nepali woman holding a cowpat, dried and ready for her fire. A sweat-soaked Marcus was triumphantly doubled-over. Finishing this race in under fifty minutes was essential for aspiring Gurkhas, but it still didn't guarantee your entry to the brigade.

I won't share my own effort; suffice to say that I won't be joining Her Majesty's finest any time soon.

7 October 2019: Kathmandu, Nepal
Expedition Day 44

The road to Kathmandu was the most breathtaking to date, a welcome distraction from my latest crippling bout of Oxforditis. Across the convoy the team were unusually quiet, awed as I was by the Himalayan foothills. Below, rivers frothed and foamed like a painting come to life. Above, vertical cliffs sprouted fantastical forests, framed by waterfalls that appeared as if by magic. Soon, however, the telltale signs of a city appeared. Foremost were enormous billboards depicting China's president, Xi Jinping, alongside the squat figure of Bidhya Devi Bhandari, the president of Nepal, celebrating the imminent arrival of President Xi, which was scheduled for the day we were hoping to leave for Tibet.

We entered Kathmandu in the late afternoon, with flimsy red-and-white archways strung across the streets proclaiming: 'Nepal–China Friendship is Great, Deep and Unshakeable!!'

'I've never trusted the double exclamation mark,' muttered David, beside me in Oxford. 'Smacks of desperation.'

Speaking of desperation, the looming verdict on our passage out of Nepal was now dominating our thoughts. We could distract ourselves from it no longer. Marcus's weeks of phone calls and emails to British, Nepali and Chinese embassies had resulted in nothing but deafening silence. Marcus was now planning to take the only course of action left – turn up on the doorstep of the Chinese embassy in Kathmandu.

Leaving Marcus to work his magic, I headed from our guesthouse to meet a journalist contact, Kunda Dixit, in the heart of the old city. We guided our convoy slowly through the maze of backstreets. A devastating earthquake had struck Kathmandu in April 2015, reducing the city's palaces and temples, some of which had stood for a thousand years, to rubble. Through the scaffolds, we caught glimpses of squares still filled with debris. However, as we pulled up to the edge of the city's famous Durbar Square my heart rose to see what had been achieved in just over four years.

The red-brick sixteenth-century Jagan Narayan temple, for example, built to honour a manifestation of Vishnu, had risen completely from the wreckage. It was almost impossible to tell it had been rebuilt as I climbed the steps between its two guardian elephants. It was the Nepal I had hoped to see, that I had always imagined.

Waiting for Kunda in the setting sun, I ambled beneath the eaves of a palace built by the Malla kings, who had ruled this valley for 500 years. Two fierce leogryphs guarded an ornate sandstone doorway, flanked by a pair of enormous, intimidating stone eyes set into the wall. Dark, shiny red footprints peppered the threshold.

As I entered, the sharp smell of blood filled my nostrils. Inside was a scene straight from Dante's *Inferno*, and a stark contrast from the pleasant early-evening bustle in the square outside. Great pools of gore flowed into a channel running four-square around the courtyard. Chattering Nepalis milled through, as if nothing were amiss, the gaps between them revealing the source – two great black buffalos, their headless corpses bound at the feet. A man in a red sarong was skinning one, its head – tongue-lolling – propped on a post behind him.

The stench of blood, faeces and animal fear filled the air, turning my stomach. Despite the gore I couldn't tear my eyes away, darkly fascinated that this could happen in a twenty-first-century city.

'You're enjoying the "Black Night" of Dashain, I see,' said a tall Nepali, his soft accent betraying many years spent outside his homeland. I knew at once it must be Kunda Dixit, the urbane, silver-haired editor of the *Nepali Times*. He'd clearly had little trouble picking my pallid face out of the crowd.

'Durga is a bloodthirsty goddess, Alex. Many here believe if she's not offered animal blood, she will take human blood instead,' Kunda explained, with a slight chuckle. Guiding me outside into fresher air, Kunda informed us that he had scheduled some overdue spiritual maintenance for the expedition.

'This is a time to pay tribute to the tools we rely on, like ploughs or even cars. I've organized a sacrifice especially for yours. Given what lies ahead, I think you'll need it!'

Seeing shock cross my face at the thought of bull's blood all over Oxford's windscreen, Kunda pulled a small, green coconut from his satchel.

'Don't worry! It's perfectly acceptable to sacrifice fruit and vegetables; nothing in the scriptures mandates animals. Some of us are working to stop what you just saw, but the old ways die very hard.'

My relief was palpable as I joined the team now gathered in the square. We lined up Oxford, PAC and Enterprise beside the square, bonnets open. Kunda handed out red and yellow paste to daub the parts of our engines that needed special attention. The Doc and Nat took forensic care painting almost every component under Oxford's bonnet, while Larry and Marcus saw to their own trusty steeds.

'And now, the sacrifice,' announced Kunda, passing a sheepish Nat the coconut. He tried and failed to smash it on Oxford's front bumper, before a wiry man from our growing audience stepped in to deliver the deathblow, sprinkling the milk liberally across all three cars.

'The final offering,' said Kunda, passing three small bananas to Nat, Marcus and Larry. Nat and Marcus tucked theirs into Oxford and PAC's front bumpers, but Larry began fumbling in the boot of his car. He emerged with a much larger banana from his stores.

'Size matters,' Larry grinned, tucking it under the winch like a pair of fruity bullhorns.

While the team headed off for our guesthouse, I sat with Kunda, keen to get his opinion on our China visa hopes without being overheard. Just twenty-four hours from our planned crossing, the Chinese embassy was still stubbornly shut.

'It's unlikely you'll get your visas, now or in the next few weeks,' said Kunda, calmly sipping sweet masala tea. 'With the seventieth anniversary of the Communist Party last week, and the visit of President Xi tomorrow – you couldn't have picked a worse time. The Chinese are on highest alert. The last thing they'll want is a load of foreigners capering around Tibet.'

My heart sank. What would we tell the others? We could either risk Pakistan, turn back and drive for weeks to cross into China via Laos, or sit in Nepal until we were finally let through. There was no good choice.

'Xi's visit is a big deal then?' I ventured.

'Very. The Chinese are promising to spend trillions of dollars on infrastructure. Without new roads and railways through the Himalayas, Nepal will always be too dependent on India. Courting China is all we can do to assert our independence, but it's a dangerous game. China and India are always sabre-rattling around us. We're all still squabbling over lines on the map drawn by you guys!'

I smiled weakly. It was becoming a familiar story.

The next morning, I found myself in a battered little taxi headed to Kathmandu airport. Not to throw in the towel, but rather to send an all-important cargo of hard drives containing all the film footage from the journey so far. Back in the 1950s, BB would do the same, posting his film reels back to an expectant David Attenborough in London.

While the worries about getting into China had been dominating our minds of late, it hadn't quite crowded out my deeper concerns about what might happen to us if we did successfully cross the border. Tibet, and even more so Xinjiang, were the two most politically sensitive provinces of China. Our travelling film crew could attract unwelcome attention, and filmmakers Leo, David and I were now putting plans in place on the assumption that our hard drives could be seized and erased at any time.

I'd offered to make the journey to the airport myself, as I wanted a little time on my own. Today, more than 11,000 kilometres (7,000 miles) away as the crow flies, I knew that my grandad was about to make his own final journey to a crematorium on the outskirts of Manchester. Although my family had told me not to come home, I still felt the guilt of not being there with them to say a last goodbye. In that strange confessional booth that a taxi sometimes becomes, I found myself saying as much to my driver, Bimal.

'We Hindus believe the body is nothing,' he said, pinching his bicep for emphasis. 'It's just a prison for the soul.'

For years now Harold's body had been his prison, behind the bars of which he'd steadily retreated from all who loved him. His failing brain tissue had leaked a lifetime of memory and let a body he'd tended to so carefully wither and fade.

'Here in Nepal, we burn it quickly, to set the soul free.' Bimal continued, catching my glassy eyes in the mirror. 'Today, he will be free.'

Bimal's words unleashed a final wave of grief that I had felt building these last few days. Tears fell, but this time they were tears of relief. However hard it had been to watch his decline into dementia, experiencing it from within must have been more difficult still. But he was free from that now, I realized, and free to roam wherever he liked. Free, I hoped, to find Joyce's hand, and perhaps the forgiveness he'd needed for so long.

As I wiped the final tears from my eyes, I saw the towers of the city airport approaching through the taxi's windscreen. I watched a plane landing on the runway, realizing it was the first plane I'd seen up close since leaving Singapore. It had taken almost seven weeks to reach Kathmandu from Singapore, a journey that would have taken only six hours by air.

I suddenly felt ridiculous at instigating this inefficient, uncomfortable and ruinously expensive journey that now kept me away from my nearest and dearest. I could pack it in now, I thought, grab a flight and be back in Manchester to hug my mum before the sun went down.

But as I looked down at the callouses on my hands, flexed the sinews in my forearms, and felt the length in my beard and hair, for the briefest moment I could smell my grandad's old leather jacket in a rainy English wood. In that moment, I felt the sadness lift, and in its place came a surge of gratitude along with a rush of memories: of Vicky, Aleena, Sithu, Rajan, and countless others who had cared for and guided us so far. I saw the sunset in Alor Setar and the sunrise in Sagaing. A tidal wave of sounds, smells and faces enveloped me, fragments of a life-changing journey only possible over land.

Of course, choosing to make this journey over land might be filled with difficulty, but therein were its rewards. No plane could take us from here to western Tibet; no railway reached Xinjiang beyond – the only way to get where we were going was to drive one of the highest roads in the world, and the car we were going to do it in was a battered, sixty-four-year-old museum piece. I looked again at the photo of my grandad as a young man, a man fascinated by all things mechanical, and had little doubt he would have approved.

On my return, I almost bounced into the guesthouse garden to find Marcus in what looked like a similar state of euphoria. I quickly discovered his glazed expression was down to his finally passing through extreme panic to the Elysian Fields of calm beyond. We had still had no news from the agency organizing our Chinese visas for our border crossing scheduled tomorrow.

'There's really no need to worry,' he said, every cell under the calm exterior vibrating with concern.

'Why's that?' I asked, hopefully.

'Because there's absolutely nothing we can do about it.'

Finding solace in my old friend's newly discovered zen philosophy, we settled in to wait.

It was 11 October, our forty-eighth day on our long journey home to London. As I stepped out into the cool morning air, I was all too aware that it could be our last. After days of tense waiting, it was D-Day. The Chinese embassy in Kathmandu was finally reopening, and we prayed that top of the embassy's list would be our expedition's fate. We were already two weeks behind schedule because of the embassy's impromptu closure, and the Chinese authorities' refusal could bring our journey to an embarrassing and premature end.

Despite my renewed sense of faith that it would somehow all work out, I couldn't deny Kunda's warning still weighed on me.

The rest of the team packed, oblivious that our fate rested with an unknown Chinese bureaucrat. Eager to find a distraction, I sought comfort in *First Overland*. Tim and co had skirted the Chinese border while in Burma:

> Henry and Pat had found a small raft, and poled themselves across the Bamboo Curtain to exchange views with a peasant on the far side. They gave him some cigarettes as a token of goodwill and then returned to the free world a few minutes later. Pat suggested that

he might one day write a book called *Ten Minutes in China*.

We might go down in history as having spent less time in China than Henry and Pat, I realized with a shudder. If we crossed as hoped, however, we would depart from their tyre tracks for thousands of kilometres, crossing entirely new territory for Oxford until we re-joined the First Overland route in Turkey.

Tim could help me no longer. It was time to consign my faithful companion to my backpack for now, reflecting that of all the change the world had witnessed since that book was written, China's rise was the most extreme. Little did he know, but the peasant with whom Henry and Pat had exchanged pleasantries was about to witness one of history's most ruthless, breathtaking acts of state-building.

Mao Zedong's victory in a devastating civil war established a new Communist republic in 1949. After consolidating power, in 1958 Mao announced China's 'Great Leap Forward' – a cocktail of disastrous economic and social reforms that, within three years, killed somewhere between 15 and 45 million people. Worse followed with Mao's 'Cultural Revolution' in 1966, leading to tens of millions more deaths, widespread terror, famine and cannibalism.

After Mao's own death in 1976, much of his calamitous vision for China was quietly shelved. The Communist Party he had brought to power, however, lived on. Now celebrating seven decades in power, it exercised near-total control over a population that had ballooned to 1.4 billion and ran the world's second-largest economy. In every country we'd passed through so far, we had witnessed a complex combination of hope and suspicion at their giant neighbour's power. That concern was shared in distant Paris, London and Washington.

As I pondered just how radically China had changed within the space of one lifetime, the tranquillity of the guesthouse garden was shattered by a delighted cry. Marcus burst into the early-morning calm of the garden bearing eight brown envelopes as if they were the FA Cup. All thoughts of China's looming threat forgotten, I jumped up and hugged him, spilling chai everywhere. Weeks of graft had been rewarded – we were behind schedule, but finally on course. Our own, entirely new course.

We were going to China.

PART 2

NEPAL TO THE CASPIAN SEA

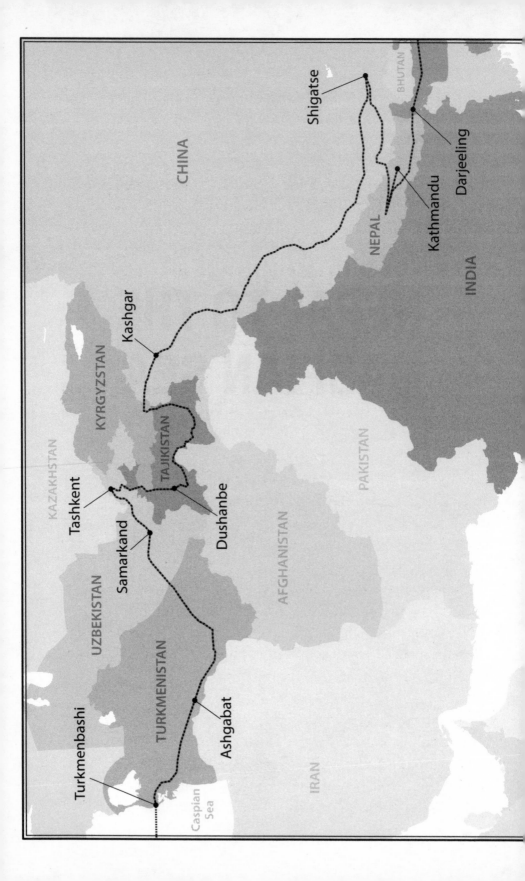

12
The Saga of Saga County

11 October 2019: Kathmandu, Nepal
Expedition Day 48

Even though we now had official permission to enter Tibet, there was still the small matter of almost 160 kilometres (100 miles) of terrifyingly steep, earthquake-damaged roads from Kathmandu to the Chinese border that needed crossing first. Persistent rain had turned whole sections into raging rapids; the team was tense and severe as we crawled sluggishly upwards.

Nat was beside me in the passenger seat of PAC, pale, drawn and with eyes closed. Perhaps, I thought, it was from the lingering after-effects of the food poisoning that had struck half the team down in Pokhara. Or possibly from the severe vertigo that a glance out of the window brought on.

'Your grandpa always thought his descendants would be immune from carsickness after he completed his journey,' I said.

Nat's raised an eyebrow in protest, but his eyes remained firmly closed. Up ahead I watched Marcus piloting Oxford only inches from the edge of a sheer drop, and tried not to let my stomach turn too.

To stop my imagination getting carried away with thoughts of Marcus's imminent demise, I pictured President Xi cruising sedately overhead and looking down on our progress. We'd heard sceptics mutter about the sinister intent behind China's trillion-dollar 'Belt and Road Initiative' to revolutionize the road and rail connections up here – right then, I wished they'd hurry the hell up.

The temperature dropped rapidly as we climbed ever higher towards the border, and layers were donned as we left the lowland heat behind. Snow-capped mountains surrounded us, and somewhere up ahead lay Everest – the greatest of them all.

At last, the road signs heralded the border crossing and the road began to level out. Our collective relief was soon dimmed, however, by two Nepali policeman at a makeshift roadblock.

'Out!' barked the taller, holding a large, battered rifle. We complied.

'Off,' he snapped, indicating the scarves tied to Oxford's front wing mirrors; gifts from our many hosts in West Bengal and Nepal. Larry explained they could be interpreted as support for the Dalai Lama, the exiled spiritual leader of Tibet. The police were vigilant for any sniff of anti-Chinese sentiment during President Xi's visit. Now free to enter China, we had tasted how careful we had to be to ensure we could leave again.

'German?' asked the policeman, tapping Oxford's bonnet.

'British,' I said. He raised his eyebrows, waving us on.

We were leaving behind the Land of the Land Rovers, and Oxford's celebrity. With new terrain came a new phenomenon – no one had a clue who we were. The feeling was weirdly refreshing, and in that moment exhilaration trumped any fear. By crossing into China, we were about to make our own piece of history, showing Oxford her first new country in sixty-four years.

Around the next corner was the final Nepalese customs house, but it could have been easily mistaken for a mining shack. After all the drama around this moment, it felt like we were now sneaking out of the back door. Chickens scratched while we emptied the cars for what would be the first thorough inspection on our journey. Our packs of camera equipment raised surprisingly little alarm. After checking again to see if we had any images of the Dalai Lama, or anything suggesting Tibet should be 'free', the guards seemed most preoccupied by Marcus's jar of Marmite, hidden in his rucksack for emergency use.

Marcus's precious yeast extract recovered, a short road took us to the entrance to China. Rounding a cliff face, we were suddenly in a narrow valley, bisected by a frothing river. A wide, tarmacked bridge crossed to an enormous building of pale-grey stone and darkened glass. Huge Chinese characters were emblazoned on it, and red flags streamed from the ramparts.

A final detachment of Nepali border guards waved us through to the bridge, where imposing Chinese guards in black uniforms, facemasks and dark glasses signalled us to park up. All passengers were ordered to step out of the car and walk across the bridge, while the three drivers slowly advanced behind them. I watched guiltily from Oxford as Nat, Leo, David, Tibie and the Doc marched ahead, squinting in the harsh sunlight and pulling their jackets close to shield from a biting crosswind. Reaching the imposing gatehouse building at last, the contrast to the Nepali exit was staggering. We were about to go backwards two and a half hours in time, but at the same time go forward by what felt like decades.

'The Chinese like a statement piece,' whispered Larry, as we emptied the cars of every bag and box under the impassive stares of the Chinese border guards. We lugged them into the main hall of the gatehouse, a colossal marble room equipped to hold hundreds of visitors. Our bedraggled, dusty crew weaved absurdly through the carefully demarcated queuing corridor, watched by poker-faced border officials in pristine black uniforms.

We placed our passports in a machine that automatically spoke in our native language. Fingerprint and iris scans were followed by the machine declaring: 'Biometric acquisition complete'. It felt straight out of Orwell. When presented with the final on-screen question, 'How was your experience?', I hurriedly pressed 'Greatly Satisfied', as if my entry depended on it.

Every bag was unpacked and searched. David, Nat and Leo were pulled into side rooms for questioning. Larry was locked in a bad-tempered exchange with a guard who wanted to confiscate a kukri knife he had bought in Pokhara, while the Doc hopped from one side of the border to the other, singing, 'Nepal, China! Nepal, China!' Looking back, the mixture of underlying tension, frustration and absurdity in that moment was an omen for things to come.

A tide of relief washed over me as eight people and three cars thankfully emerged intact. Leo and David noted with particular relief the surprising lack of questions about our bundles of camera equipment.

'They seemed to be more intrigued by our haircuts,' confessed Leo, whose thick black mane was starting to develop a life of its own.

Stylish or not, at last we had made it to China, our seventh country. It was an achievement in its own right – now all we had to do was both cross and leave it. The man responsible for that was leaning on a large Toyota Land Cruiser, dressed in black with matching sunglasses. Born and raised in Tibet, Lhakpa was handsome, soft-spoken and – I would quickly come to learn – completely inscrutable. He was one of only two guides in the whole country sanctioned to bring foreigners driving their own cars through China overland, and I immediately wondered what compromises and limitations he'd had to make to secure such a treasured status in a region as sensitive as Tibet.

He shook hands with us all, before beckoning us to follow him on to the smooth black tarmac that wound ever upwards onto the Tibetan Plateau.

Within moments of entering China, the bone-breaking, axle-rattling roads of northern Nepal were a distant memory. Oxford sang as a rejuvenated Nat powered her onwards and upwards on slick, black roads entirely free of other cars, until an immaculate traffic light stopped us in our path.

'You know, I think those are the first working ones we've seen since Mandalay,' said Nat, waiting patiently for the lights to change.

I thought of the arduous kilometres this old car had crossed since then, and the many, many more to come. As we climbed ever higher, the green, forested slopes that had surrounded us since making for Pokhara began to recede. In their place were steep slopes brushed with yellows, browns and greys, a semi-lunar landscape that heralded our arrival onto the Tibetan Plateau.

Our first night in China was spent in the town of Gyirong, about 30 kilometres (20 miles) from the border crossing. I hadn't known what to expect of Tibet, but Gyirong certainly wasn't it. The town was immaculate, as if built last week. It had the feel of a deserted Alpine ski resort, with surgically clean supermarkets and spotless public squares.

Next morning, Lhakpa guided us through tidy backstreets in total darkness, bundled up like polar explorers against the cold, close to minus-ten degrees. Even though it was almost 9 a.m., the sun had yet to make an appearance.

'Why is it so dark?' asked Tibie, voicing what we were all thinking.

'China has only one time zone,' Lhakpa replied, 'Beijing time. The sun will rise after 9 a.m. today; at some times of the year it sets around midnight in western China.'

During my research for the journey, western China had taken up a lot of my attention. I had read much about the efforts of the central government to impose their writ on Tibet and the neighbouring province of Xinjiang in recent decades. Successive Chinese governments from the Ming to Mao had seen these two westernmost territories as the 'natural' western frontier of the country – often only theoretically, and always at the intense displeasure of the local inhabitants – but it was in the last half-century that central power had become so evident here.

The central time zone, the importance of which I had overlooked until now as we stumbled through Gyirong's dark streets in search of breakfast, was the prime example of the central government's high-handedness in dealing with their westernmost and traditionally most restless citizens. It was brought in by Mao in 1949 to promote national unity, and like many of his dangerous whims, had come at the expense of the people who had to live with it.

Separated in the darkness, Nat, David and Leo had disappeared into a side street, where they erupted into a tide of giggles. The source of the fuss turned out to be a large, spot-lit vending machine filled with a range of colourful and highly inventive sex toys.

'That is not exactly the image I had in mind when I pictured Tibet,' I admitted.

'You have to keep an open mind in China,' Larry chuckled, as Lhakpa ushered us through a doorway covered with a thick hanging carpet. As he heaved it aside, a waft of delicious smelling steam filled my nostrils, my stomach quickly taking control over my struggling eyes.

After a delicious breakfast of soup dumplings and tea, I jumped into Enterprise alongside Larry. The poker-faced Lhakpa was proving to be predictably cagey when I posed questions outside of basic logistics, so I was reliant on Larry – our resident Chinese speaker – to understand this brave new world.

'We're supposed to be heading north-west, towards Xinjiang,' Larry explained. 'But first we have to drive 600 kilometres the other way to register the cars in Shigatse. It's the nearest large town to here.'

Looking at the maps unfolding on his various dashboard screens, the sheer scale of Tibet was clear. Between us and Shigatse was one of the world's highest roads. Over the next two days we crossed passes as high as 5,200 metres (17,000 feet), more than halfway up Everest. Indeed, we stopped at a sign directing us to the Everest Base Camp, where we took in that famous pyramidal mountain on the horizon. I was struck by a feeling of spiritual awe, probably encouraged by the altitude, whose effects were starting to be felt across the team.

'You all need to be more careful, take it slower,' Larry warned, advice we would soon regret ignoring.

Back in Enterprise, Larry was in his element. He chattered enthusiastically about this country, from which both his parents had emigrated to Singapore, where he was later born.

'Many criticize China for annexing Tibet,' he explained. 'But the government has invested a fortune here – look at these roads, and there's 4G signal everywhere you go! They get nothing in return, there's barely any revenue.'

We would occasionally pass villages of neat houses, flat red roofs visible over low compound walls.

'When I drove through in 2007, none of these were here,' he explained. 'Now these villages get electricity, schools, good roads. All thanks to the central government.'

This rose-tinted perspective was new to me. We talked about the Dalai Lama, who had been forced to flee in 1959 along the same road we'd taken through north-east India. I argued that surely forcing the rightful ruler of Tibet into exile wasn't a good thing.

'The Dalai Lama abandoned his people,' Larry countered, uncharacteristically emotional. 'And maybe it was for the best. Tibet under the Dalai Lamas was so poor, all the money went to the monasteries. There's a joke among Tibetans – the last place on Earth you'd want to be reincarnated is here. Now they have a better way of life.'

It was tough to square what Larry was saying with the idea of Tibet's status that I'd grown up with in the UK. At university, I had sometimes seen 'Free Tibet' protests among the endless cycle of causes we students were incensed about, and I had once attended a seminar given by the Dalai Lama in London, where he'd talked movingly about his and his people's disastrous treatment at the hands of the Chinese government.

Instinctively, I felt the Tibetans had every right to feel aggrieved by the removal of their independence, and the exile of a leader of the calibre of the 14th Dalai Lama; but having barely seen a Tibetan to ask directly as we sped through this beautiful, spartan wilderness, it was hard to truly know.

Shigatse, Tibet's second-largest city, hammered Larry's point home. Almost entirely rebuilt in the last fifteen years, neat shops selling every mod con imaginable lined spotless pavements. Squint, and it could have been Singapore.

Lhakpa pulled up alongside to make a rare offer of information from behind his opaque glasses. Larry, Marcus and I, the registered drivers, needed to register ourselves and our cars as fit to drive in China. The fact that we'd already been driving in China for three days was, apparently, irrelevant.

Lhakpa joined me in Oxford as we headed to the local registry office, and I realized that this was the first opportunity I'd had to talk to him alone. Given Lhakpa was a native Tibetan, I was keen to check whether what Larry had said was felt by Tibetans themselves.

'Since 2008, the Chinese have transformed Tibet,' Lhakpa intoned, with little feeling.

'What happened in 2008?' I asked innocently.

'There was a lot of unrest, but now it's ended,' he said, turning his head away to look out of the window.

He clearly didn't want to divulge about the violent protests that had unfolded here, with Tibetans angry at the increasing numbers of mainland Chinese moving in. The uprising sparked sympathetic protests across China and the world, but was ruthlessly stifled. Foreign media were evicted in an effort to kill the story while China was hosting the Olympics in Beijing. It was simply the latest in a series of uprisings by Tibetans deeply unhappy with the formerly independent country's integration into China, a project that had been started only a few years before Oxford's last great adventure. Now, the central government seemed to be doing all it could to bribe and cajole the Tibetans into accepting their fate.

'Turn left,' said Lhakpa, relieved to change the subject. Over the next few hours, the cars would be inspected for roadworthiness, taxed and insured.

'Next,' Lhakpa announced, 'you must pass your Chinese driving tests.'

'But I don't speak or read Chinese!' I exclaimed, omitting that I'd also disastrously failed my UK driving test first time round, and that was in English.

'Don't worry – I've arranged for an English-speaking instructor.'

The cars, even Oxford, breezed through their road checks. The only query was why our engines were daubed with coloured paint, the remains of the blessing Kunda had organized in Kathmandu. My explanation was met with mild indignance. In strictly secular China, it seemed spirituality was as welcome beneath the bonnet as it was out in public life. Oxford was getting a lot of attention, as mechanics from across the inspection centre came to take a look at their first Series I Land Rover. One began to punch the door while another kicked the wings furiously while pulling heavily on a cigarette.

I moved to intervene, but Larry held me back.

'It's okay, here in China to hit is to love.'

The two men started laughing to one another, before giving me a delighted thumbs-up.

Now for the humans to be deemed roadworthy. After fifty days on the road since leaving Singapore, my battered, pudgy body didn't seem much good for anything else.

Luckily all we were required to do was pass an eye test and prove that we had eight fingers and two thumbs to properly hold the steering wheel. The latter was done via my brand-new Chinese driving-licence photo, in which I held out all ten appendages in gormless jazz-hands around my grinning face. I'll treasure it for ever.

Finally, the theory test. Marcus, Larry and I waited in a long queue to enter a neighbouring building, as Lhakpa went to track down our specially assigned English-speaking instructor.

'This is when your English tradition of never learning other languages is really going to catch up with you,' joked the capably bilingual Larry. I couldn't argue.

After an uncomfortably long wait, Lhakpa returned looking uncharacteristically sheepish.

'Good news – you've passed the theory test.'

Marcus and I exchanged puzzled glances.

'The English-speaking instructor is on leave today,' Lhakpa explained, with a shrug.

Marcus and I both sagged with relief. It turned out to be premature.

'Bad news – I've just heard from the police that Oxford is too old to drive in China. Forty-four years too old, to be exact.'

My mouth hung open in disbelief, while Marcus flushed with fury.

'What?! How could you not know that! We told you months ago how old the car was!' he hissed in a stage whisper, trying not to make a scene while being apocalyptically furious.

Lhakpa shrugged. 'This is China. Rules change. You were lucky to get in at all.'

'But how do we get out?!' I asked, my temper now flaring.

'Drive,' Lhakpa responded, his face impassive once more. 'We leave right now, the police will look the other way. Just don't hit anything until you reach Kyrgyzstan.'

The news in Shigatse left us shaken. Oxford was now driving without Chinese plates, which meant if we were stopped at any point over the next 2,900 kilometres (1,800 miles), we could be fined or arrested. Lhakpa decided that evening to suddenly become more communicative, holding a team meeting in our hotel lobby. What he had to say was no more encouraging.

'Firstly. The border crossing from China into Kyrgyzstan is closing, so you have to speed up your drive or you will be stuck. It will mean longer drives, fewer stops – you will need to plan fuel intake carefully.'

Marcus, who was still recovering from the afternoon's revelation, began to simmer back to a boil.

'Second. Until Xinjiang Province, we are going to be driving and sleeping at very high altitude, up to 4,500 metres. Some of you are struggling already. It is going to get worse.

'Third thing. We are getting higher, so it is getting colder. Down to minus twenty at night. Final thing. The accommodation. We are going into the most remote part of Tibet – it will be very bad.'

We sat in silence.

'Well,' I said, looking for the silver lining, 'if the accommodation's terrible, it's freezing cold and cripplingly high, at least it's a good thing we're in a rush?'

Larry turned to me sternly.

'We must take the altitude seriously. It's very dangerous. So far you all seem to think it's funny. It's not. You must hydrate lots, sleep often, move slowly.'

'What about Viagra?' asked Nat, equally seriously. 'My grandpa told me we should take it up here to combat altitude sickness.'

'Did you bring any?' I asked.

He shook his head.

'I did,' grinned Larry, 'but it's for personal use!'

In response to our accelerated schedule and the harsh conditions, this little team – many of whom had never met each other before Singapore – developed a focus and steel that only shared endurance can forge. We would need it. The week-long journey from Shigatse was the most brutal of our journey.

An intensely dry cold played havoc with lips and fingertips, which cracked and bled as layers came on and off. Oxford's lack of any heating or insulation made it torture to drive in the early morning, but even in PAC and Enterprise, you struggled for warmth. Nat adopted a cunning trick of sneaking hard-boiled eggs – a Tibetan staple – up his gloves to warm them.

The altitude too was punishing. During the day I felt like I was living in a freezer while someone sat on my chest and stuck needles in my heart. At night, headaches and shortness of breath disturbed my sleep, leaving me with a hangover without the joy of drinking the night before. And I wasn't the worst hit.

On 16 October, after an eleven-hour, 400-kilometre (250-mile) drive, we arrived in the appropriately named county of Saga. Leo fell first, slurring his speech and leaning on David – also struggling – to reach his bed. The Doc hooked our formerly invincible film crew to an oxygen machine, and both lay on their beds sucking through plastic nasal tubes.

'Don't let me die here,' joked Leo half-heartedly.

'You have to keep him awake,' the Doc warned, instructing me to stay. Seeing Leo laid low like this was worrying. He and I had been on many a reckless adventure together in the wildest corners of Myanmar, and this hardy Parisian was always the last to make a fuss. I knew it must be serious.

Nat, meanwhile, was vomiting in a room down the corridor. Tibie looked on with concern, battling her own thumping headache while offering a nauseous Nat a cocktail of pungent essential oils that she swore by.

The critical patients stabilized, I joined Marcus and Larry in the lobby. Both were faring relatively well and, true to form, were hungry.

'Where's the Doc?' I asked.

'He's checked himself into hospital – suspected acute mountain sickness,' said Larry.

Larry had been right. We'd not approached the Tibetan altitude with the seriousness it deserved, and now in the land where – despite official efforts – karma was still stitched into the national fabric, we were getting our just desserts.

Luckily the next morning the Doc was safely discharged, and Leo, David and Nat began to improve as their bodies slowly adjusted. We had been humbled by Tibet, and set off that day with the respect that this terrain and its inhabitants demanded. Given our relentless pace, interactions with Tibetans were few and far between. I suspected it was by design, and Lhakpa was still reluctant to help translate in the few occasions when we had people willing to talk. In the few interactions we were lucky enough to have, I learned that to call Tibetans hardy was to do them a disservice –

they were tougher than the mahogany to which the burning sun turned their skin. I'll never forget our first stop in a Tibetan village for lunch.

We were quickly mobbed by men, women and children, each wrapped in their traditional *chuba*. This long-sleeved loose coat was adaptable for the wildly swinging temperatures and doubled as a huge pocket for carrying anything from personal items to small livestock. Most were topped with fetching, felt cowboy hats, perched on long black hair, sometimes rolled into thick curls around fragments of wood, coloured stone or bone.

Both men and women were jangling with amulets, jewellery and all manner of trinkets hanging from their belts and necks. They were a feast for the eyes, making them so disarmingly charming that five young men were able to force us gently out of Oxford, before asking us to take their photos as they clambered clumsily over the roof, windscreen and bonnet.

For the most part, however, we saw Tibetans at great distance from our windows, leading animals in the desolate expanse that stretched for miles before curving up to distant mountain ranges or threshing thin yellow corn. I struggled to think how I would describe the country or city in which I lived; it would be so alien to everything they knew.

Every few hundred kilometres, the parched tundra was occasionally pocked with a lake of the most dramatic, eye-watering blue. There were no trees, making pee stops problematic for Tibie, who – unlike her uncouth male companions – always preferred decent foliage to hide behind.[7]

Given Lhakpa's reluctance to offer up context, I spent the few precious hours each day when I wasn't too cold or delirious to think clearly, drowning myself in the beautiful bleakness of Tibet.

---

7   We had tried to brave Tibet's infamous pit latrines at its few-and-far-between petrol stations, before being completely overcome by the intense, noxious gas. I quickly learned why Tibetans preferred to shit outside.

I still struggle to describe it. It was something like the Scottish Highlands, if they were a hundred times larger, or perhaps the Tora Bora mountains, only a hundred times wider.

While dawn brought shades of brown, grey and yellow, sunset was met with a kaleidoscope of blues, reds and golds. It was simply magnificent. The Chinese had tried to tame Tibet with this highway, but it was merely a thin black line in this colossal canopy of colour. Within it, our convoy looked like Matchbox cars on a planet far from Earth.

After three days' drive from Saga, Lhakpa pointed to a solitary, granite mountain standing proudly ahead with a curious four-sided peak. I had been awaiting this sight ever since Marcus, Tim and I had first sketched a route through Tibet.

'Mount Kailash. We will stay the night here.'

I've always been fascinated by holy mountains. I had trekked to see the silhouette of Mount Olympus in Greece, and hiked overnight to see sunrise from Mount Sinai in Egypt. While you feel an echo of the divine at each one, the ease with which they can now be climbed has in part shattered their mystique.

Kailash, however, was different. It's the mother of all holy mountains, standing at over 6,500 metres (21,300 feet) and sacred in not one but five religious traditions. For millennia Buddhists, Jains, Hindus, Bons and Ayyavazhi pilgrims have made the arduous journey to this most remote of earthly shrines, believing it to be home to their gods, a font of divine knowledge, and the centre of the universe.

Dripping in divinity, it has never been climbed. Legendary climber Reinhold Messner warned, 'If we conquer this mountain, then we conquer something in people's souls.' Unlike the famous peak of Everest not so far from where we stood, where climbers queue to take a selfie on the summit, it was somehow comforting to think that no human feet had touched the peak towering over my eyeline.

We passed through the town of Darchen, lying in the shadow

of the mountain. As the mountain drew closer, I spotted several strange bundles of wool and rags crawling like caterpillars on the path to the base.

'Pilgrims,' said Lhakpa.

We followed on behind as they made their way to a small fire where more dusty bundles were unpacking thermos flasks and food. They were Tibetans who had come from a village 65 kilometres (40 miles) away. One, who introduced himself as Tsering, explained this was his fourth pilgrimage to Kailash.

'We must travel fifty-four kilometres to circle the holy mountain,' Tsering explained via Lhakpa. 'It will take eighteen days.'

'You can walk around in maybe three or four days,' Lhakpa explained, 'but for the very devout it takes much longer.'

He indicated the tattered padding strapped to Tsering's knees and hands, then asked Tsering to demonstrate how he prostrated himself flat, marked a line with his fingers, rose to his feet, walked to the line, then fell to his knees and started over again.

'He just told me they've been going for ten days already, and this is the *fourth* time he's done it,' Lhakpa added. Even our usually stoic guide seemed genuinely impressed.

'Can I ask why?' I said.

Lhakpa translated as Tsering explained.

'We're paying homage to the deities and praying for all sins to be released. Not just ours, but all sentient beings'.'

It was an astonishingly unselfish feat of endurance in pursuit of spiritual purity. Simply walking around the mountain at this altitude was difficult enough. More than that, to me Tsering and his companions were also a living, breathing testament to how the efforts of the Chinese government to erase the old ways of thinking and believing here in Tibet had yet to win out entirely.

Nestled around a weakly smouldering fire, the flames gasping for air with the rest of us, Tsering offered me a cup of salty butter tea, and asked about our journey. As Lhakpa explained our drive from Singapore to London, Tsering's wizened, sunburned face lit up in admiration. Here at Mount Kailash, we were about 7,200 kilometres (4,500 miles) from London, and 4,000 kilometres (2,500 miles) from Singapore by crow's flight. As I showed him the map, I thought how even if everything went to plan, we still had another two months of driving ahead of us, and right down the road, the most politically challenging section of our journey lay in wait.

For one brief moment, however, Tsering's enthusiasm washed all my doubts away. He thumped me on the back, conferring hearty approval from one dusty, weary pilgrim to another. 'Singapore' and 'London' were no doubt just words to someone who lived up here on the roof of the world; but after all we'd been through to get here, the admiration of a man who spent his holidays crawling marathons filled me with a deep and reassuring sense of purpose.

As we turned to leave, I took one last, lingering look at the mountain and clenched my mind, hoping to fix that haunting profile there for ever.

13

Fear and Loathing in Xinjiang

18 October 2019: Darchen, China

Expedition Day 55

In the dawn twilight, happily wrapped in the six layers I had slept in, I sat on the guesthouse doorstep drinking in the holy mountain one last time. Reaching Mount Kailash felt like a milestone. For six days we had endured Tibet. Now, we were enjoying it. The altitude, cold, sleep-deprivation and rugged digs had bonded our overlanding family closer than ever.

I could see it in the little things – the bag gently helped on to tired shoulders, the packet of biscuits carefully shared eight ways, the hugs and jokes exchanged before we set off on yet another stretch of Tibet's seemingly endless roads. Of course, there were fractious moments too – cross words had and pet peeves pushed – but they were always overcome by a shared, unspoken understanding: nothing could endanger the goal we had set.

Larry emerged beside me, stemming a nosebleed; even our veteran overlander was feeling the altitude. The Doc checked him over.

'You're bleeding … it means you still have blood. Good!' He waltzed away, cackling.

Besides human bodies, Adam had warned that altitude and cold could play havoc with the cars, particularly starting in the thin oxygen. He was right – the hills were alive with the sound of Larry and Marcus failing to start their engines.

To my delight, Oxford started first time. The fact she ran on petrol, which vaporized at much lower temperatures, was to her advantage. I drove magnanimous circles around the two diesel cars, trying to raise morale. Mine, not theirs.

As I waited for Larry and Marcus, I looked afresh at the battered old car that had carried us so capably thousands of kilometres through some of the toughest terrain on Earth. She was filled with trinkets from her journey, each bringing back a rush of memories. Where else but in Oxford would you find a waving cat from Singapore, Thai toll-gate tickets, and a plaster bust of Myanmar's democratic icon, Aung San Suu Kyi?

For the first six countries on our journey, Oxford had been on a comeback tour. The grand old dame had been on what felt like a swansong along the roads of her youth. But here in China, it was as if she was born again. Every kilometre under her wheels was new, the dust that gathered in every nook and cranny completely fresh. And the seven countries that lay between us and Turkey were all waiting to be driven for the first time. She was on a brand-new adventure, and from the way she was chewing up the road, I felt she was enjoying it as much as we were.

I saw that Larry too, once we got back on the road, was in his element. I was glad for it, as I know he had been hard hit by Tim's departure from our overlanding family. The chance to overland with the man who had inspired him had been the reason he'd signed up to join us, but instead he himself had become the accidental elder statesman. It was a role he was growing into now; and, although he was a cynic by nature, Tibet brought out a softer, more philosophical side in him. As vast expanses unfolded all around, he talked movingly about love, marriage and family. He had brought his wife Simone and daughter Lucy on his last great overland in 2015, and fondly recalled how Lucy had seen snow for the first time in Tibet.

Above: Marcus (L) and I flank lead trainer Santosh at the finish line of the infamous Doko Run – the final stage in the selection process for the British Army's fearsome Brigade of Gurkhas.

Below: The Last Overland team join British charity the Gurkha Welfare Trust on a visit to the Nepalese village of Arthar, home to many serving and veteran Gurkha soldiers.

Above: PAC, Enterprise and Oxford eagerly await their spiritual blessing – or *puja* – in the Nepali capital, Kathmandu.

Below: The expedition crosses the vast expanse of the Tibetan Plateau, with the Himalayan mountains up ahead.

Above: David, Nat and Tibie and I start to feel the dizzying effects of driving at over 5,000 m (16,400 ft) in Tibet, while expedition manager Marcus looks impatiently on.

Below: Oxford cautiously navigates the winding mountain roads north of Kathmandu, Nepal, on the way to an uncertain reception at the Chinese border.

Above: A chilly Doc tends to his favourite patient in Xinjiang Province. A blocked fuel line has brought her to a halt, but a quick manual siphon should do the trick. Where's Nat …?

Below: No man's land. Heading through the 14.5 km (9-mile) buffer zone between the borders of Kyrgyzstan and Tajikistan, and to the start of the infamous Pamir Highway.

Above: The colossal dome of the Turkmenbashi Ruhy Mosque, outside Ashgabat, Turkmenistan. Built by and named after Turkmenistan's first post-independence leader to fit 10,000 worshippers.

Left: When the wheels – quite literally – fall off your expedition. The Doc surveys the damage after Oxford's rear wheel removes itself while I was driving full speed in eastern Turkmenistan.

Below: Less weight, more speed! Nat and I test one of Oxford's nifty 1950s customizations near Murghab, Tajikistan, as we prepare to take on the Taliban-haunted road along the Afghan border.

Above: Back on (very) dry land. Fresh from crossing the Caspian Sea, Oxford and PAC cross the desertscapes of Gobustan National Park in Azerbaijan.

Below: Laughter is always the best medicine. Larry, the Doc and Nat monitor Oxford's dicky alternator on the road in Uzbekistan.

Above: Oxford prepares to set a world record – for age, not speed! – at the Istanbul Formula 1 Racing Circuit in Turkey.

Below: The Last Overland team after trying and sadly failing to recreate the iconic First Overland 'brew-up' at the foot of the Eiffel Tower in Paris, France.

Above: Reunited at last:
Nat and Tim embrace
in Folkestone, England.
Mission complete.

Left: Reunited at last:
Harold and Joyce at
home in Manchester,
England.

'I don't have a lot of money, but I can leave her rich in memories. Maybe in sixty years' time she'll drive Enterprise back to Singapore!' He patted his beloved steering wheel. 'Do her dad proud.'

Later that morning, Larry and I waited for a herd of goats, goaded gently by a shepherd bundled in countless multicoloured layers, to slowly cross the immaculate tarmac. It was the first sign of life we had seen in hours. A broad grin spread across Larry's face.

'When you're in Tibet, with the cold, the altitude, the long driving days, you'll often find yourself thinking, why on Earth did I come? But trust me, one day you'll find yourself thinking, when can I go back?'

From Darchen we continued north to Gar, another neat new town. Passing a hardware store, I spotted a window full of enormous camouflage jackets trimmed with fake fur – the kind worn by Tibetans we had seen working outdoors in this harsh climate. The Doc, Nat and I had underestimated quite how cold Tibet would be and had packed too light, so we bought one each for the price of a pint in London. The fact that we now looked like a ragtag militia didn't matter – for the first time since being in Tibet, we were truly warm.

Even though our overnight accommodation in much of Tibet became little more than a room to lie flat in, I was starting to sleep more deeply than I had in days. Learning never to undress was a crucial survival trick, and only a fetching new Tibetan cowboy hat differentiated my indoor and outdoor look. We began to live like the Tibetans, lounging in the sun whenever we could find it before retreating through thick-carpeted doorways to huddle around iron stoves, the staple noodle soup in hand.

On our final day in Tibet, I was sitting beside Nat in Oxford, following our blue dot on Google Maps. Zooming in and out with my grubby fingers, I marvelled at how far we'd come, how far we had to go, and how far we were from absolutely everywhere.

Suddenly, the yellow road line we had followed since Shigatse vanished. I looked up.

'The road's disappeared,' I said, baffled.

'That looks like a road to me,' said Nat gesturing ahead. He was now fully adjusted to the altitude and cold, and capably chewing up 80 kilometres (50 miles) of the immaculate tarmac an hour. 'Altitude getting to you?'

I looked up – the road was definitely still there. On the map, however, it disappeared, re-emerging 160 kilometres (100 miles) ahead. Zooming out, I realized why: we had crossed a dotted line into an area the size of Switzerland labelled Aksai Chin.

Ever since crossing into north-east India, we had skirted similar dotted lines diplomatically drawn by Google, marking the disputed border between India and China. The two countries share a 4,000-kilometre (2,500-mile) border – but given the extreme, empty terrain through which long stretches of it pass, the two gigantic neighbours have never quite got around to agreeing where it is.

Imperial British cartographers, once again, carry some of the blame. China recognized a line put forward by a Mr Johnson in 1865; India preferred another proposed by Messrs Macartney and MacDonald in 1899. In 1962, China's construction of the road we were (or perhaps weren't) traversing sparked an inconclusive war. Neighbouring troops have skirmished ever since, the most recent clash only a month before, a few kilometres from where we were driving.[8]

I wondered how many of the political and military leaders in India and China who had sent soldiers to die for Aksai Chin had ever been here. There was absolutely nothing worth

---

8   Not long after we passed through the border, tensions in this barren moonscape escalated to their worst in decades, bringing the two Asian superpowers close to all-out war. In June 2020, more than twenty Indian soldiers were reported killed in fighting with sticks and clubs, and in September 2020, shots were fired for the first time in forty-five years.

fighting over. Mostly sitting above 5,000 metres (16,500 feet), the terrain is flat and barren, a fact the name – meaning 'white stone desert' – suggested.

Its only apparent use to China was to provide the shortest route between Tibet and Xinjiang. Not that people flocked between them; we had seen a mere handful of cars all day, but that hadn't stopped the Chinese government installing speed cameras.

Thanks to the overdrive[9] Adam had installed during Oxford's restoration, we had been nudging Oxford's top speed of 96 km/h (60 mph) on these flat, immaculate roads. But every 60 kilometres (35 miles) we would slow sharply to 32 km/h (20 mph) for fear of getting a ticket. Nat and I giggled at the thought of Adam back in York translating a fine from Aksai Chin.

'I reckon he'd only agree to pay once China and India decided once and for all who owned it,' said Nat.

'A proper Yorkshireman,' I added in agreement.

Marcus's voice crackled on the radio:

'We're leaving Tibet.'

A blue road sign appeared. I had grown used to Chinese characters twinned with the swooping, elongated Tibetan alphabet. Now, distinctive, right-to-left Arabic script accompanied Chinese logograms. We had entered the Xinjiang Uyghur Autonomous Region – our journey's most politically sensitive leg. While Marcus had sweated for weeks over getting us *into* Tibet, I had fretted over getting us *out* of Xinjiang.

The relationship between China's westernmost province, Xinjiang, and the Chinese centre has always been fraught. Bordering Afghanistan, Russia and Kazakhstan, and home to a large Muslim

---

9   While Adam had tried to be as faithful as possible to Oxford's original condition, the installation of an overdrive unit was a very welcome anachronism (as any Series Land Rover owner will agree.) Popularised in the 1970s, this unit acts a like a bonus fifth gear for the four-speed Land Rover, reducing fuel consumption and engine noise when driving at speed for long periods (which road conditions in the 1950s rarely allowed for!).

population – the Uyghurs, who speak a Turkic language – Xinjiang briefly aspired to be an independent republic in the chaos of early-twentieth-century China, before Mao tightened his grip in 1949.

Xinjiang's estimated 10 million Uyghurs have since simmered with rebellion, seeing a Chinese government determined to erase their cultural, linguistic and religious identity. The Chinese government sees a religious minority threatening national order via separatist movements and terrorist attacks.

While Islamists claiming to represent the Uyghur cause have killed many innocents in recent years, the central government were now accused of terrifying state coercion. It turned out the building spree we had seen in Tibet was not unique – investigations by the BBC and others in 2018 revealed the detention of hundreds of thousands of Uyghurs for 'voluntary re-education courses to combat terrorism and religious extremism'.

Journalists and NGOs documented testimonies of Uyghurs detained without trial for 'crimes' including contacting relatives overseas, praying, or missing a water bill. Age and gender meant nothing; old women followed young men behind bars. Former detainees recounted beatings, brainwashing and humiliation. The Chinese government countered with a bluster of denials, harassing any journalists attempting to dig deeper.[10]

There was no escaping the fact that we were at real risk of falling foul of the authorities solely by being here. There had been no point applying for filming permits for Tibet and Xinjiang; the entry of a multinational film crew (with David, an American, and myself, a Brit who'd worked with the BBC) would have been flatly denied.

---

10   Only a few weeks after our journey through Xinjiang, the International Consortium of Investigative Journalists (ICIJ) published leaked Chinese-government documents revealing the scale of the sites, with up to 1 million people thought to be detained, and 15,000 being detained in one week in 2017 alone. The Chinese government responded with allegations of 'fake news', while pointing to the decline in terrorist attacks in recent years.

A sweep of the cars would reveal copious cameras and hard drives belying any pretence that we were simply tourists.

Leo, David, Marcus and I had discussed the risks at length, and decided our only defence was the truth: we were documenting Oxford's historic journey home, not seeking (as much as we might have wanted) to expose any alleged government barbarity. We had been warned to expect a thorough search through our phones, laptops and hard drives by government officials for anything that undermined that story. Given we had been filming for weeks already, the process could take days or even weeks. It was a risk we had no choice but to take if we wanted to pass through China.

I suddenly pictured Tim and Nat's parents – Kate and Lionel – back in London, and the rest of our families in Singapore, the UK, US, Belgium, and Indonesia, and envisioned their reactions to our indefinite detainment in Xinjiang on spying charges. Even though every one of the team had signed up knowing the risks involved, I couldn't help but feel nauseous.

Oxford, it seemed, sympathized. Having been uncharacteristically reliable across Tibet, her engine spluttered out on a bleak, empty highway not far from the provincial border with Xinjiang. Our convoy, the road, and a line of wooden poles stretching into the distance were the only signs we were not on some distant, deserted planet. Clouds had gathered overhead for the first time in days, removing the brief respite the midday sun usually gave our frozen bones.

'It can't be fuel,' shivered Nat, 'the second tank's full.'

The Doc waddled over, dressed like a decadent Ewok in an oversized camo coat, bright-yellow ski trousers and an orange thermal hat, and somehow coaxed Oxford to life.

'The fuel line's blocked,' he yelled over the struggling engine, before driving Oxford at speed onto a pile of gravel, leaving her left wheels higher than her right at a precipitous angle.

'Nat!' The Doc summoned his erstwhile assistant mechanic. Nat and the Doc's relationship had blossomed over the last few weeks, as together they took charge of Oxford's daily maintenance routine. Watching their morning ritual checking Oxford's vital signs started my day with a smile.

'Suck!' the Doc shouted through his scarf, offering a hose he had fed into Oxford's reserve tank. I couldn't see his mouth, but his eyes belied a mischievous grin. Nat, similarly wrapped up like a frogman, slowly unwrapped his hood and scarf and placed the tube in his mouth, daring me to laugh. I did. Moments later, Nat's eyes bulged before he spat out a great cloud of fuel.

'Euuuggghhhh!' he spluttered, wiping his tongue with his glove. The Doc, chortling uncontrollably, fed the dripping hose quickly into Oxford's main tank.

'Very good! Five minutes. Then we go.'

An hour on was the day's first sign of civilization. A line of HGVs queued for our first checkpoint in Xinjiang. The HGVs plates showed they were coming from all across China, Larry explained on the radio, from as far afield China's most north-easterly province, Heilongjiang. It was a journey of more than 5,000 kilometres (3,000 miles) across a single country, eight hours by plane but likely a fortnight by road.

'These drivers spend their whole lives on the road,' Larry explained. 'Look, they bring their families with them.'

Sure enough, inside the cabs were women and children, little hands and faces pressed against windows as we drove past in a lane reserved for smaller cars. It was humbling to see. For us this drive was a once-in-a-lifetime adventure, and the hardships we endured up here were all part of the excitement. For these drivers and their families, however, it was their means of existence.

'They're heading to Kazakhstan or Kyrgyzstan,' Larry explained, 'then Europe, even London! We're at the start of the Silk Road.'

Larry's words sent a zap of excitement down my spine. It was hard to believe this desolate, dusty, frozen road was the far-eastern end of a network of historic trade routes that had linked the East and West for centuries, and for me conjured images of camel trains, bazaars and adventuring heroes. Now I was about to be a tiny part of that rich tapestry of perpetual human movement from East to West, a tapestry whose first stitches were sown millennia before.

A few hundred kilometres further on lay the ancient city of Kashgar, one of the most important Silk Road cities, where we would be resting for several days. First, however, we'd be stopping in what Lhakpa informed us was the small barracks town of Sanshili, a place we struggled to find on Google Maps.

As we approached the checkpoint, I saw my first real sign that we were entering a different corner of this country. The gun-toting, navy-uniformed guard approaching our car looked as if he had just arrived from Eastern Europe. His swarthy Caucasian look jarred with the Mandarin tumbling from his mouth. His colleagues, loitering or cooped in pillboxes around us were similar in appearance, many with a thick, single eyebrow giving them a deeply menacing air.

We were ordered to get out of the cars, ready our documents, and were then led away by what looked like a fourteen-year-old girl in the same blue uniform. He, or possibly she, chivvied us on to a Portakabin in a high-pitched voice.

'They must be struggling to recruit, given all the people they've locked up,' Leo muttered darkly at my shoulder.

A disgruntled senior officer – notably Han-Chinese – emerged from a side room, an automatic shotgun strapped across his back. He and Lhakpa began a heated discussion. Lhakpa was unusually deferent and tactful, which made me nervous.

'They want to see three Chinese licence plates,' Lhakpa explained guiltily, 'we only have two.'

It was just as we had feared ever since leaving Shigatse in a car four decades beyond legal. We were marched outside, where Enterprise was meticulously unpacked. Lhakpa, meanwhile, headed back inside to parlay with the officer. The guards found a small bottle of propane Larry had packed for his camping stove. One held it aloft, as if he'd won the lottery.

'They're saying I could use this as a weapon,' an exasperated Larry explained, while pleading with the guards to see reason. They didn't, and the propane was confiscated. Satisfied with their haul, their search of PAC (stuffed to the gills with camera kit) was blissfully cursory.

Moments later the officer marched out, Lhakpa trailing in his wake. He beckoned me to open Oxford's rear door. Nudging me aside with the butt of his gun, he looked briefly inside with angry eyes, before gesturing to Lhakpa, who after a muttered conference turned to me.

'We can go.'

I sighed with relief.

'It would be too much paperwork to detain us', Lhakpa explained. 'We're lucky he was lazy.'

It was almost dark when we arrived at Sanshili. A huge set of gates were up ahead, beyond which a platoon of soldiers was marching in drill formation. Our passports were checked by a very large man with high cheekbones, wearing green camo and a black bearskin hat, a perfect Soviet Bond villain.

'We are on the edge of a military base,' Lhakpa warned on the radio. 'No cameras.'

Down a small slope, a car park was filled with dozens of green trucks, each carrying a mobile missile unit. It reminded me how close we still were to the disputed border zone. We crossed another set of gates before Lhakpa's car signalled for us to park. Our home for the night was a petrol station opposite a disused barracks; a single-storey block with an undeniable slaughterhouse vibe. Fluorescent lights flickered, sporadically revealing damp-streaked walls and bedding. I surveyed the faces of my exhausted companions, trying to communicate a wordless apology.

Before we could turn in, Lhakpa signalled us for one of his rare team briefings. I had learned they heralded only bad news, but ushered the team to stay upright a little while longer. We huddled around a table on which Marcus had unfolded his paper map of China.

'Tomorrow, we drive to Kashgar – it will be a long day,' he announced, impassively. 'Our planned overnight in Yecheng is cancelled due to civil unrest.'

'What's going on?' I asked.

'Civil unrest,' he repeated, tersely. His bloodshot eyes showed he was as exhausted as we were after the grilling he'd sustained at the checkpoint. I decided not to argue.

'Because we cannot stop, we will have to drive seven hundred kilometres without a break.'

Marcus looked alarmed. 'The longest we've ever managed with Oxford in a day is just short of five hundred kilometres.'

'We leave early – five a.m. If we cannot reach Kashgar before nightfall, we will sleep in the cars.'

Now it was my turn to look alarmed. Driving in Oxford in these temperatures was tough; sleeping in Oxford in these temperatures was suicidal.

The one comfort was – absurdly – the electric blankets on our beds that looked like they'd come from a Victorian prison. Given the freezing temperatures even indoors we all – bar Marcus – switched on. As we bedded down, I could hear Marcus shivering in the bed next to mine.

'Turn your blanket on, fool.'

'I can't. If I wet the bed, I'll be electrocuted.'

Too tired to enter the long debates usually provoked by my old friend's peccadillos, I switched off the flickering light and drifted into a dissatisfying, short sleep.

It was bitterly cold when my alarm rang. Marcus, who had survived the night without electrocution, fumbled for the light switch, spluttering. He'd developed a nasty, hacking cough in recent days, which was worsening in the harsh conditions.

Driving Oxford in these conditions was torture, but without

hesitation Nat volunteered for the first shift, his tired eyes steeled with a determination far removed from the nervous kid who climbed on stage in Singapore. I knew Tim would have been bursting with pride to see the determination his grandson was showing today. I certainly was. My pride didn't provoke chivalry, however, and I let David take the co-pilot position while I clambered in the back of PAC. Even with the heating on full blast, it took a good hour to bring any feeling back to my hands and feet.

The neat tarmac of the G219 that had carried us all the way from Shigatse was no more; loose gravel roads kicked up dust clouds as we descended the Tibetan plateau. Eventually, dawn's first light streaked pink across the horizon. I imagined we were inside a Martian rover exploring entirely new worlds, and drifted into a doze, until I was rudely woken by an argument between Tibie and Leo in the front of PAC in their native tongue.

'*C'est un aigle!*'

'*Non, ça ne peut pas être, c'est un yak!*'

'*Un yak! Non – c'est absurde!*'

They were craning to see a hulking shape on a hilltop overlooking the road.

'*Mon dieu – c'est un chameau!*' Tibie exclaimed.

She was right – it was the first of a herd of camels that soon crested the hillside. Not the scrawny dromedaries I had once ridden on a holiday in Egypt. These were Bactrian camels – massive, twin-humped beasts with shaggy brown hair. At first, they studied our convoy stoically, then began to jog alongside. When picturing China from afar, I had never imagined camels. Xinjiang was full of surprises; this was a rare pleasant one.

Perhaps Oxford was as keen as we were to cross Xinjiang at speed, and over the sixteen arduous hours it took to reach the city of Kashgar, she performed her longest drive yet without a fault, even with the additional stress of crawling through eleven different checkpoints. It was a sign of how sensitive the security situation in Xinjiang was, and the frustrating routine of presenting paperwork, unpacking and repacking began to undo even the calmest among us. It did, however, give us plenty of time to take in the scenery changing dramatically around us.

Gone was the harsh, lunar landscape of Tibet; greenery was returning. This was the Tarim Basin, the southern lowlands of Xinjiang. The Westerners among us were hypnotized by a landscape that looked, for the first time since arriving in Singapore, a little like home. We saw compounds covered in creeping vines that reminded Tibie of holidays in Italy; orchards of tall, thin trees that, to Leo, could have stood in the south of France. Leaf-dusted sidewalks reminded David of Massachusetts in the fall.

The spell was broken when we limped with dangerously empty fuel tanks into a fuel station on the outskirts of Kashgar. Razor-wire fences were dismantled to allow us through, and as I filled Oxford, a woman in a Kevlar vest looked on, stroking the trigger on her AK-47.

To me, the word 'Kashgar' always evoked images of palm-lined oases, but the reality was closer to a Chinese Las Vegas, with wide boulevards and flashing neon lights. I realized it was the first taste of big-city life we'd had since Yangon seven weeks earlier. Sadly, there was to be no lavish letting down of hair. The streets were quiet due to a city-wide curfew, which meant the only place to feed our weary bones was in a twenty-four-hour hospital canteen.

There, beneath the harsh halogen strip lights, we parted with Lhakpa. It was a fittingly austere place: we had spent more time with him than any of our guides to date, but he was the one we had struggled to really connect with. I felt the same about Tibet – this desolate place remained a mystery to me. Lhakpa seemed relieved to have completed his job. Taciturn and inscrutable, his job had seemingly been to whisk us through from the Nepali border to Kashgar experiencing as little as possible. For the rest of our stay, we would have a local guide from Kashgar.

Abdul came to collect us from our hotel the next morning. He was a portly, middle-aged man with kind eyes, and clean-shaven except for a neat little moustache flecked with grey. Had I not been in China, I would have placed him as Turkish. I shouldn't have been so surprised – look on a map, and you realize that such is the scale of China, Kashgar is closer to Istanbul than it is to Beijing and for 2,000 years had been a melting pot of religion, art and ideas. Because of its pivotal place on the old Silk Road, Kashgar, I had read, was steeped in a rich Turkic and Islamic heritage. Stepping out with Abdul into Kashgar in the daylight, however, I was struck not by the heritage, but by the silence. Despite the throngs of pedestrians and traffic, there was an eerie quiet. It was like a city with sound dampeners on.

Passing a huge statue of Mao festooned with flags and lanterns to mark the Party's seventieth anniversary, Abdul explained reluctantly in accented but otherwise impeccable English the laws in place to combat 'terrorism': sweeping restrictions on gatherings and traditional Uyghur dress. Beards and other signs of Islamic piety were suspect, and there were reports of men having their facial hair forcibly shaved off. I lost count of how often he ended his cautionary advice on what we should or should not do in Kashgar 'because the cameras are watching'.

While I was trying to allow what I could see take precedence over what I had read, I began to feel that Kashgar was a city of quiet fear. I had heard about the smartphone and facial-recognition software the government was reportedly deploying to monitor its own citizens here and nationwide. Foreign journalists increasingly referred to the 'open-air prison' the Chinese were building in Xinjiang.

Abdul was leading us to the 'Old City'. He explained how Kashgar had been ruled by Buddhist kings, Arab warlords and Mongol hordes. Its narrow streets had hosted Genghis Khan, Tamerlane[11] and Marco Polo, and in the nineteenth century they

---

11   He can't have enjoyed them much, however, because when he arrived in 1389, he razed the city to the ground.

were a den of conspiracy for Russian and British spies engaged in a covert imperial wrestling match known as the Great Game. Its iconic mud-brick buildings had housed Chinese and Armenians, Christians and Muslims, Kyrgyz and, of course, Uyghurs, for whom the city was their cultural heart.

That made the sight ahead especially troubling. Abdul pointed to a battered group of beige, three-storey mud-brick buildings that looked as if they had endured an artillery siege, separated by tall fencing, abandoned and off-limits.

'The "old" Old City,' Abdul explained. 'There is little left now, since 2009 the government has demolished and rebuilt almost everything.'

'Why?'

'Many reasons,' Abdul continued, looking down. 'There are earthquakes here, the old buildings were unsafe. The sanitation, heating, electricity all needed upgrading. The "new" Old City will be much safer for us, and for tourists.'

His heart clearly wasn't in the explanation he was offering, and I knew why. In 2009, Xinjiang had witnessed a series of deadly secessionist uprisings. Hundreds were killed, and the government responded by shutting off the outside world. Many found the timing of the rebuild highly suspicious, seeing it as an erasure of Uyghur history and identity. My mind turned back to what Larry had said in Myanmar about the world becoming safer but less free. It seemed that the Uyghurs were doomed to be the exception that proved the rule – in trying to take on the sinister might of the Chinese State, they were both less free, and less safe.

'The "new" Old City is here,' said Abdul, indicating a glittering gate.

Up ahead, three Han Chinese policemen were standing in an awkward triangle by the gateway facing outwards, dressed in blue uniforms topped with yellow hi-vis vests. One held a riot shield, another a gun, and the third – bizarrely – an enormous trident. Another officer approached them, barking a series of orders that caused the three stooges to shoulder their weapons, form in single file, and jog past us. It was like a British Changing of the Guard ceremony, with fewer funny hats.

It marked the start of a depressing experience. The streets beyond were lined with immaculate concrete buildings, filigreed archways and domes that hinted at the city of old. Like an out-of-town shopping centre, identical shops sold identical tourist tat. Nat, walking beside me, had a quizzical look.

'I've never been to Morocco,' he said, 'but I imagine this is what it looks like.'

The curiously faux-Arabesque streets teemed with Chinese from the interior, shopping and taking photos dressed in newly purchased 'ethnic' costumes.

'This year tourism from inside China has increased 40 per cent,' Abdul explained. The government's 'improvement scheme' was clearly hitting its goal of attracting more tourists to China's most westerly city, but I felt they had reached a place stripped of its soul. Those selling the tat looked very similar to those buying it, attesting to accusations from local citizens that the economic boom was being enjoyed only by other Han Chinese.

The one saving grace was the food. After ten days spent sifting fragments of boiled meat with our teeth from unchanging bowls of Tibetan noodle soup, Kashgar's cuisine was delightful. Abdul ordered lavish mutton kebabs, flavoured rice, and wheels of hot flatbread – food I would expect in London's better kebab shops. Despite what I'd read about the region, I confessed I found it strange to see it here in China.

'The Turkic peoples originally came from here in western China!' Abdul chuckled, happier discussing the past than the present. 'We've been moving west for centuries. You'll follow our footsteps until Eastern Europe, so I hope you like kebabs!'

On 24 October, after twelve long days in China, we were finally preparing to leave. The combination of Tibet's suffocating altitude and Xinjiang's equally suffocating politics had wrung the team dry. Spirits were low, and tempers short. Ahead lay the exit customs checkpoint and – we'd been warned – the most thorough search we could expect on our entire journey. My fears of being detained on some sort of trumped-up spying charges resurfaced.

We had tasted everyday life here in Xinjiang, and I was exhausted by it. The constant need to watch your words and actions, and the worry at who was prying into your phone or laptop, was physically, mentally and spiritually draining. Abdul advised me not to contact him after leaving, and our security team in London had warned us that our hotel rooms were probably bugged. To add to the underlying tension, the hotel had been playing the first four bars of 'Moonlight Sonata' on a loop since we arrived in an act of gruelling audial torture. I would be happy never to see Xinjiang (or hear Beethoven) again.

We left for country number eight: Kyrgyzstan. With more than 160 kilometres (100 miles) to cover and a long wait at the border, warned Abdul, we left at a weak sun's first reluctant light.

We reached the Irkeshtam border crossing just in time for opening. What Abdul called the 'border port' looked like an abandoned industrial estate. Guards dressed in black carried batons as tall as themselves. As our passports were handed over, we settled down to wait.

After almost an hour, Abdul returned sheepishly.

'There's been a power cut. The X-ray machines for scanning your cars are not working. You will have to wait.'

We waited seven hours, time enough to go through our phones and identify any contentious photos, and to delete the VPN apps we had used illegally to circumnavigate the Chinese firewalls. We had no reason to suspect that the rumours we'd heard of the intense scrutiny weren't true. A friend who'd been here a few weeks earlier warned that he'd had special apps installed in his phone to scan for 'suspicious material' that could undermine China's national sovereignty or dignity. I hesitated over a photo of Nat sneaking warm boiled eggs into his clothing and decided it could stay.

The sun was setting when Abdul motioned us forward. We were

rushed through the imposing X-ray buildings, and the human surveillance stations, all still powerless. I visibly sagged with relief. We were safe. We were leaving. In a stunning stroke of luck, due to the power cut, not a single phone or hard drive had been checked.

Abdul could barely hide a smirk as he said goodbye.

'The world fears China the great superpower ...' he whispered, 'and they can't even keep the lights on!'

I returned a small smile. I liked Abdul, a man doing a tough job in a difficult time. I couldn't share his joke though. From what I'd seen in the last fortnight, the ambition and power of the Chinese state was as awe-inspiring as it was disturbing. Today's China was unrecognizable from the impoverished, conflict-torn nation in which Henry and Pat had spent ten memorable minutes. Given another sixty-four years, I suspected China would learn much more than how to keep the lights on in Xinjiang.

14

The Heroin Highway

24 October 2019: Irkeshtam, Kyrgyzstan

Expedition Day 61

Gold teeth glinted from a beetroot-red face, thrust without warning through Oxford's window after freewheeling several hundred metres down a dark track lined with razor wire. We had exited China, but I wasn't yet sure we had entered anywhere else.

The guard spoke rapidly in a language I only knew wasn't Mandarin. One word resonated, however.

'Passports.'

As Nat retrieved them, I radioed David. I had recruited him for his camera skills, but as the child of Russian-speaking Georgian emigrants, his second language was about to come in handy.

David spoke sparsely and gently, as if remembering how to form the words. I realized that although he'd been raised speaking Russian, this was possibly the first time David had spoken it outside his family home in New York. It did the trick, though, and the guard's sour demeanour lifted. He sprang uninvited into Oxford alongside Nat and me, slapping the dashboard.

'Go!'

Passing mercifully fast through customs, where enormous men in fur hats thumped sausage fingers on tiny keyboards, we were set free into Kyrgyzstan.

We'd arranged to meet the fixers here who would take us across Central Asia. Since Myanmar, all of us had been preoccupied with getting into and then through China. It only struck me now that the most physically dangerous section of our journey was still ahead of us. Suddenly, the radio crackled with an almost cartoon Russian accent.

'Larry! This is Alex. Do you copy?'

'This is Larry, copy!'

The bald, bearded man-mountain Alex Fedin, highly recommended from Larry's previous overlands through Russia, lumbered grinning into our headlights. Well over six foot and broad-shouldered, he effortlessly scooped up Larry's sizeable bulk into a crushing bear hug. From what I'd heard and now seen of Alex Fedin, and his equally enormous driver Vladimir, I had a strong feeling he was the right man for the job ahead.

'You must be starving!' Alex said, enveloping each of our hands in turn. Let's drive!'

He hopped into a white Mitsubishi van alongside Vladimir and tore away.

'My call sign is Zubr,' he explained on the radio, a Russian name for an enormous breed of bison. Fitting, I thought.

That night, in a cosy homestay in the village of Sary-Tash, was one of the happiest so far. Over smoked yak shoulder, soft cheese and a little too much excellent vodka, we got to know Alex and Vladimir. Both had served in the Soviet armed forces, with Alex having deployed in Angola during the 1980s.

'I still can't move my little finger,' he raised his left hand with a chuckle. 'One of those Angolan bastards almost cut it right off.'

Now both retired from service, they ground a living from the growing tourism in Central Asia. While Vladimir lived in Kyrgyzstan, Alex was returning to this corner of the world for the first time since the 1990s, shortly after the collapse of the Soviet Union and the independence of the Central Asian republics, including Kyrgyzstan.

'It was a free-for-all,' he sighed. 'Everybody was out to make money; Communism was dead, business was booming. It was not for the weak. I made enemies, and had to head back to Russia very quickly.'

I wondered how we would fare on the road ahead, if a man Alex's size was spooked by what he'd found there.

Vodka, an open fire and good food all contributed to one of the best night's sleeps in days. In the pre-dawn calm, I felt closer than ever before to our little band of travellers, bunkered down in the same room for the first time on the journey. I imagined it must have been the same warm feeling Tim and the gang had felt on so many mornings, waking up all stacked together under canvas, or in whatever shelter they'd been able to find.

While Alex and Marcus double-checked the mass of paperwork we would need for the roads ahead, I decided to make use of the crisp Kyrgyz morning to fix a great wrong. Despite being almost halfway through a historic overland journey, one of our team had never once driven a car.

'Only idiots and billionaires have cars in New York!' David explained, as I marched him to Oxford.

After a few false starts, I watched proudly as David completed lap after giddy lap of the house, Mount Lenin's frosted peak brooding on the horizon. The memory of Lenin and Russia loomed large here; Russia had controlled the territory now called Kyrgyzstan from the late nineteenth century right up to 1991. The influence of the old colonial power was still felt clearly, and not always welcome. The story would be similar until we reached David's native Georgia in around three weeks' time. While the Soviet Union had always felt distant and disconnected to me, I realized that David – the twenty-five-year-old child of Jewish emigres from the former Soviet Union – symbolized just how close we were to the ripples of the Union's collapse.

Sadly, I couldn't scratch my itch to dig deeper into Kyrgyzstan. We were spending less than twenty-four hours here before our route took us south into Tajikistan. After teaching David to parallel park (the only remaining skill he deemed necessary to survive in New York), we were driving in convoy under a clear blue sky. With only a thirty-minute drive to the border crossing of Kyzyl-Art, I was sad to say goodbye to Kyrgyzstan. The roads had a rugged charm, the houses we passed even more so, and everyone we saw waved with genuine affection.

The border post was small but well staffed. We were directed to a razor-wire gate, overlooked by a Portakabin manned by a huge Kyrgyz soldier.

'The road ahead is very popular with smugglers – weapons, drugs, whatever,' Alex informed us, handing back our passports.

'Some call it the "old Silk Road", others the Pamir Highway. Heroin Highway would be better!' he laughed, folding his huge form into his little van.

'We have fourteen kilometres of no man's land, then we reach Tajikistan. Let's go.'

Apparently not looking like would-be smugglers, we zipped through the Tajik border into country number nine. After spending a fortnight crossing China, covering two countries in two days felt dizzying.

We drove on through hills blanketed with fresh snowfall. We had seen snow on distant hilltops since West Bengal, but this was the first time we'd been able to get among it. Nat and I couldn't resist speeding ahead in Oxford to lay snowball ambushes for the rest of the convoy. It was a playful mood that we knew we'd soon have to rein in on the road in front of us.

Back when our dream was merely another line on a map, Marcus had described the Pamir Highway with a mix of dread and awe. Those that knew it spoke of epic scenery through the Pamir mountains, skirting Afghanistan. Our security team at AKE, however, warned of the deadly attack on a group of Western cyclists by Tajiks claiming allegiance to Islamic State in August 2018. We had taken the best advice, and recruited a trusted guide, but once out on the road we would be a long way from help.

Given Tajikistan's contorted shape, you could be forgiven for concluding it was formed from whatever its larger neighbours didn't want. This wild corner of the map had been fought over and ruled by Russian tsars, Uzbek khans and Chinese emperors, almost as an afterthought. Britain, predictably, had a hand in its bizarre cartography, carving out the Wakhan Corridor from its southern border in 1893 and giving it to Afghanistan, creating a buffer between British India and the Russian Empire. Stalin had served to complicate the picture even more when it became part of the Soviet Union, deliberately wiggling the Tajik border to prevent any one ethnic group gaining a demographic advantage.

Stalin's schemes would sow tragedy for the people of the newly independent Tajikistan. After 1991, Tajikistan imploded into a brutal five-year civil war costing tens of thousands of lives. The Pamir Highway struck south through the heart of the old battlegrounds – the autonomous region of Gorno-Badakhshan – a desolate, mountainous area forming almost the whole eastern half of Tajikistan, but home to only 3 per cent of its population. These people – many of them ethnic Pamiris, not Tajiks – had tried to break away from Tajikistan but were roundly defeated. Today it remains the poorest region in Central Asia's poorest country.

We were now onto the Pamir Highway proper, and it was as beautiful as promised. Either side, as far as the eye could see, snow-capped mountains watched over lakes of deepest aquamarine. We were climbing again to around 4,000 metres (13,000 feet), close to Tibetan levels, but by now we were hardened to the altitude. The cold when combined with higher humidity was merciless, and as darkness fell, just after 5 p.m., it really began to bite. Even Larry, who in Tibet had sported shorts in fifteen degrees below, trousered up. Through wind erosion, extreme cold and poor maintenance, the road felt like badly fitted carpet, reducing us to a 25-km/h (15-mph) crawl to avoid tumbling nose-first into a ditch.

Well after dark, we arrived at our night stop, Murghab. Nat dryly recited the Lonely Planet entry: 'Utterly isolated … the desolate town of Murghab fascinates as an example of life lived in extremis. The people here are used to a hard life.'

Our beds for the night were in the Pamir Eco Resort, a scruffy, single-storey building behind mud-brick walls looking ripe for a US Special Forces raid. Its only eco credentials were the lack of any working electricity.

Once inside, by the light of a dung fire, Alex informed Marcus and me of rumours he had received.

'There's Taliban reported on the road ahead. We don't know exactly where, but we have to be on our guard.'

'Why would Afghans be attacking here?' I asked.

'Killing foreigners makes headlines. Plus, lots of Tajiks left to fight for Islamist groups in Afghanistan, Syria, Iraq. Now they're coming home. But don't worry, Vladimir and I will keep you safe.'

Once again, we were all in one room, and as I was last to turn in, the only bed was a small child's bunkbed adorned with paintings of Winnie the Pooh. Drifting into uneasy sleep, I quietly willed that if jihadists were to murder me in my bed, please don't let it be this one.

Thankfully, Pooh was spared bloodshed and we rose intact. An inverse link had developed between the quality of accommodation and speed of exit, and the team readied to leave quickly. Donning my Tibetan camo coat and huge fur hat recently purchased in Kashgar, I looked like a stumpy Chechen warlord. I went to wash my face and examined it in the mirror for the first time in days.

I looked tired, old and dishevelled, the streaks of dirt I had managed to move around with the ice-cold water only accentuating the lines. In all my years travelling, I had pointedly avoided areas where people might remove my head simply for its colour. But beyond the fear of starring in the latest ISIS hostage video, looking into my own exhausted eyes that morning, I realized there was nowhere I would rather be. Thanks to the sense of purpose this journey had given me, even with its draining twists and turns, I was more at peace than I'd been in years.

Outside, I found Nat trying to scrape away a paste of brown

dust that had formed on Oxford's windscreen. Vladimir, spotting Nat's struggle, approached us brandishing an improbable pack of ladies' sanitary pads and mimed the act of putting one on. Wheezing hysterically at the confusion on our faces, he removed one and wiped it on the windshield. Moments later he stood back theatrically, revealing a now completely grime-free window.

'Did you learn that in the army?' asked Nat, before accepting a fresh pack and setting to work.

For nearly 320 kilometres (200 miles), the Pamir Highway wiggled along the River Panj, part of Tajikistan's 1,300-kilometre (800-mile) border with Afghanistan. We were instructed to keep our headlights on at all times to avoid the attention of Tajikistan's crooked traffic police – and even then, we were stopped on numerous occasions. I only wish I'd learned the Russian for 'They didn't have seatbelts in the 1950s', as this would have saved an awful lot of time.

True to Abdul's prediction in Kashgar, at simple roadside cafés we discovered the food here was similar to the Turkic cuisine we had enjoyed so much in Kyrgyzstan and Kashgar. At every stop we were spoiled with freshly baked flatbreads, succulent grilled meat, and delicious salads to share, and we'd pigged out at every opportunity. Alex was particularly keen we tried a local Tajik delicacy called *osh*, considered to be Tajikistan's national dish (although the neighbouring Uzbeks claimed the same, calling it *plov*). It could be found in most local eateries bubbling away in the back, a delicious mix of rice, carrots, onions and a meat of your choice.

'Lamb is usually the main ingredient,' boomed Alex, shovelling great mouthfuls beside Nat, who was doing the same. 'But I've always enjoyed it like this one, with horse.'

Frenchman Leo nodded his agreement, but Nat stopped shovelling and slowly lowered his spoon.

Whether it was the horse meat or another local delicacy, our gluttony soon came back to haunt us. Nat and I had to pull Oxford over repeatedly to scuttle into ditches and relieve ourselves. I had long dreamed of setting eyes on the famed Hindu Kush, that noble 800-kilometre (500-mile) range of mountains that stretch through Afghanistan, Pakistan and Tajikistan, but I never imagined I'd be getting my first glimpse trouser-about-ankle.

We stopped to swap drivers at a rickety tea shop overlooking the Panj into Afghanistan, a country that had dominated the headlines during my formative years. Unfortunately, my awe was overshadowed by yet another pressing need for the lavatory. I searched unsuccessfully around the back, before hearing a whistle from the clifftop above. A heavily armed man's rifle pointed right at me. My bowels' disquiet intensified, before I realized he was indicating a tumble-down pile of wood further on, which served as a rudimentary toilet. Alex explained later that the Tajik government had posted soldiers all along here to keep tourists safe from jihadi attacks. They were really going above and beyond in that service, it seemed.

Returning to the tea shop, I found David deep in conversation with a wizened, mahogany-skinned man in an oversized black coat. Leaning on a wooden stick taller than himself, he regaled David with a toothless lisp.

'This is Abdullah,' David explained. 'He was born here seventy-five years ago.'

Abdullah scanned me with one working eye, before continuing in a breathless stream of Russian, as if he'd had no one to talk to in months. David translated.

'During the Soviet times, we would never see foreigners here like you! The world has changed so much, my life was better in the USSR. I was a mechanic, I could travel across the USSR for work, no need for permits and passports. Now there are *sixteen* different republics, it's such a shame. I'm Pamiri, but they tell me now I live in Tajikistan – it was simpler when there was one Soviet government. The road was much better, for sure. I've been walking it my whole life.'

As a Brit born as the Cold War was ending, to hear someone mourn the Soviet Union's downfall was novel. Life within that totalitarian structure had, for Abdullah, been more safe and more free.

David filled Abdullah in on where we had come from, and where we planned to reach. His one working eye widened. 'Oh, that's a very, very long road!' He chewed thoughtfully. 'It will take you another three months to reach London, I think.'

I told him we were hoping to make London in six weeks, shortly before Christmas. It was met with a snort of disbelief.

'Is the road ahead safe?' I asked, remembering our discussion with Alex.

'Of course! We are Muslims, just say *as-salamu alaykum* [peace to you] and we are duty bound to look after you. But whatever you do, don't cross the river,' he warned darkly, pointing to Afghanistan.

'Have you ever been?' I asked.

'No! Never, in seventy-five years. Too dangerous.'

We thanked him for his advice, and Abdullah cast an experienced eye over Oxford's battered shell.

'*Land Rover*.' He chewed the unfamiliar words on the badge. 'Don't break down. You'll struggle to get fixed out here. I've never seen one before.'

Alex was anxious to move on. He stressed the need to keep almost bumper to bumper as we tracked the Afghan border for the rest of the day. We hugged the river, the light fading. On the opposite bank appeared a pickup truck, stuffed with standing men watching us closely. My mind began to race with the worst possible outcomes, but after mirroring our progress for 9.5 tense kilometres (6 miles), the truck pulled away.

Even though the road seemed to be gradually improving, Oxford was still far slower than a modern car. It meant we were making less progress than Alex had anticipated, forcing a night stay on the border itself. Darkness had fallen when we pulled into the guest house, nestled on the banks of the Panj in the town of Ruzvat. The setting was suggestive of the English Lakes or the Swiss Alps, but knowing Afghanistan lay across the way gave it a sinister edge.

Since Alex's 'Heroin Highway' quip, I had been reading more closely about the local drugs trade. Twenty per cent of Afghanistan's booming illicit industry was estimated to cross this border on its way to the West, fuelling a third of Tajikistan's GDP. The highest levels of government were supposedly in on the bonanza. The system exploited desperately poor people, both sides of the border, who were preyed upon to smuggle the drugs past corrupt guards at the few official crossings. Depressingly, money sent by Western powers to help Tajikistan in its 'war on drugs' was allegedly used to improve the traffic's flow.

So, I chuckled darkly when I saw the Sharq-Darvoz Hotel's sign proclaiming that its construction was 'supported by the Government of the United Kingdom'. Even smugglers need to rest their heads, I suppose. The owner, a swarthy, skinny man, introduced himself as Sher Ali and settled us in for a delicious meal with the now obligatory lashings of vodka. As the night grew later, and charmed by David's increasingly confident Russian, Sher Ali joined the table.

'Welcome to the Gates of Badakhshan,' he said, gesturing through the window to Afghanistan. 'I know everything that crosses the border here,' he added with a knowing smirk.

'All these are *businessmen*,' he declared, indicating the men lounging around us on raised platforms, picking at platters of food as they watched 'Tajikistan's Got Talent' on the TV. A huge roar of laughter erupted as a band of male contortionists came on screen.

'They're laughing at the homosexuals!' Sher Ali snickered, before continuing his story.

'That man there – he is a *very* rich man from Afghanistan,' he pointed to a diner in a shiny tracksuit, sniggering with the rest. A woman in a short skirt with a bored look sat close by his side.

'I am a rich man myself,' he ventured, with a sniff.

'From the guesthouse?' I asked, thinking back to my fellow taxpayers' money that helped build the Sharq.

'Oh no. From marble! There are good deposits near here. Allah puts it in the ground, and from his grace I make a good living.'

I wondered how many of my fellow diners were also making a killing from nature's bounty. I noticed it was close to midnight, and I started to excuse myself. I had a feeling Sher Ali was only just getting started.

'I'm sorry for keeping you, Alex. Then again, this is my house,' he said, his tone darkening. 'You will talk to me if I want to talk to you, and you will leave if I let you leave!'

He roared with laughter at his own joke. I stayed.

'Oh fuck, Afghanistan,' grumbled David, appearing vodka-eyed beside me the next morning as I sat fixing another horizon in my mind.

I nodded. We had survived a night on this troubled border with nothing more than a bad hangover. Our reward was the view in front of us, which by dawn light was stunning. Below us the river ran in startling aquamarine, and above the sun picked out delicate strands of green and orange on the sheer grey rock face, stabbing starkly upwards into the clear blue sky. It took an effort to remind myself we were looking into the Afghan province of Badakhshan, where Talibs were known to lurk.

We breakfasted on fresh pomegranates, a fruit that I'd read Americans had been trying – largely unsuccessfully – to bribe Afghan farmers to grow instead of opium poppies. Our host loaded us with bags of them for the road and waved a cheery goodbye.

As we peeled away from the Afghan border, it felt like a lingering menace had been lifted. The road became greener, houses more frequent. We were 400 kilometres (250 miles) from our next destination, Dushanbe, the Tajik capital.

Marcus crackled on the radio: 'Dushanbe marks the halfway point! We're almost halfway home, everyone!'

'Not if you live in Singapore,' said Larry.

Accepting Larry's valid point, I allowed myself to reflect that it was one hell of an achievement. After months of preparation, Tim's dramatic illness, a cantankerous old car, the stresses of China and the morbid threat of jihadis, we were still moving forward, largely intact. Caught in the moment I swelled with pride, before swerving Oxford out of the path of a limousine careering towards us.

'Must be a "pomegranate" salesman,' said Nat on the radio.

From Ruzvat we continued our careful, wiggling progress along the border with Afghanistan. Nat driving PAC behind was so keen to follow Alex's rule of keeping close formation that I could see the whites of his eyes. I was reminded that when we'd first spoken, he had picked out Tajikistan as the place he was least keen on crossing, and I felt a deep sense of responsibility for him now that I was here dragging him through it. Yet to his credit I had never heard him express a single worry or complaint. While we still held out hope Tim would join us, he – and indeed all of us – couldn't have asked for a better man to step off the bench.

Marcus, beside me now in Oxford, watched quietly as cloud-ringed mountains emerged across the frothing Panj. We had both come of age in the aftermath of 9/11, masterminded by Osama Bin Laden, who had hidden for years in the wild country now only metres away. Friends of ours had served in the grinding war that followed, and for what?

Back in the 1950s, the First Overland had driven through Afghanistan with ease. The country was experiencing a rare window of peace and prosperity, as Afghanistan's Shah cleverly courted both Soviet and American aid. Tim wrote of long, peaceful days driving through Afghanistan's 'slowly changing loneliness', and of camping out under the stars.

After departing from their route in Nepal, even though we were driving the same old car, it had been hard to feel the connection to the First Overland that had pulled us so firmly through South Asia. Here, for the first time in weeks, we were in touching distance of them again. Staring now across the Panj on our left, I could see in my mind's eye a sixty-four-year-old dust trail still rising into the pale-blue sky.

After decades of civil war, foreign invasions and extremist rule, Afghanistan today is the poorest country in Asia, thousands die yearly in communal violence, and right now the Americans were putting the final touches to a 'peace deal' with the Taliban – the very people who had sheltered Bin Laden in the first place.

'Pass me a sanitary pad,' said Marcus, 'I want a better look.'

Even after de-steaming the window, our curiosity was undimmed. The Panj calmed and widened; a sloping pebble beach appeared, the water only ankle deep. We pulled the convoy over.

Sensing this might be our only opportunity ever to step into Afghanistan, Marcus and I trod gingerly across the stones. Nat, suddenly flushed with bravado, jogged to overtake us:

'I'm going to Afghanistan, boys!'

As the three of us scrambled down the scree into the riverbed marking the border, a heated conversation began above.

'Be careful! They shot!' shouted Tibie, mixing her tenses in her panic.

'What?!' shouted Nat.

'They can shoot!' yelled Alex, pointing to a border guard in green, who had appeared on the opposite bank. Nat suddenly hit reverse, jogging past us in the opposite direction.

'I'm not going to Afghanistan,' he shouted as he passed in a blur.

Realizing our stupidity, Marcus and I also retreated, but only after I'd grabbed a stone to remember my first foolish near-visit to that troubled country. There was nothing special about that stone, I realized, looking back across the river. It was identical to those on this side of an invisible line, the division between one imagined nation and the next.

But soldiers now spent their lives ensuring no one crossed that line, while drug smugglers risked their lives to do so. Most people, like Abdullah and us, would never try. For us that line had become something greater: a mental wall, beyond which lurked only danger and devils. As we finally parted ways with the border to head north to Nurek, I was not sad to say goodbye.

15

Halfway Home

29 October 2019: Nurek, Tajikistan

Expedition Day 66

From Nurek we were making the 100-kilometre (60-mile) dash to the Tajik capital of Dushanbe, and spirits were soaring. No longer creeping along crumbling roads, haunted by the spectre of jihadis, we cruised through the flat, sunlit plains of western Tajikistan.

The surroundings seemed quintessentially Soviet era. Villagers in neat but well-worn clothes managed roadside stalls stacked with autumnal vegetables; battered old Lada cars ferried anything from a family of twelve to a small mountain of onions. These boxy little vehicles, proud symbols of Soviet engineering and egalitarian ideals,[12] had outlived the ideology that spawned them.

Present-day Tajikistan's 'frozen-in-time' feel might stem from the old Soviet apparatchik who had gained power following independence and held it ever since. The humourless, black-suited bulk of President Emomali Rahmon, officially 'The Founder of Peace and National Unity, Leader of the Nation', had glowered from countless billboards and murals ever since the Pamirs. He was now the longest-serving leader in the former Soviet Union, and with eye-watering electoral majorities and a hamstrung opposition, he didn't look like shifting.

---

12   That is, the egalitarian ideal that everyone should own cars of equal ugliness.

Traffic police in absurdly wide hats grinned at Oxford chugging through road stops. And chug she did, increasingly loudly, until 50 kilometres (30 miles) short of Dushanbe, she conked out. The Doc, shrunk in half by shedding his cold-weather gear, popped his favourite patient's bonnet.

'Battery dead ... because dynamo dead. Alternator, I think ... dying. Spark plugs ...' He grimaced, examining a cracked, stained spark plug – a victim of the questionable fuel we had been taking on in the Pamirs (more often than not, the fuel-station attendants came out brandishing a sieve to filter out the twigs, and that was only the more fastidious).

The spark plugs were easily replaced from our supply of spares, but not so the knackered dynamo and alternator – which kept the lights and other electrical parts on. With no backups, we would have to ask Adam to send them from the UK. Meanwhile, we'd need a patch. The Doc and Larry – our mechanical brains trust – convened. Oxford's battery was swapped from PAC, and both cars were restarted.

While I was concerned about Oxford's current state, I was quietly pleased we had managed to get this far without calling Adam back in York for help. Not that I could take much credit for Oxford's surprising endurance – it was entirely down to the wisdom and experience of the jolly little man whose head was now buried deep under Oxford's bonnet. I'd learned so much from the Doc in the last few weeks about Oxford's multiple foibles and how to address them, but as I watched him at work, I knew I still had an awful lot to learn.

'First problem: solved. Now second problem ...' The Doc scratched his chin. 'We need a workshop.'

The closest we could find was 40 kilometres (25 miles) away on the edge of Dushanbe, and it was already afternoon. We had no choice but to soldier on. Her successful heart transplant notwithstanding, the patient was still very sick. She wheezed and jolted like an asthmatic frog, barely managing 25 km/h

(15 mph). Vladimir motioned to pull in at a nearby town, where after a few minutes he returned carrying what looked like a spray can of deodorant attached to a long black hose. Usually sparse with words, Vladimir started communicating enthusiastically to me via Alex.

'The engine is not getting enough fuel, because the fuel pump is getting no power. We need to get more fuel into the engine, and the quickest way is injecting propane gas,' Alex translated, tapping the spray can. 'Like a DIY LPG conversion.'

He fed the hose through the ventilation hatches beneath the windscreen, into the engine's air intake. He started Oxford up, prompting a lurching growl. Wincing, Vladimir turned the nozzle on the propane. To my delight and surprise, the engine purred like a contented kitten. The propane-ventilator was a success, but I had a burning question.

'Is this safe?'

The Doc shook his head, uncharacteristically graven. Vladimir had conducted the whole operation with a lit cigarette in his mouth. A vote of confidence, I thought, or suicidal bravery?

'Please,' said Vladimir, inviting Nat and me to re-embark.

I gingerly took the wheel, Nat clutching the can. Leo, who usually jumped at the chance to film our foolish antics from inside the cab, was noticeably absent. Tibie watched with an air of deep concern, holding a fire extinguisher. As Nat fed propane into the engine, we pulled away.

'This might be the stupidest idea yet,' I observed, before breaking into a fit of giggles, almost certainly sparked by the cloud of propane leaking into the cab. Nat, giggling alongside, agreed. Luckily, neither of us smoked.

Our mobile Molotov cocktail miraculously reached Dushanbe's outskirts without spontaneous combustion, and Alex pulled the convoy into a roadside car wash.

'No dirty cars in the city. President's orders.'

I thought Alex was joking, but he clearly wasn't. Rahmon's eyes bore into me from a billboard across the road; not a man you wanted to upset. Due to her sieve-like condition, Oxford had to be emptied completely before going under the hoses. There was something deeply therapeutic about watching huge lumps of dirt – rich with fragments from Singapore, Thailand, Burma, India, Nepal, China, Kyrgyzstan and Tajikistan – tumble from Oxford's nooks and crannies. The eight of us stood side by side, mesmerized and lost in thought.

Many of my colleagues, I guessed, were dreaming of being as clean as Oxford. I certainly was. For the past two months we had all become used to undressing only as much as we needed, and to showering on special occasions. The bright lights of Dushanbe offered a much-needed rest for humans and vehicles alike. The Doc and Larry disappeared with Oxford to their happy place – a nearby workshop – to have Oxford's bodywork looked at. The bone-rattling roads we'd been driving on ever since leaving Thailand had taken their toll on the old girl, and without urgent welding on her bodywork she was at risk of becoming a hatchback – or, worse, a convertible.

Once we reached our guesthouse, we did our best to scrape off the worst of the dirt as we'd been invited for lunch with the British ambassador, Matthew Lawson. His residence, a dainty mock-French chateau hidden behind a high wall was, I thought, a suitably glamorous way to mark our journey's halfway point. Matthew and his partner Enrica were elegant and impeccably dressed, quite at odds with our dusty rabble. I sat guiltily on Her Majesty's spotless sofa, eating Tajik delicacies from bone china.

Britain's network of embassies and consulates had been invaluable for the First Overlanders back in the 1950s. Letters and telegrams between these far-flung postings had greased the wheels of their journey at a time when Britain was one of the world's foremost political and military powers. While we'd had valuable offers of help from Matthew and his counterparts all along our route, today we were driving through a very different world. China, the US, Russia, Brazil, and even Italy now had a greater diplomatic footprint than Britain today, its middling status on the world stage increasingly apparent.

'Some people here think Britain is still pulling the strings, playing the "Great Game" with Russia,' Matthew chuckled.

Back at university, I'd read an awful lot about this episode of imperial willy-waving between the British and Russian Empires that ran through most of the nineteenth century. Driven by Britain's (arguably unfounded) fears of Russia coveting its precious Indian empire, the Central Asian plateau became a shifting 3D chessboard for generals and mandarins in London and St Petersburg to plot their intrigue. Afghanistan, and parts of modern Uzbekistan and Tajikistan, were seen as the central battleground, with both Brits and Russians wanting to prevent the other from gaining too much control, lest it tip the global balance of power.

Like the Cold War of the twentieth century, it was a conflict defined by little direct action between the forces of the two main protagonists, but it would come to have direct and deadly impacts on the peoples of Central Asia through whom a proxy war was fought. The Great Game is generally seen to have been brought to a close by the creation of the cartographical oddity we had driven past on our way here – the Wakhan Corridor, a thin sliver of land tacked on to Afghanistan that separated Tajikistan from Pakistan.

As I listened to Matthew describe Britain's benign presence here today – supporting poverty reduction, promoting trade – I could see that like in Malaysia, Myanmar, India and Nepal, Britain's legacy was still being felt long after the Brits themselves had retreated.

'Despite what I say, there's always a feeling that Britain is still up to its old tricks. But from what I can see,' Lawson concluded, 'the only thing that remains true from the Great Game era is that Tajikistan is still seen as a barrier by the Western powers. Not between empires, but between the West and the jihadists and drugs pouring from Afghanistan.'

After lunch I stood beneath a glowing portrait of Queen Elizabeth II, wondering what to write in the guestbook. If, sixty-four years ago, I'd told Her Majesty three of her subjects would be on a jolly jaunt in Tajikistan, being guided by two Soviet soldiers and driving an icon of British engineering fresh from the roads of China, I suspect she would have raised a regal eyebrow. Stalinabad, as Dushanbe was then called, would have been unthinkable territory for Brits in 1955. Now here we were, in the far recesses of the old Soviet empire, halfway on our journey across a world that had turned in more ways than one.

I put my pen to the page.

See you in 64 years? Lots of love, Oxford.

1 November 2019: Dushanbe, Tajikistan
Expedition Day 69

The first of November marked the start of our fourth calendar month since leaving Singapore, and passage to our tenth country. Uzbekistan shares with Liechtenstein alone a 'double-landlocked' status,[13] and as we prepared to cross the border it felt as if we were finally reaching the arid heart of the vast Central Asian Steppe.

It struck me on the road north from Dushanbe towards the Uzbek border that I'd forgotten what it was not to be on the road, not to eat three meals a day with the same people, not to drive a car without power steering, waterproofing or insulation. To be honest, I didn't want to remember. This *was* my life now, the life of pure adventure of which I'd always dreamed. There was a blissful, zen-like state to it, one in which cares about the past and future

---

13   Surrounded entirely by other countries that are themselves landlocked.

couldn't interfere. All that mattered was the few metres of road in front, and the next destination on our list.

The morning was chilly, but for the first time in weeks I was driving Oxford without thick gloves, and only a light jacket. In many ways, Oxford was still being held together by the mechanical equivalent of sticking plasters, and would be until Adam's care package arrived, but the Doc's devoted tinkering in Dushanbe had restored her to reasonable nick. Now that we'd been able to abandon Vladimir's propane hose, the air in the cab smelled crisp and reassuringly inflammable.

Next stop was Tashkent, Uzbekistan's capital, which for us would represent another less celebratory watershed moment. That morning at our daily breakfast briefing, Marcus had confirmed a sad state of affairs that had been looming before us for some time. When we reached Tashkent, we would be temporarily saying goodbye to one our team, our now inseparable little wheel-bound family that had overcome so much.

The visa regime for Turkmenistan, our next country after Uzbekistan, was to blame. It had proved the most painful (even above China) for Marcus to navigate. The Turkmen authorities had allowed us to swap Nat in for Tim at short notice but had done so by inexplicably removing Tibie. We had been warned that appealing the decision would likely see our entire convoy rejected by the prickly Turkmen authorities, halting our expedition at the Turkmen border. Tibie, while devastated to be breaking ranks, had nobly fallen on her sword.

She would board a plane in Tashkent and, within a few hours, land in Georgia; if all went according to plan, we would re-join her there in just over two weeks.

'Just make sure you get Oxford – and Nat – to Georgia in one piece, please?' she said with mock severity, as I hugged her goodbye at the airport. It was like losing the little sister from my overlanding family. Sensing the malaise left by losing one of our own, Alex rallied the crew.

'I've organized a surprise, a night out just for the *boys*.'

His fiendish look haunted me across the 320 kilometres (200 miles) from Tashkent, via the Uzbek border, to ancient Samarkand. One of the region's oldest continuously inhabited cities, Samarkand draws its historic wealth and importance from its position at the centre of the old Silk Roads and therefore, for many centuries, civilization.

Ever since our decision to deviate from the First Overland's original route and traverse Central Asia, my inner historian had ached to better understand the nations Tim, Marcus and I had crudely lumped together as 'the Stans'. Rather than the 'middle of nowhere', as they can seem when viewed from Britain, for centuries they have been the crossroads of the known world.

Civilizations were born and the world's great faiths and languages cross-pollinated here. History's mightiest empires battled for the riches of its trade routes linking East and West. It was through here that my famous namesake, Alexander the Great, had made his easternmost foray on his world-conquering road trip, and where that insatiable glory hunter was said to have wept for having no more worlds to conquer.[14]

While we had been driving through the driftwood of Britain's fallen empire for most of our journey, it was worth noting that for a major part of Central Asia's long and illustrious history, it was we Britons who were at the wild fringes, inhabiting a dark, heretical island on the edge of the world.

That night, however, it was not the footsteps of Alexander or the ruins of the famed fourteenth-century Islamic architecture that Alex was keen to show us. He instructed us to drop our things and meet him at a mysterious location in the backstreets. Bundled up against the biting night-time cold of Uzbekistan, we followed

---

14   Okay, so the historian in me will have to make clear he almost certainly never said that, and it's not even clear what he might have been weeping about, but it's a fable that's too poetic not to repeat.

Alex's directions, arriving at a gate where a squat, expectant old man beckoned us in.

We descended a maze of stairs, passing strange, conical brick structures resembling antique pizza ovens. Arriving at a room of tattered old lockers, realization dawned on David.

'*Eto khamam?*'

'*Da!*' said our guide. '*Teper snimi odezhdu.*'

'Welcome to the Hammam,' said David. 'Get naked, gentlemen.'

Minutes later, our mottled physiques followed David deeper down into a honeycomb of brickwork with slick, tiled floors. The temperature and humidity, and a fug of man-sweat and menthol, rose with each step.

'What took you so long!' boomed a familiar voice, punctuated with slapping and grunting.

Around the corner appeared the enormous, sweat-slicked hulk of Alex Fedin, naked but for an overworked towel. He was face-down on a white marble podium, a tiny, hairy Uzbek man in black Y-fronts pummelling and squeezing his back and shoulders while riding him like a horse. The sight quickly burned into my retina.

'Relax … get warm …!' Alex instructed between beatings.

We each took turns to be manhandled by the tiny Uzbek, whose hands, assisted by the heat, found the stresses and strains of more than two months on the road, teasing them out to groans of pain and relief.

Afterwards, one of his equally tiny, hairy colleagues had the unenviable task of scraping away our dead skin, then rubbed the fresh skin with ginger, as if readying us for the oven. A glorious spectacle of homoerotic healing that I think, on balance, Tibie would have been glad to miss.

Next morning, looking years younger, we were free to see Samarkand. As I had daydreamed my way through the history books back in the school library in Manchester, Alexander's description of Samarkand after he seized it in 329 BC had stuck with me: 'Everything I have heard about Marakanda [Samarkand] is true, except that it's more beautiful than I ever imagined.'

Now it was my turn to gawp. Stepping onto Samarkand's Registan, the ancient central square, I could almost feel Alexander standing shoulder to shoulder beside me. On three sides rise towering, arched doorways, twenty metres (sixty-five feet) high and flanked by even taller minarets. Samarkand had played host to Sogdians and Seleucids, Sassanids and Umayyads, Abbasids and Samanids, Seljuks and Mongols, and had been the spiritual home to Zoroastrians, Manichaeists and Nestorians, although it was Islam that shaped the bedazzling city standing today. The oldest of these *madrasas* – schools of Islamic learning – date to the mighty Timur, or Tamerlane, in the fourteenth century.

Timur, who claimed descent from Genghis Khan,[15] resolved to rebuild his forebear's gargantuan empire. Through genius tactics and orgies of blood-spilling (he's rumoured to have slaughtered 5 per cent of the world population at the time), Timur achieved his goal, securing his place in the warlord hall of fame alongside the Great Khan.

Samarkand had already been a wealthy trading city on the crossroads of China, India and Persia for centuries, but from 1370 Timur rebuilt it entirely. Plunder from his campaigns funded a whirlwind of construction and artistic patronage, and he brought the finest thinkers from across his new empire to bring his vision to life.

Timur's madrasas had been painstakingly maintained more recently under Uzbekistan's first post-independence leader, Islam Karimov. The blunt might of their profile was softened by intricate, geometric tile work in dazzling blues, greens and golds, glittering as if laid yesterday. Inside, however, the hallways

---

15   Probably wrongly, but given Tamerlane's reputation I'd be reluctant to disagree with him.

and corridors no longer rang with discussion of the Qur'an or recitations of the Hadiths.

Karimov, who had held control of the newly created Uzbekistan from 1991 until his death in 2016, had harnessed the memory of Timur and his empire for a new nation in need of an identity. However, like most old Soviets, he suspected Timur's religion – Islam. Despite his first name, Islam Karimov considered the faith and its increasingly politicized adherents a threat. The madrasas were restored to their former glory but, rather than the faithful, they housed souvenir stalls selling tourist tat. My mind cast back to Kashgar, another 'restored' city where the only approved religion was retail.

Timur's tomb, contrastingly, was a place of deep, almost religious reverence. Situated near the Registan, the heavily restored *Gur-e-Amir* boasted the now familiar looming arch with accompanying minarets, topped with a huge azure dome: a distinctive style that would be copied far and wide, including by the Mughal architects behind the Taj Mahal.

Inside, hushed silence surrounded the tombstone of a man whose empire had stretched from Russia to India, from Mongolia to the Mediterranean. Timur personified an age when this windswept, barren spot was the centre of the civilized world. He had died, aged almost seventy and doubtless exhausted from four decades' marauding, leading an enormous army to conquer China.

'Given the chaos he caused, I'll admit I'm amazed I'd never heard of the bloke until coming here,' said Nat. I nodded in agreement.

Legend has it that Timur's legacy was not consigned to history. In June 1941, Stalin's researchers opened the tomb to take Timur's remains to Moscow for examination. Allegedly, they found a warning inscribed on the coffin:

Whosoever disturbs my tomb will unleash
an invader more terrible than I am.

Two days later, Hitler invaded the Soviet Union, starting a conflict that would cost more than (a Timur-beating) 25 million Russian lives. Stalin, not famously superstitious, learned of the curse and ordered Timur's remains returned and reburied with full religious rites in November 1942. That same month, the Soviets turned the tide of the war at Stalingrad. Superstitious nonsense or not, I'd wager that few could suppress a shiver down the spine standing by Timur's tomb.

Foremost on my mind, however, wasn't Timur, but Tim. We had last spoken by phone shortly before entering Nepal, having since been stymied by Chinese firewalls and shoddy signals in Kyrgyzstan and Tajikistan. I had also been reluctant to call him until I'd delivered his grandson through our most dangerous leg. With Nat now safely through Xinjiang, the Pamir Highway and the Afghan border, I felt it was time to set up a video call to London.

The First Overlanders were amazed they could get a letter from almost anywhere in the world in seven days. In emergencies a cable was quicker, but ruinously expensive. Video conferencing from an Uzbek café to Wimbledon would, I am sure, have provoked scoffs of disbelief from Tim in 1955.

Now, in 2019, it seemed the effect was not lost.

'Goodness gracious, modern communications!'

Tim's voice was followed by his face fuzzing into view, my first sight of it since the hotel in Singapore. He looked frail, but a damn sight better than he had on that awful morning.

'Instantaneous picture and sound, marvellous! How far have you gone now?'

'Ten thousand kilometres,' I answered, proudly.

'You mean six thousand miles. None of that bloody kilometre nonsense!'

I was happy to be corrected, and even happier to see Tim approaching his old, cantankerous self. I still lived in hope that Tim would re-join us; and seeing him today had fanned the flame. He had proved everyone wrong once already, so why not one more time?

'How are you, Nat?' asked Tim, leaning in to get a better look at his grandson.

'Very well, thank you, they're looking after me quite well.'

'Glad to hear it. What country are you in now?'

'Uzbekistan.'

'Uzbekistan! An improvement on Tibet, I hear?'

'Massively.'

'And Oxford?'

'Coping better than we are, I think.'

Listening to Nat navigate his grandpa's mechanical, geographical and logistical interrogations, I felt a twinge of sadness. Tim had been giddy tracing his fingers through 'the Stans' on his living-room floor map. His dream to see these madrasas before it was too late had brought us to their doors without him.

But I understood now that my sadness was unjustified. I could see first-hand how much Nat taking his place clearly meant to Tim, and how privileged the two were to share this adventure. In the days before and after my grandad's death, I had envied them. I would have given anything to have that bond with my own grandad. But today envy was giving way to gratitude, and a realization of how lucky I was to be able to help bring a grandfather and grandson together closer than ever before.

'Is he pulling his weight, Alex?' Tim's question jolted me back to the present.

'Just about!' I joked.

'Good. Well, I'll say goodbye and we'll talk soon. Oh, Nat, your mother says, "Get a haircut!"'

Our last stop in Uzbekistan was Bukhara, another once-booming Silk Road city and pillar of early Islam, about 320 kilometres (200 miles) due east from Samarkand. Home in its pomp to philosophers such as Ibn Sina, and the poets Rudaki and Firdausi (the Persian-Islamic world's Newton, Milton and Shakespeare), a millennium of decline had reduced it somewhat. A quick loop of its old city – preserved in similar souvenir fashion to Samarkand – was sufficient. Evening's Arctic chill returning, I returned to our guesthouse opposite the intimidating bulk of Bukhara's most famous site: the Ark.

The massive fortress, first founded in around AD 500, had formed the city's military, administrative and cultural heart ever since. I had read about the Ark years ago at university, but back then, to me it was simply another beguiling name in a far-off place. That wasn't always true for my fellow Brits – however, the events that transpired here in 1842 horrified Victorian Britain and marked a major milestone in the 'Great Game'.

Right here, possibly where I was standing, two British officers were made to dig their own graves in frozen earth before being beheaded, while the Emir of Bukhara looked on. Colonel Charles Stoddart had been a prisoner of the Emir for four years, after a diplomatic mission intended to sway him from Russia to Britain's side had gone badly wrong. Captain Arthur Conolly had been sent to save Stoddart but had been sentenced by the Emir alongside him.

Despite outrage in the British press, their deaths signalled the beginning of the end of Britain's ambitions to control Central Asia, ceding it to Russian control, which – as it only formally ended in 1991 – could still be felt today. Back in the 1840s, Britain was too busy fighting a doomed war in Afghanistan (sound familiar?) and forcing the Chinese to buy opium at gunpoint to care about this godforsaken place, or the two imperial sons sent to die here.

Since leaving Singapore, we had driven through the driftwood of Britain's imperial project. In Singapore, Malaysia, Myanmar, India, Nepal, Tibet and now Uzbekistan, the legacy of my tiny island home's hubristic idea could still be seen in bricks and mortar or felt just beneath the surface – like the skeletons of Stoddart and Conolly – in the cultural, political and religious conflicts left in its retreating wake.

As I sat on Oxford's bonnet, greedily soaking in the last sliver of sun outside the lobby and chewing over the miserable fate of the two British officers only yards from here, I noticed a battered Toyota Land Cruiser pulling up nearby. I say noticed – it was impossible to miss. It was painted bright yellow, with the words 'LANDCRUISING ADVENTURE' in large sweeping font on the flank. It was equipped with a large snorkel on the right side and four mighty spotlights above the windscreen; and was stacked on top with all manner of crates, cans and canvas bags, as if ready to take on a crossing of the Amazon.

This was an unwittingly astute observation, as I was about discover when the car's two occupants – immediately drawn in by Oxford – introduced themselves. I listened with amazement as I learned that Karin and Coen, both from the Netherlands, had been living, working and travelling together across the world in this Toyota for the last sixteen years.

'I thought four months was a long time!' I confessed, as Karin invited me to join them both for coffee that she was prepping on a little stove in the back. As we sipped on the scolding brew, they started to share their story.

'We sold everything we had and set off to drive from the Netherlands to Singapore back in 2003. The Singapore journey is the big one – as you know!' said Karin.

'We originally gave ourselves two years,' continued Coen, 'but then once we reached Singapore we thought, why stop? After driving all around Asia, we shipped the car from Malaysia to Argentina, and spent nine years driving to the remotest corners of South America. Then in 2016, we shipped the car from Suriname to South Korea, and we've been working our way back east ever since!'

'We're probably the slowest overlanders in the world!' chuckled Karin. 'We only average about fifty kilometres a day! For us that's the only way to truly see the world – how can you make genuine connections to a country, to its people, moving at fifty kilometres an hour?'

As she opened the back doors of the car and I saw the entirety of their little mobile world, I recalled with regret Kyrgyzstan, Manipur and Malaysia – all places I had technically been to, but yet I knew so little about. Then I remembered Xinjiang – sometimes you can't go fast enough.

'Everything has its place,' explained Coen, gesturing me into their neat little capsule, 'and we keep nothing that is not completely necessary.' It was totally adapted to their needs, and they pointed out the tiny alterations – a black-out blind here, a carefully placed wodge of insulation there – that had come from thousands of days and nights together in here. I thought guiltily of the clutter and mess we battled to control in PAC and Oxford every day.

As the temperature plummeted with the setting sun, I invited them into our cosy hotel lobby, where Coen cracked out a precious bottle of cognac – clearly one of the scant luxuries that was allowed. I told them about our story, and they listened intently. They were both in their early fifties, apparently, but there was something about the pair that made them hard to age. Karin's shoulder-length white hair sat at odds to a face free of worry lines, and Coen's grey flecks and stubble served to frame eyes filled with youthful mischief. They were clear that tensions arose between them, but the way they held hands while they thought no one was watching, and never once spoke across the other, told of a deep and abiding connection forged through countless trials over the years.

'Overlanding for us,' said Karin, 'is not about getting from A to B as fast as possible. Nor is it a competition where you tick off as many countries as possible. There's no winners and losers in overlanding. We *live* on the road, this is not a one-off challenge, a holiday or a sabbatical – this is our life. For us it's about learning, sharing, and most of all connecting with those we meet along the way.'

Given the mad dash across the world we were currently on, and all the media attention that had gone with it, I couldn't help but see an implicit criticism of our endeavour in Karin's description of what was and wasn't overlanding. In some ways, I thought, she was right. To truly *live* on the road really was another life entirely, and not one I had ever considered until meeting them. The conversation turned to home, and what it meant to those who had chosen to live as nomads. For the first time, I saw an area of disagreement between the pair.

'I would be happy to never go back to the Netherlands,' confessed Coen, 'but Karin – she has family, she has roots. Her mother, her sisters … at some point they will need her to go home.'

Karin nodded slowly, and I felt that the cognac was leading us into terrain that was not mine to tread. I understood their predicament, however – I felt I had shades of both Karin and Coen in me, and that at some point it was a conflict that would have to be resolved. To change the subject to lighter matters, I gestured to the hulking shadow of the Ark outside and retold the story of Conolly and Stoddart's grisly fate.

Karin shook her head with a smile.

'Well, that's what you get from wanting to write yourself into the history books, Alex!'

We said an emotional goodbye. Brief though it was, the meeting would be one of the most memorable on my long journey. When I got to my room at last, for the first time in weeks I found it had a bath, and despite the brown-tinged water that came from the taps, I submerged myself in its piping heat. The tendrils of steam carried away the fleeting feelings of homesickness and doubt that Karin and Coen's words had left me with, and I trembled with excitement at the thought of the next country to come.

It was by far the most reclusive, peculiar, and for me downright beguiling on our journey: Turkmenistan.

16

The Turkmenator

6 November 2019: Bukhara, Uzbekistan

Expedition Day 74

On a cold, clear morning we motored west out of Bukhara towards the border with Turkmenistan, our eleventh country. Oxford was running surprisingly well – as was I, thanks to the new diet of yak meat and fine Russian vodka. Marcus and David, beside me in Oxford, were on similarly effervescent form. In fact, they looked fit to burst.

Ever since we'd settled on our Central Asian route, Marcus and David had been obsessed with the bizarre, reclusive dictatorship we were about to cross, and I had heard snatches of them compiling their favourite Turkmen trivia for weeks now. Now the time had come for them to let it loose.

'Are you ready?' Marcus asked, giddily.

'Go on then …' I replied, hiding a smile.

So, he began.

'Turkmenistan is roughly the size of France, but mostly desert, and home to less than 6 million people. It has the fourth-largest natural gas reserves in the world, most of which it exports to China. Since independence from the Soviet Union in 1991, it was run by the same man for twenty-five years – Saparmurat Niyazov – or, as he called himself, "Turkmenbashi", or "Leader of the Turkmen". Now …'

He paused, handing the baton to David.

'Turkmenbashi declared himself President for Life in 1992, and it went to his head. He built the world's largest white-marble city, with an *enormous* gold statue of himself in the middle, which rotates to face the sun; wrote a semi-autobiographical book, the *Ruhnama*, that became compulsory reading for all citizens (including as part of the driving test); renamed the days and months after himself and members of his family, and the word "bread" to the name of his mother ...'

Marcus, unable to resist, jumped back in.

'He banned opera, the circus, ballet, spandex, lip-synching at concerts, and beards on men under seventy; he declared national holidays for both melons and carpets; he banned smoking in public because he was trying to quit ...'

David wrenched the baton back.

'Then in 2005 he closed all hospitals and libraries outside the capital, deeming them unnecessary; finally, gold teeth were made illegal – those wanting stronger dentures were officially advised to chew on bones, as the president saw dogs doing that when he was a child and it seemed to work for them.'

'Finished?' I asked.

'No!' they replied in unison.

'We haven't even started on his successor!' said Marcus.

'When Turkmenbashi died in 2006, his dentist – Gurbanguly Berdimuhamedov – took over. He prefers to be called "Arkadag", meaning "Protector".'

David picked up seamlessly.

'So, people thought he would be a breath of fresh air, but no. This year Turkmenistan ranked bottom in the world for press freedom, and apparently has only *one* working journalist; taking a leaf out of his predecessor's book, Arkadag is building a massive gold statue of himself on horseback; he makes patriotic rap videos; and, finally, he's been dubbed "the Turkmenator" for his love of shooting at things with big guns.'

While awaiting a blockage of horses and carts to clear ahead of us, to prove David's point, Marcus treated me to a video of the president riding slowly past a series of targets on a bicycle, hitting the bullseye on each, to the riotous applause of watching soldiers. Despite the hardship through which he was putting the long-suffering Turkmen, it was impossible to not be intrigued by the scale of the man's preposterous ego.

As we approached the Turkmen border crossing, it was time to say an emotional goodbye to Alex and Vladimir. I was sad to lose the reassuring bulk of our two guardians, who had kept us safe during the most dangerous stretch of our journey, but this parting also marked a major spirit-lifting milestone for our crew. While Turkmenistan was deeply odd, at least it wasn't dangerous for foreigners. With China and the Stans now safely traversed, the toughest sections of our journey were behind us: as soon as we crossed through Turkmenistan and towards the edge of Europe, it felt as if we were home and dry.

As Alex and Vladimir's waving forms shrank in our mirrors, we pulled through a series of forbidding barbed-wire fences topped with sniper posts, towards a large immigration building, where a severe, muscular man of about forty waited. Alex had recruited this replacement guide to meet us on the other side, but such was Turkmenistan, neither he nor Marcus had ever communicated with the newcomer directly before. The mirrored sunglasses and blocky head, clean-shaven but for a strip down the middle, gave the impression of an Action Man figurine come to life. Climbing from Oxford to greet him, I noticed a livid scar stretching from his left earlobe to the corner of his mouth.

'I am Tashmurad,' he said, crushing my hand and grinning to reveal strong white teeth. 'Welcome to Turkmenistan!'

We followed him into a neat building, where the Arkadag's image adorned every wall.

'You mustn't point at pictures of the president,' whispered David, sharing another finding from his extensive homework.

'Who? Him?' said the Doc, pointing directly at a painting of a fur-clad man on horseback, cuddling a puppy. David winced.

Tashmurad ushered us to a line of officials overseeing a byzantine system of taxes and fees. For an hour we bounced back and forth between them to purchase insurance, scan passports, pay road tax, bridge tax, tax for crossing military areas, and various other fees and subsidies. Seeing my growing frustration as our precious reserves of US dollars rapidly depleted, Tashmurad shrugged.

'Turkmenistan doesn't need tourists, we're rich.'

I raised an eyebrow. From my own research, I knew that wasn't true. Despite the natural gas bonanza, the average Turkmenistani was around six times poorer than the average Brit. We would soon discover where the money went.

As we waited, Tashmurad embarked on an impassioned lecture on the history of Turkmenistan. Into tales of its twenty-four ancient tribes, or the importance of the beautiful Akhal-Teke horse to Turkmen culture,[16] Tashmurad interwove stories of his own life. While enlightening us about the virtues of Sunni Islam, he excitedly shared videos of himself bending frying pans, crowbars and other lumps of metal with his bare hands. He had tried everything – soldiering, teaching and even, for a fortnight, accountancy. 'It didn't suit me,' he admitted, to no one's surprise.

'Now, final stage,' announced Tashmurad, 'car inspection.'

One of the bureaucrats guided the convoy around the building to another band of uniformed officers thawing in the sun. Their leader, apparently irked, accosted Tashmurad. After an angry exchange, Tashmurad turned to me, furious, 'He's asking what took you so long? You're making his officers look bad by moving so slowly through immigration.'

Seeing the confused look on my face, the officer started to laugh.

'Conor McGregor!' he shouted at me, beckoning his colleagues

---

16 So precious are these horses in Turkmen culture that Turkmenistan is the only Central Asian nation where horse is not on the menu. I didn't have the nerve to tell Tashmurad that we'd been chewing on a fine stallion steak only a few days before.

over for a closer look. My apparently passing likeness to the Irish cage-fighter seemed to soothe tensions, and he shook my hand heartily. Just as I began to relax, he snarled again at Tashmurad. I looked imploringly for help.

'He said Conor McGregor insulted Islam greatly, and you should apologize,' explained Tashmurad. I turned to the officer, looking for signs in his narrowed eyes that this was a joke. Nothing.

'I'm ... sorry?'

He stared back at me, then grinned and slapped my arm.

'Conor, good fighter, come!'

Apparently, Turkmen small talk was a verbal fistfight in which McGregor himself would struggle.

After a perfunctory search, Nat and I jumped into Oxford and made to pull away just as her window was grabbed by a gigantic hand, attached to one of the largest humans I had ever seen.

'Conor. Leak,' said the camo-clad giant, pointing to a pool of green-black liquid on the inspection platform.

'She's just marking her territory, all old Land Rovers do it,' I joked, stealing the Doc's standard explanation for Oxford's regular incontinence. With our passage almost complete and the Turkmen tarmac stretching out in front, I was riding high and refused to let Oxford spoil the moment.

Tashmurad translated, and the officer-giant shrugged before letting us loose. Thinking no more of it, I revved Oxford hard and pulled away into the open roads of eastern Turkmenistan.

'In Asia there is usually only one road, and if you're not on it, you're in the desert.'

Nat read aloud the very appropriate words of Pat – the First Overland's navigator – as we cruised across the slick tarmac of the M37, the east–west highway connecting most of sparsely populated Turkmenistan's major cities. To my right the Karakum Desert, a vast expanse of sand constituting 70 per cent of Turkmenistan, covered the fossil-fuel riches on which its elite, at least, thrived.

I felt a jolt of pure, selfish excitement that came with breaking new ground. I had last felt this rush crossing into Tibet almost a month ago, after all the border drama. I thought of the First Overlanders driving their way into history all those years before. Now here we were in one of the most inaccessible countries on Earth, making history of our own.

I looked to Nat, who was staring pensively into the desert. No longer 'Tim's grandson' standing in for his famous grandpa, he was an overlander in his own right. I realized that once we were out of Turkmenistan and its onerous visa regime, the door was open for Tim to return as soon as he was ready. From the emails I'd had from Tim and Kate, he was growing stronger by the day. I daydreamed of the moment Tim and Nat were reunited on their grand adventure, perhaps in the streets of Baku or Istanbul, and it left me drunk with joy.

In the endless expanse, my mind wandered to our next destination – the town of Mary, 240 kilometres (150 miles) further west. Today Turkmenistan's fourth largest city, in the twelfth century it was one of the greatest on Earth, a dazzling pearl on the ancient Silk Road until our old friend Tamerlane flattened it. Here, too, in 1885 the Great Game reached its final crescendo. Britain and Russia teetered on the brink of war after Russia annexed Mary, which Britain considered uncomfortably close to India ...

CLUNK.

'What was that?' squeaked Nat, both of us snapping from our daydreams. I looked backwards at the tarmac, clear but for Enterprise on the horizon.

'Pothole?' I ventured, unconvinced. Oxford had become an extension of my body over the last seventy-three days; both Nat and I could read her every creak and groan.

'That was definitely a new one,' said Nat as we accelerated back to top speed on the three-lane highway.

The radio crackled with the cries of an unusually animated Larry.

'STOP!!!'

'What did he say?'

'Stop!'

'Why?'

'STOP!' both Nat and radio-Larry shouted in unison.

I slammed the brake pedal, which went straight to the floor. Oxford raced on, accelerating to 96 km/h (60 mph) as the road hit a decline.

'STOP!' shouted Larry again.

I pumped the brake frantically, but it was futile. Desperate now, I grabbed the handbrake and wrenched as hard as I could. Nothing.

'No brakes!' I shouted to Nat, whose ashen face showed he already knew.

I was powerless. My only option was to pitch Oxford into the metal barriers to my right before we hit another car. Nat gripped the dashboard. The faces of Tim, Kate and Lionel flashed again, this time cursing me for killing their beloved on this vainglorious adventure. There was nothing else for it – I moved to bury Oxford's nose in the barrier, when suddenly she swerved left as another clunking thud filled the cab.

'The wheel, the *wheel!*' screamed Nat, as Oxford's back-left tyre complete with half-axle span off into the road behind us like a giant, rubber spinning-top. Sparks flew as her newly naked wheel bearing scored a thick groove in the tarmac. At the expense of her undercarriage, Oxford ground to a shuddering halt beside the road. Even once we'd reached a standstill, I struggled to prise my leaden fingers from the wheel, and to stop my heart hammering in my mouth.

Slowly Nat stepped out, and I followed. The team came running down the road, shouting and waving. Even as they drew close, I could barely hear their cries. A pool of red-tinged axle fluid was spilling from Oxford's open wound, now flowing down the groove she had carved in her death throes. Our giant Turkmen friend had clearly spotted the first signs of a problem back at immigration – and in my hubris, I had ignored him.

Larry brought a jack from his car, and the Doc was soon under his critical patient, Nat on standby to pass any tools he needed. Excruciating minutes passed as the Doc assessed the damage.

'The pothole broke the wheel bearing … Then the half-axle came out … The brakes with it. I can put the half-axle back in and she will roll, but I think the rear differential is damaged. If it is, she will not drive any further.'

Fearing the worst, I stood looking on dejected, the hopes of realizing mine and Tim's dream reduced to roadside scrap. I watched in a daze as Tashmurad radioed for a flatbed truck, onto which Oxford's carcass was loaded. Not content with depriving us of our expedition's little sister before we even crossed the border, now Turkmenistan had claimed our wizened matriarch too.

Marcus came over, placing his hand on my shoulder.

'The good side …'

'What's the good side?' I said, with barely concealed frustration.

'The good side is that you're alive. Imagine if that had happened coming down a mountain.'

I nodded, grateful for my old friend's cool head.

'I'm glad you're alive,' he continued matter-of-factly, opening a bag of crisps.

'I'm glad that this episode has given you an opportunity to say that,' I replied.

After this uncharacteristic exchange of affection between two male Brits, I found myself sitting in the stifling cab of the flatbed truck, the full enormity of the crash dawning.

First came a wave of relief that no one was hurt, and that the bearing had cracked on the flat highway, rather than – as Marcus had said – atop a Nepalese mountain. Next, the shame of defeat, our famous antique broken and potentially unfixable.

After that came panic – what on Earth would we do? With phone and internet reception censored out of existence by the Turkmen regime, we were completely cut off from support. We had five days left on our Turkmen visas; then, with or without Oxford, we had eleven more countries to cross. Without Oxford, we were just a bunch of grubby idiots who should have caught a plane.

As we approached the outskirts of Mary a few hours later, it wasn't relief, shame or panic that plagued me. It was something deeper, darker that remained. I kept replaying the moment in Oxford when the brakes had failed to work, and reliving the look of blind panic on Nat's face. I had believed then it might be the last look I ever saw on a face that had so many years to live, and for the first time in weeks I thought of my grandad. I remembered the car crash that had killed my grandmother and collapsed his world. I saw then how easily one brief moment of bad luck can dictate the rest of our lives.

With Oxford's demise, my belief in a life made meaningful only by going on a great adventure had died with her. I wanted to shrink into the seat, vanish into nothingness – we had failed, I had failed, and now I had to face the consequences of my own foolish ambition.

After dozens of calls, Tashmurad had found a workshop that would agree to inspect a car that no Turkmen mechanic seemed to have heard of. We pulled into the compound. It was a place where cars went to die, their rusting innards spilling across the floor.

Only the gaggle of oil-stained men inspecting a decrepit Toyota revealed it might be more than a scrapyard. Tashmurad sought the owner, a squat man with close-cropped hair, who on seeing foreigners insisted we take no pictures or video of him or his crew. We sat in dejected silence on a clutch of old tyres while Tashmurad joined their huddle, under clear instruction to establish how bad the damage was, whether it was possible to get Oxford back on the road, and if not, how we could get it out of the country.

After ten minutes' heated exchange, Tashmurad returned.

'Is it dead?' I asked.

'We haven't discussed that yet.'

'What have you been talking about all this time?!'

'They want to know why you're here. They don't understand.

I tried to explain, but they keep asking – "Who is paying for this? Don't they have wives and families? Don't they have jobs? Does their government know where they are? It makes no sense to travel just to *travel*." Don't worry, I explained you are gypsies.'

Almost boiling over, I sent Tashmurad back into the fray. We needed to make decisions fast; the clocks on our non-extendable visas were ticking. This time, the head mechanic disappeared beneath Oxford. More bickering ensued, and Tashmurad returned.

'He doesn't know Land Rovers. He wants to know why you didn't bring a Toyota, much easier to fix. Even BMW – he has loads of BMW parts. Why didn't you come in a BMW?'

Anger flashed across my face. Tashmurad raised his hands for calm.

'Okay, okay, we will have to wait while they open up the rear differential; only then can they say if they can fix it.'

Like a group of nervous fathers in a maternity ward, we discussed our options in the fading sun while the mechanics set to work.

'We have to be in Ashgabat tomorrow, 400 kilometres away. We can't break the schedule we gave the government,' Marcus explained. 'Plus, we're due on state TV the day after. It'll be very awkward if we don't show up.'

'More awkward if the famous overlanders turn up in a taxi,' said Nat.

'In the worst case,' Larry weighed in, 'we could ship Oxford out of Turkmenistan as freight.'

'All the way to London?' said David.

'We could jump in with her and mail ourselves home,' suggested Leo. 'Much less embarrassing.'

After an eternity, the head mechanic barked to Tashmurad. My heart pounded as Tashmurad translated the prognosis.

'You are very lucky. The axle is not broken, it is … what is the word … *dislocated*. They can reassemble it, but it will take two days.'

Before relief could sink in, Marcus chimed, 'So the risk now is relying on this guy to deliver Oxford to Ashgabat as promised. If he doesn't, we have to leave Turkmenistan without her?'

I nodded. We would have to continue to Ashgabat without Oxford while the work was done, leaving the world's most famous Land Rover alone with these strange men, in a strange town in an even stranger country. We had no better option.

I could try to capture Ashgabat in a sentence, but the famed travel writer Paul Theroux will always do it better: 'An example of what happens when absolute political power, money and mental illness are combined.'

Only a city as bizarre as the Turkmen capital could distract me from the nagging fact that our most treasured possession was now in the hands of a man who thought me an idiotic nomad. Given the expeditionary purgatory we found ourselves in, there was no place more fitting to be than this sterile vision in dazzling white marble. Ashgabat resembled an architect's fevered sketching of 'Earth 2300' brought to life.

'Welcome to Ashgabat, which means the City of Love! It holds the Guinness world record for the most marble buildings, all finest Italian stone, designed by the best French architects.'

That wasn't the city's only record. The next day, Tashmurad showed us, among other marvels, the world's largest star-shaped building, the most fountains in a public space, and the world's largest indoor Ferris wheel.

'Why build the world's largest indoor Ferris wheel?' I asked.

'Why? That is the wrong kind of question.'

We moved on.

'This *was* the world's largest flagpole,' Tashmurad said mournfully, 'now it's only the fifth tallest.'

I put my hand on his shoulder in sympathy.

When they weren't building big, it seemed the Turkmen liked to build obvious.

'There is the Ministry of Foreign Affairs,' he pointed to a building topped with a giant globe.

'There is the hospital of dentistry,' indicating a building in the shape of a giant molar, 'and there is the Ministry of Carpets.' This was, of course, a gigantic building fronted with a huge ornate carpet.

'Only a French architect would be cool enough to keep a straight face when that commission came across his desk,' I whispered to Leo, who nodded calmly in agreement.

'Of course, here in Turkmenistan we have the world record for the biggest carpet.'

'Of course,' I replied.

'It's all so clean,' marvelled Nat.

'The roads are scrubbed with soap every night by local women,' explained Tashmurad. 'Some roads also have underground heating to prevent them icing up in winter.'

We all nodded, genuinely impressed.

'Over here is Central Asia's largest airport, capable of handling 16 million passengers per year. There are direct flights to your country, Birmingham.'

This struck me as odd. Among Marcus's trivial Turkmen titbits had been the fact that the country admits only a few thousand tourists a year – fewer than even the famously hostile North Korea.

'It is designed like a falcon.' The swooping marble form of the airport was undeniably breathtaking but prompted a question that had bugged me all day.

'Tashmurad, where *is* everybody?'

Despite travelling around the city for several hours, we had seen only a handful of people in the streets and even fewer cars on the road.

'Working probably,' Tashmurad shrugged.

I had read that due to Turkmenistan's severe repression, anyone who could leave had done so. Severe brain-drain was blighting the country, and despite the Turkmenator reversing his predecessor's disastrous policy of closing schools and hospitals across the country, insufficient teachers and doctors remained to fill the reopened buildings.

The whole experience was made more surreal by the fact that

our tour was being beamed live to the nation via a Turkmen TV crew, following our every move. When we arrived at a pristine golf course designed and opened by golfing legend Jack Nicklaus (who later admitted he had no idea why, as no one here plays golf), I was asked to say a few words on behalf of the expedition.

'If you can be as grateful as possible, and please do up your shirt,' the Turkmen producer warned.

As I looked down the camera lens of the lady I assumed was Turkmenistan's only working journalist, I found myself struggling. Ashgabat was undeniably beautiful, but the whole place gave me the creeps. It felt like one ghastly, desolate vanity project, built at the expense of its long-suffering people, who thanks to the previous president's policies, now had to walk hundreds of kilometres to go to the dentist. I didn't mention that, of course; I think I said something about the lovely horse-free *plov*.

Having paid my non-consensual tributes to the 'esteemed president', we were on the move again. I watched Nat taking in the city, a look of concern on his face. He was a man of few words, but I'd come to learn they were always worth listening to. 'I read Turkmenistan has one of the highest infant-mortality rates in the region,' he said, taking in the vista of white marble all around. 'It feels like money could be better spent.'

Our tour concluded with the tomb of the country's first, thoroughly peculiar president. We had earlier passed his gargantuan, rotating golden statue, as well as another one commemorating his bizarre self-help book, the *Ruhnama*.

Niyazov's final resting place sat beside an enormous mosque, unsurprisingly Central Asia's largest. With capacity for 10,000 worshippers and underground parking for 400 cars, it caused outrage when it opened in 2004, as Niyazov had inscribed its walls with quotes from his *Ruhnama* alongside Qur'anic excerpts. Perhaps that explained the total dearth of Friday-afternoon worshippers.

What makes a man do all this? Inside the tomb, noticeably an almost carbon-copy imitation of that other gigantic ego, Napoleon's in Paris, I glimpsed answers. Niyazov's black marble sarcophagus, inscribed with heavy gold lettering, lay in the centre of a sacred, eight-pointed Islamic star. Around him were four identical sarcophagi for his mother, father and two infant siblings. All were dead by the time he was seven, his mother and siblings killed in the earthquake that had flattened Ashgabat in 1948. Their bodies were not even here.

In a story almost a cliché among despots, this orphaned nobody had thrived in adversity, and had gone on to write himself so crudely onto the world that no one could forget him, or his family, ever again. If he hadn't done it by becoming a maniacally repressive bastard, I'd almost have pitied him.

Few men in history have been as delighted to see a truck as I was when one bearing a four-wheeled Oxford arrived at our hotel. I hugged her battered bodywork in childlike delight, drank in the smell of leaking fuel, and gave her restored tyre a testing yet affectionate kick. With her, my dreams of a life of adventure were restored. I felt invincible, divinely protected by the motoring gods, and it was time to leave this crackpot country and head on to London, and to glory. I'd grown begrudgingly fond of the spartan, scrubbed-out people of Turkmenistan, and was thrilled that – thanks to the heavily subsidized fuel – we could refill all three cars for roughly the price of a large coffee. But given the near disaster we had faced here, there were few countries on the journey I was keener to leave.

PART 3

AZERBAIJAN TO LONDON

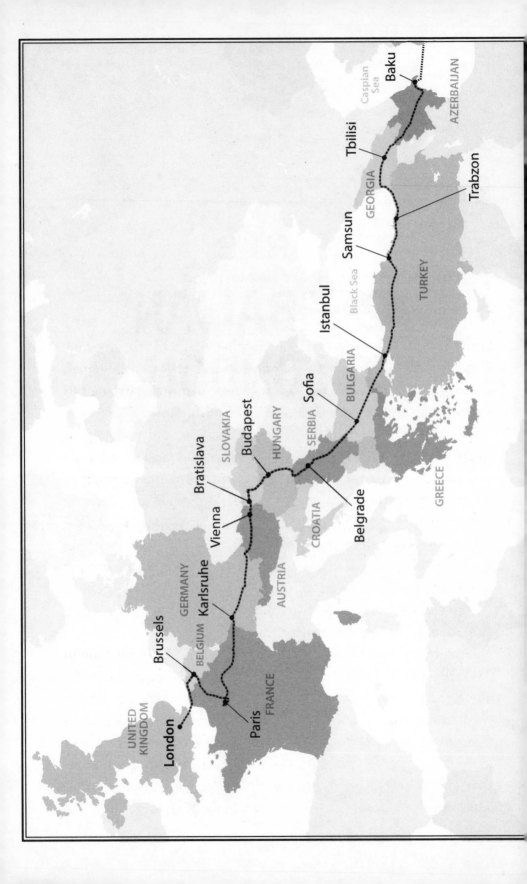

17

Roots

12 November 2019: The Caspian Sea

Expedition Day 80

I breathed the salty winds of the Caspian Sea, tonic for my soul. The sun, rising slowly over turquoise water still as a millpond, shimmered on the *Besterkar Fikret Emirov* car ferry carrying our seven bodies and three cars to country number twelve: Azerbaijan.

Catching the ferry had meant heading west from Ashgabat to the port city of Turkmenbashi – named, now predictably, after the first president – on the shores of the Caspian Sea. The prospect of boarding a ferry – however unavoidable, in light of our decision not to attempt retracing the First Overland route through Iran – had still felt incredibly odd. The team were below deck, enjoying the sleep of the dead in cosy bunks, the only sound being the occasional twang of an ancient mattress spring. Beneath them in the bowels of the ship were Oxford, PAC and Enterprise, safely stowed and, likewise, slumbering.

Despite my own exhaustion, I was too rattled from our time in Turkmenistan to sleep. It was the first time I had been able to be alone and still in what felt like weeks; the terror and relief of the crash, the agonizing wait for Oxford's diagnosis, and the lingering fear our great adventure might all come to nothing had taken more of a toll than I realized. But as I warmed my bones, lizard-like, on the ferry's prow, relishing the novelty of moving under someone else's steam for the first time in eighty days, I felt the tension begin to slowly ease. Phileas Fogg had circumnavigated the world in eighty days, I thought, a little ashamedly. Then again, he was fictional, so screw that comparison. Like Phileas, however, I had wagered everything on a long, arduous journey for reasons that were still elusive, and only days earlier it had seemed all for nothing.

In the disaster of Turkmenistan, the nagging question had reared its ugly head. Why the hell was I doing this? Without Tim, whose dream this journey had been, and then for a time without Oxford, what was the point?

I pictured Tim, gnarled fingers skittering across his globe, fervently listing all the places he still planned to visit. A fierce lust for life radiated from him, lust that had driven a man approaching ninety to embark on a journey that many thought might kill him.

Then I saw my grandad stretched on his tiny bed, a shadow of his former self, humanity robbed by the cruellest of diseases.

While I yearned to live and grow old like Tim, I still feared I had my grandad's fate in store. However irrational, I knew it was the fear of Harold's end that had brought me here, to the middle of the Caspian Sea. In the face of oblivion, I wanted to live a life so rich with incredible memories that they couldn't be taken from me. But in Turkmenistan that desire had seen me endanger the life of a dear friend.

Unsettled, I rooted for my ragged copy of *First Overland*. We would soon re-join their tyre tracks in eastern Turkey, marking the beginning of our journey's end. A rush of sadness struck me; this would all be done in a month. What came next, who knew?

I opened the first page, to find Tim answering the question that nagged me: 'Why did we go? I am not going to be drawn into a discussion of whether we did anything useful. We went because, if I may coin a cliché, we wanted to.'

A smile crossed my lips, knowing both Tims, young and old, would belt me round the ear for wallowing.

I flicked to Tim's triumphant arrival in Singapore and the

achievement of their great dream: 'We had reached the far end of Asia, and, by land, we could go no farther … And it was most satisfactory.'

That wasn't the end though, was it? After reaching Singapore, they had turned around and driven all the way back. The book's epilogue finds Tim in Oxford somewhere in Afghanistan, on 'an endless strip of corduroy, of rocks and holes and dust'. After reaching London, Tim barely rested before driving back to Burma for a new TV programme, beginning a life of perpetual motion in pursuit of adventure. More than sixty years later he was still willing to risk it all writing a brand-new chapter in the remarkable story of his life. He wasn't ready to put this story down, because he wasn't ready to put life down – not yet.

In this uncertain place – not quite a lake, not quite a sea – it hit. Tim had never stopped moving because moving mattered most. When you're on a journey and you haven't arrived, you're really alive. It was something Tim had discovered out in the middle of nowhere, a realisation Karin and Coen had stumbled upon too; now it was my turn.

I resolved to email Tim as soon as we were back on land. Now we were seemingly through the worst, it was high time to arrange his return to the mad adventure he had started. Feeling lighter than I had in years, I climbed quietly down to my bunk among my crewmates, and finally slept.

'What's she saying?' I asked, blearily, as a stocky woman in an apron burst into, then out of, the car ferry's bunkroom, blaring Russian like a foghorn.

'Breakfast,' David translated, fumbling for his glasses.

In the dining area we were revived with hot, sweet tea under the gaze of Ilham Aliyev, President of Azerbaijan, whose portrait adorned the wall. Aliyev, with the look of a predatory door-to-door insurance salesman, had inherited control of the oil-rich former Soviet statelet from his father in 2003 who in turn had crushed numerous coups to seize it in the chaos following the collapse of the USSR. Tiring of his stare, we retreated to the prow to admire the Baku skyline.

'We're on our own from here; no more guides,' Marcus warned, shading his eyes. 'And no more accidents!' Nat and I exchanged a guilty look. 'We can't afford any delays; there's zero wiggle room in our schedule if we want to be home on December the fourteenth.'

We would stay just two nights in Azerbaijan, and only then for vital repair work that Oxford still needed. This rapid pace would become the norm for the final month of our journey. I was determined to enjoy every minute of it and ensure the team who had come so far with me did too.

Exiting the ferry, we fell into the waiting arms of the Land Rover Owners Club of Azerbaijan in a flurry of horns and flags. Since leaving Nepal, we had not seen another Land Rover, let alone one of our growing online community of fans. Having initially appreciated the respite, being swamped for selfies and team photos by people who had followed our progress from the start was a much needed, if conceited, shot in the arm.

The Doc, Larry and Nat followed the club to a nearby workshop to install Oxford's new dynamo and alternator, posted to Baku by Adam. I was delighted she would get some much-needed TLC after her ordeal, from people who actually knew what a Series I was.

Meanwhile, Marcus and I made for one of Baku's glitzy cafés to talk tactics. Unfurling his trusty map, he traced a line westward from Baku.

'From here we head to Georgia, then into eastern Turkey, where we re-join Tim's old route. After that, Bulgaria – back into the EU! Then, Serbia – where we leave the EU – Hungary (EU again), Slovakia, Austria, Germany, France, Belgium … home! Eleven countries in one month. Final sprint!'

Despite the excitement in my old friend's voice, his face betrayed his deep exhaustion. I realized now I had withdrawn into myself following the crash, leaving him the burden of keeping us moving.

I resolved to retake my share and get him to the finish line smiling.

Having covered the previous eleven countries in three months, spending weeks crossing one or another, this final stretch would feel very different. I studied the scrunched-up continent of Europe. Before moving my life to Burma, this crinkled patchwork of nations had been my universe. Now, having crossed the length of Asia to reach it, I had a new appreciation for exactly how small Europe was.

Her higgledy-piggledy national borders speak of a crowded, fractious continent whose eternal infighting had exploded onto the rest of the world, until the age of empires had been mortally wounded just as Oxford began her maiden voyage. Sixty-plus years later, we had driven through the wreckage of that world, and the Cold War that followed, while watching the foundations of a new order being laid. Having seen up close the might of the Chinese state, and the reach of its tentacles, there was little doubt that the new order would be Asian, not European. Though I was heading home at last, I felt I was driving away from the future, and into the past.

We started early on 14 November. To keep to Marcus's schedule, we had to cross Azerbaijan and reach Georgia's capital, Tbilisi – nearly 650 kilometres (400 miles) north-west – in one day. We had additional pressure of being on time for Tibie, who would soon arrive in Tbilisi. It had been a tumultuous two weeks without her, and I was eager to reunite our little family. Luckily, after a day of pampering in Baku, Oxford was back to her best. Well, almost.

We were apparently playing the vehicular equivalent of a whack-a-mole game, and after the latest round of repairs Oxford had started sounding her horn without the button being pressed. A car already bursting with personality now had a voice of her own, leading to some awkward encounters. As we waited in a lengthy line to cross the Georgian border, Oxford began sounding her frustration. A rain-sodden guard tapped on my window as Nat tried to silence her.

'*As-salamu alaykum*,' I said automatically, my standard Arabic opener to the countless policemen who had stopped us through Central Asia.

'This is Georgia, we are a Christian country,' he spat. Luckily, Oxford stopped blaring long enough for me to apologize.

It was my first reminder of the Georgians' fierce, prickly pride. This plucky little nation has been defined by the great-power rivalry of its much larger neighbours – Russia, Turkey and Iran. My first encounter with Georgia was in 2008, when I watched live on BBC News as this country of less than 4 million people declared war on Putin's mighty Russia. I had longed to know more ever since.

For our filmmaker David, however, Georgia held a deeper allure. Back on the Afghan border, David had opened up to me about his past. The Jewish families of his great-grandparents had settled in Georgia from Belarus, Ukraine and Poland after fleeing pogroms and civil war in the wake of the First World War. But on 27 October 1990, his extended family had escaped the turbulence of Georgia, on the periphery of the collapsing Union, to start a new life in Queens, New York, where David was born in 1994. In all his twenty-four years, he had never visited and his parents had never returned.

'People forget everything when they move to America,' he told us over breakfast on our first day in Tbilisi. He was busy devouring *khachapuri*, a cheese-filled pastry and a traditional staple of Georgian cuisine that his parents had raised him on.

'This place was collapsing, there was no food, life was bad. America was the land of opportunity. They never had any photos of this place, nothing,' he murmured, cheese dripping onto his plate. To a man who had dedicated his life to the camera, I could tell this was troubling.

David had wasted no time getting out into the world, and had already visited many of its weird, wonderful corners when we first met in Myanmar. Here, however, my old friend was strangely reticent. Leo and I coaxed him into exploring the city in which his parents were born and raised, and with the help of a hand-drawn map from his aunt in New York, he agreed to take us digging into his past.

Tbilisi has a strange combination of feeling decidedly European, with a subtle twist of Central Asian. Brimming with tumbledown charm, futuristic buildings of steel and glass neighbour thirteenth-century fortress-churches, like alien craft parked up on a visit.

'Those were the streets where my mother was born, my father was born, my grandparents, great-grandparents. Somewhere is … I don't want to say our house, it's not our house … it's not our house anymore.'

We followed David's hand-drawn map through closely packed streets, kicking through autumn leaves, winding closer to his family's old neighbourhood. As we walked, he explained that though there had been Jews in Georgia for more than 2,500 years, they had been singled out by the Russian Tsarist regime and, later, the Soviet authorities.

Waves of Jewish emigration to Israel and elsewhere occurred throughout the twentieth century, but Jewish families from Georgia were distinctive in moving entire extended families in one go. The USSR's collapse triggered a vicious civil war in Georgia, the early tremors of which finally forced David's family to seek a new life in America.

Suddenly David stopped, a huge smile on his face.

'I understand why they moved to Queens; it looks identical! Little buildings, little stores, little parks.' He sped up again, rounding another corner.

'I think this is it!' he exclaimed, covering his mouth and chuckling to himself. He sat on the pavement, feet in the gutter, taking in a dilapidated three-storey building with high windows and delicate balconies, typical of the Tsarist era.

'It's eerie. Like ghosts live here.'

Inside we found a small courtyard, washing lines strung between the balconies. It was a scene that might not have changed for generations. David began fitting his parents' stories onto the bricks and mortar around. He looked unsettled.

'Are you happy to see it?' asked Leo, cautiously.

'It's not a question of happiness, really,' David replied, thoughtfully. 'You become obsessed with where you're from when you're not from there, right? And when you go to live somewhere you're not from, you become obsessed with there too, right?'

Leo and I nodded, uncertainly. He turned to us both.

'I'm a little jealous of people like you, just being from one country and speaking the same language with your parents. This is my parents' past, not mine. I was born in Long Island Jewish Hospital in New York. I'm an American citizen; I speak English.'

He stopped, struggling for words.

'Coming here has taught me one thing: I'm not Georgian in any way, shape or form. I don't speak this language; I don't know this culture. I thought maybe coming here would help me understand who I am, but really it's told me who I'm not.'

I started feeling guilty, wondering if Leo and I had forced him into something he hadn't wanted to face.

'There's just one more place I'd like to see.'

He followed his map a few streets along to a gated compound, filled with ancient trees.

'The cemetery,' he explained. 'I think my family are here, somewhere.'

He ducked under the gate and wove between the carefully curated gravestones, each surrounded by delicate wrought-iron fencing. Finally, an excited shout echoed through the air.

'My mom's grandparents!'

Leo and I joined him by a large black headstone carved with delicate writing, topped with two black-and-white portraits.

'Judah and Betty Kalinik. She looks just like my grandma!' His earlier solemnity forgotten, he began enthusiastically searching for more of his family.

'Perelman! My dad's grandparents, my other great-grandparents!'

David hopped into the enclosure, wiping dust from the small grey headstone.

'Do you want some time?' asked Leo, as David stared at his great-grandfather's final resting place.

'No, it's okay. I don't know how to pray,' he joked, bashfully. Instead, he rooted for a pebble in the debris, and according to Jewish tradition balanced it on top of the headstone.

'My parents have always sought out other Jews, felt an affinity to them,' he said. 'I never quite understood, but I think I get it now. When you live somewhere like this and you're the minority, always singled out negatively as Jewish, then other Jews are your people. But when Jews move to America you can almost forget you're Jewish. You can't here.'

He took one last look at the tombstone.

'I've met my great-grandparents at least. Before now I always felt like my history stopped with my grandparents who came to America. Not anymore.'

I had spent a sleepless night thinking hard about what David said on our tour through his family's past. As quickly as my epiphany on the importance of perpetual movement had come, David's words on the importance of roots had begun to unravel it. His words mixed with the contrasting thoughts of Karin and Coen's on the draw of home, and I found my own feelings hard to pin down. Luckily our own family reunion put paid to the tumult in my head for now.

True to form, Tibie bounced enthusiastically out of arrivals. Not one to be kept idle, she filled me in on her two weeks' driving a van around Ireland, ensuring she kept her overlanding muscles tuned. It was as if she had never left. My heart rose; except for Tim we were a full team again, and I felt my confidence return. Stopping by the hotel to gather the others, we set off for the 400-kilometre (250-mile) drive to our final night stop in Georgia, Batumi.

That drive was one of the most memorable of the whole journey.

Georgia in November is breathtaking, with the frostbitten red, yellow and gold of autumn leaves cascading all around us as we weaved up and down the hills of the Borjomi National Park. Even Oxford's continual glitches couldn't spoil the mood. When black smoke started rising from her wheels, signalling the brakes were overheating, the Doc, Nat and I burst into fits of giggles while relieving ourselves on them.

'No need to waste good water!' the Doc advised with a toothy grin.

We reached Batumi in a pink-tinged dusk, pulled down its neat promenade and looked out over the seafront.

'Welcome to the Vegas of the Black Sea!' trilled Marcus on the radio.

I suspected Georgia's most infamous son, Iosif Dzhugashvili – better known by his catchy rebrand 'Stalin' – would not have approved of the comparison. Stalin cut his political teeth here in the early 1900s as Batumi grew rich on oil from Azerbaijan. He became a thorn in the side of the Tsarist regime through a campaign of arson, mass strikes, and deadly riots. That ruthless skill set served him well in later life.

Stalin would also have viewed that night's dinner venue dimly. Spying their first McDonald's since leaving Thailand, Marcus and Nat insisted on scratching the itch. Even Leo, who as a Frenchman viewed McDonald's as something close to a war crime, tucked in. I looked with pride at the team who had been through so much, daring to think the worst was behind us.

All that remained now was to find Oxford's old tyre tracks in neighbouring Turkey, and from there follow them to London.

18

Turkish Delights

18 November 2019: Trabzon Province, Turkey
Expedition Day 86

'Twenty-three thousand, one hundred and forty-seven!' shouted
Nat. 'That's how many days since Oxford was last on this road!'

'That economics degree's coming in handy,' I replied, squeezed
between him and the Doc.

Two months ago, we had departed the First Overland route to
traverse Central Asia. Now we had finally re-joined Oxford's tyre
tracks on Turkey's balmy Black Sea coast; in July 1956 Tim and co
had driven this very road, returning from Singapore after crossing
Pakistan, Afghanistan and Iran – a feat, as David Attenborough
had predicted, that was pretty much impossible to us today.

Oxford, according to Tim's diaries, had brake trouble here, and
she seemed in nostalgic form. Indeed, since Georgia her brakes had
behaved like optional extras. This explained the Doc's presence: our
vehicular horse-whisperer would routinely take the wheel whenever
Oxford was persistently misbehaving. Nat and I remained, bravely;
I couldn't help feeling that only the Doc's devout Christian faith
explained his fearlessness in driving a brakeless Oxford down
the highway at top speed. One foot on the accelerator, one in the
afterlife, as Rajan had said.

Nat had been buried in our copy of Tim's road diary, and as we
approached the coastal town of Trabzon, he asked to pull over.

'July the fourth: Two more punctures and into Trabzon,' he

read, as we approached the shoreline where a breakwater had been constructed from large boulders, against which the Black Sea threw itself with gusto. After so long away from their original route, it felt comforting to be criss-crossing once again the ghosts of those six young men. After what we had been through these last few weeks, I felt that this time we could look those ghosts in the eye.

'They camped here back in 1956, and Adrian lost the wallet with all the expedition's money in it. They weren't perfect either!'

'Reckon it's still there?' I asked, conscious of our own reserves dwindling.

'Nah, some kids gave it back a few hours later. Different world.'

Quite. While the view across the Black Sea can't have changed much, the political landscape was unrecognizable.

On their outbound journey, the First Overland entered a Turkey on a war footing with Greece over the island of Cyprus, then still a British colony. Guerrillas claiming to represent the majority Greek population took up arms to evict the Brits and unify the island with Greece, in the face of staunch opposition from the Brits and Cyprus's Turkish minority. In response, Istanbul's sizeable Greek population suffered a series of targeted riots only ten days before Tim's arrival. Turkey today was roiling from a different cocktail of crises – a perpetual conflict with its Kurdish minority, a president with dictatorial tendencies, and an enormous influx of refugees from the war in neighbouring Syria.

Right here on the Black Sea, however, all was peaceful. The midday heat was rippling off the tarmac in front, and I began to imagine this country in the time of Alexander the Great. At exactly my age, Alexander was rampaging through here on his way to defeat the Persians. As much as his exploits had beguiled me as a child, I was secretly glad to be moving away at speed from the Persians right now. From Tim's diaries, it was clear his mind had also drifted to antiquity on his way through here.

As the young Tim passed through the ruins of Rome's ancient

empire, his diary entries foreshadowed the beginning of the end of the world order he'd been born into: '… the endeavour of the British and our resultant empire of the last century are without compare in history … but how much of us will remain in 2,000 years?'

Britain's empire would crumble faster than Tim and his companions could have guessed, lasting years, not millennia. Its ruins littered our journey, whether in the unhappy hill peoples of Burma and India, the contested boundaries of China and Tajikistan, or indeed Cyprus, where the 1955 conflict was still unresolved today.

Nat stared thoughtfully out to sea. The last time we had stopped on the same stretch of beach as the First Overland was in Thailand, mere days into our journey. He had seemed then a nervous boy, struggling to cope not only with becoming an accidental overlander, but also with filling his grandpa's sizeable shoes. Ten weeks on, he cut a transformed figure.

Self-assured, worldly wise, an indispensable and overwhelmingly popular member of our crew, he had seen Mount Everest at sunset, survived the headhunters of Nagaland and – thanks to Oxford – endured a bona fide near-death experience. As Tim had written of himself as he neared the end of his own expedition, here stood a man with 'enough recollections to make me a thundering bore for the rest of my life'.

'Do you miss your grandpa?' I asked.

'Yeah, I do. It's the longest I've gone in my life without seeing him.'

I missed Tim too, but in some way I felt as if he had never left me. His book was a nearly constant companion, and as much as technology and accessibility had allowed we had communicated throughout by email, plotting his triumphant return to the expedition he'd inspired. This morning, however, I had received news that I couldn't keep to myself any longer.

'He emailed this morning. He's not joining us.'

I read out Tim's email, in response to my own suggesting he join us in Istanbul, Budapest or even Paris to lead Oxford home.

'I'm flattered by your various suggestions, Alex, but I have decided that I don't want to be an interloper, riding on *your* collective achievement. I think that England is where I should be, on the pavement where, expedition-wise, you finally apply the handbrake. I hope you can understand. Congrats, and Bloody Marvellous. Tim.'

Nat stood in considered silence, before dipping his fingers in the water.

'Bit cold for a swim, I think.' He strode back to Oxford, then turned to beckon me.

'Come on, we can't be late to London. Grandpa will kill me.'

He slid confidently behind Oxford's wheel and signalled the convoy to prepare to move on. As amazed as I was by his grandson's calm, no-nonsense acceptance of the mantle he had never asked for, I was still heartbroken at Tim's decision. Leo, clearly reading my mind, put his hand on my shoulder reassuringly.

'Tim's right. This is Nat's story now, not his.'

I nodded, and thought of my old friend Sithu's words while we looked at his great-great-grandfather's palace in Mandalay.

You really can't bring back the past, can you?

We made for Tuzla, just outside Istanbul, for a long-planned rendezvous with the Land Rover Club of Turkey. There, we were reunited with Cervet, a charming, heavily bearded Turk we had met briefly a few days earlier at the Georgian border. Giddy at Oxford's arrival, he had driven 960 kilometres (600 miles) in one day to make sure we crossed into Turkey trouble-free; our first taste of a country whose people claimed to have a 'hospitality gene'. Cervet's total lack of English was immaterial, as he communicated enthusiastically (and mostly about Land Rovers) via Google Translate.

I still find this technology astounding. I grew up reading *The Hitchhiker's Guide to the Galaxy*, and was fascinated by the idea of the Babel Fish. When inserted into your ear, this yellow leechlike creature made any language comprehensible. Now Google had made that fantasy reality, with the added advantage of not requiring anything inserted into your person.[17]

After a comfy night's stay on our Turkish hosts, we were woken early by Cervet. I didn't need Google to translate the excitement on his face.

'We have a surprise for you, and for Oxford. Let's go!'

We formed our first proper Land Rover convoy since Thailand. The not-unwelcome sensation of being visiting royalty returned. What awaited, however, trumped any stuffy state banquet.

'No *way*,' gasped Nat, as we entered a large, gated compound. 'The Istanbul Formula One circuit! Do you think they'll let us walk on the track?'

Before I could answer, Cervet beckoned us through a gate to the starting grid itself, where a burly Turk holding a large flag leaned on a gleaming white Porsche GT3. Cervet guided Oxford into pole, while PAC, Enterprise and an assortment of Land Rovers from the Turkish club filed in behind.

Nat and I exchanged looks of disbelief. Remarkably, it was the second time Oxford had been on a Formula 1 track on this journey, but in Singapore we had been (sensibly) kept off the main track for fear of damaging the incredibly expensive tarmac. A single oil-spill would require tens of thousands of dollars of repair work; so, given Oxford's chronic incontinence, we couldn't risk it. The Turks, however, had a much more relaxed attitude,[18] and the flag bearer, a huge man who introduced himself as Bura, approached my window.

---

17   I'm sure the First Overland's navigator and chief interpreter, Pat, would have found it even more amusing. Or perhaps entirely unnecessary, as he advised: 'Those with no linguistic ability need not worry – English will get them through (though the tendency merely to shout louder when misunderstood should be resisted).'

18   That, I later discovered, was because in 2011, Formula 1 Chief Executive Bernie Ecclestone had doubled the fees for hosting the race, a price the Turkish government refused to pay. Despite Ecclestone dubbing the track 'the best in the world', it hasn't hosted a Grand Prix event since.

'Oxford will have a thirty-second head start, a gift for the Old Lady. Oh, and don't overtake my guide car,' he gestured to his Porsche, capable of 0-100 km/h (0-60 mph) – Oxford's top speed – in three seconds.

'Shouldn't be a problem,' I replied, although Oxford's temperamental brakes certainly would.

'The professionals can usually cover this five-kilometre circuit in about sixty seconds,' Bura added, helpfully.

'And in a sixty-four-year-old Land Rover …?'

'Just get round in one piece, hey? You're the first Land Rover on this track, so no matter what, you're going home with a record.' He patted Oxford's roof and returned to his Porsche.

Nat was already in the zone, revving Oxford's engine hard in a challenge to our competitors, hunched low over the steering wheel to see the bank of lights better.

'Jenson Button always complained about Turn Eight – the *Diabolica* – but it's the Turkish Corkscrew right after the front straight that you've really got to worry about. Just give me advance warning to my left and right, and I can defend the line.'

I stared in blank incomprehension before grabbing the dashboard and hoping Nat had more in common with Lewis Hamilton than his Grenadian heritage. Behind bellowed the excited engines of eight more Land Rovers, outdone momentarily by the blare of the starting hooter.

'Go-go-go!' I shouted, entirely lost in the moment and bouncing in my seat. Nat stormed out of the blocks, passing 30, 50 and then 65 km/h (20, 30 and 40 mph), as we gobbled up the smooth tarmac. Oxford screamed and shook, as did I around the Turkish Corkscrew. A burning smell filled the cab.

'Is that the brakes?!' I squealed.

'It can't be!' Nat shouted. 'I haven't touched them!'

Our thirty-second head start flashed by. Within moments the familiar outlines of PAC and Enterprise loomed behind. Months of steady, sensible long-distance driving that had brought us safely across the world were forgotten entirely – Nat, Larry and Marcus were men possessed. I had never understood the fuss around Formula 1, but there, with the adrenaline rushing, I finally got it. The thrill was electric, and we were only going at quarter the speed of the professionals.

'PAC on your left, Enterprise on your right!' I warned, as Larry and Marcus gained fast. Despite Nat's bold defensive driving, Enterprise snuck by on our inside, the Doc grinning and waving through the passenger window. Seconds later Marcus stripped past on the straight, to Nat's intense annoyance. I wondered what Adam would say if he could see his two beloved Land Rovers now. One by one the Turkish Land Rover Club zipped past. As we finally crossed the line, only a battered old Land Rover ambulance, weighing two tonnes, still trailed us.

'Five and a half minutes,' I read as we reached the finish, 'and all four wheels, at least.'

'A new world record,' said Nat. 'Turkmenistan would be proud!'

The 50 kilometres (30 miles) from Tuzla to Istanbul, though bereft of scenery, was rich with meaning; it was the final leg of our journey across the Asian continent. We had begun our journey eighty-eight days earlier on the furthest tip of the 'Far East', a geographical idea that for centuries had drawn adventurous souls from my damp little island on the edge of Europe. I had called Asia home for most of a decade, and – for better or worse – it had made me who I was today.

Behind us lay the birthplace of the world's first civilizations and great religions. As the Bosporus,[19] Asia and Europe's historic boundary, grew nearer, I was thankful that thirteen Asian countries

---

19   I later discovered that 'Bosporus' is loosely drawn from the ancient Greek for 'cattle strait', or more neatly 'Ox-ford'. I'll forever regret not being able to bore my colleagues with that little etymological coincidence at the time, but rest assured, I made up for it afterwards.

now brimmed with towns and cities that would never again simply be names on a map: Samsun and Kevron, Gyirong and Tingri, Hetauda and Kaziranga, Hat Yai and Alor Setar. Once a collection of strange syllables, they now conjured the memories of new friends, delicious meals, dubious roads, and a lifetime's supply of jaw-dropping sunrises and sunsets.

Oxford, reluctant to leave Asia, conked out on the busy expressway into Istanbul. Only a quick-thinking Tibie, shunting us safely off the road with PAC, saved Nat and me from being flattened by an HGV.

'A new problem every day!' Larry quipped, as the Doc reattached a loose wire that had stymied the fuel pump.

'We can't afford twenty-four more problems,' grumbled Marcus, scratching his long, increasingly grey-flecked hair.

Like Oxford, I felt that any of us could conk out any minute. These last few days our moods were fragile, elated one minute, cranky the next. It took little to prompt a sharp word, but even less to bring a hearty chuckle. It was a clear sign of a deep exhaustion that was affecting us all, but luckily for Marcus, and the rest of us, a final surprise awaited us as we pulled into Istanbul.

Sixty-four years earlier, Tim had entered a city under martial law following the anti-Greek riots, witnessing tanks on the outskirts, armed police patrolling the streets, and a city-wide, night-time curfew. One bright spot had been the brand-new Hilton, Asia's first five-star hotel, opened one month earlier by a planeload of Hollywood stars. The First Overlanders were invited for lunch on the terrace, their arrival staged for the cameras in the hotel's grand foyer. They weren't offered a bed, though; instead, they were billeted in a spare office at the local Mobil petrol station. Nor were they offered a drink, which the expedition considered 'dead poor'.

Hoping to right a historic injustice, I had contacted the Hilton to let them know Oxford was returning, and her current occupants might appreciate bed and board this time. The Hilton team of 2019 obliged with gusto, offering us three nights' complimentary stay and all the drinks we could shake a cocktail stick at. With reams of virtual paperwork to shuffle ahead of our homecoming celebrations on 14 December, it was the perfect recharging point.

'Without doubt the most impressive hotel I have seen anywhere,' wrote Tim in his diary as he sat on a ferry crossing the Bosporus from Europe into Asia.[20] Sixty-four years later as we crossed the Bosporus by a swooping suspension bridge (that had arrived almost twenty years too late for the First Overland), we could see the same iconic building of glass and concrete standing proudly on the skyline. After much honking and hollering at the 'Welcome to Europe' sign, we pulled up to the hotel in the evening sun, where the Hilton team waited with drinks and a press pack.

'I've thought about it. Grandpa can keep his overlander-in-chief title, I'll take the free bar in the Hilton Executive Suite,' said Nat magnanimously, before polishing off another pina colada.

Having passed through many ancient grievances on our long journey across Asia, it was nice to find one, at least, we could help put to rest.

Now a sprawling mega-metropolis of almost 15 million people, for millennia Istanbul has been the gateway between two worlds: the continent on which I was born and raised, and that on which I'd made a new life. This glittering jewel at the Silk Road's western end had been the glory of the Caesars, the beating heart of Eastern Christianity, and later the awesome capital of the Ottoman Caliphate. It had gone by many names: Byzantium, New Rome, Constantinople.

Today it is Istanbul – meaning something close to 'the city' in Turkish, attesting to the once-incomparable nature of this place.

---

20 A seminal moment on their outbound journey, for more than one reason. The First Overland's amateur doctor, BB, declared from here on out all water was to be boiled, and all uncooked vegetables banned. Still today the surviving First Overlanders recall the expedition battle-cry of, 'No lettuces beyond the Bosporus!'

One building embodied its history above all others – the Hagia Sophia. Built in AD 537 by Emperor Justinian I, it remained the largest cathedral on Earth for 1,000 years. In 1453, this bastion of Eastern Christianity was converted into a mosque by the Ottoman sultan Mehmed II. It remained so until 1935, when it was made a museum by the secular founder of modern Turkey, Mustafa Ataturk.

For me, the Hagia Sophia's towering domes, sweeping buttresses and ornate minarets symbolized the city's beautifully mongrel nature, sprung from this turbulent crucible of the world's greatest thinkers, designers and earthly rulers. As I stood awestruck in the museum's grand plaza, a small, bespectacled man sidled up to me.

'Are you looking for a guide?' he asked, almost apologetically.

He introduced himself as Mehmet, and something about him suggested I was in for more than a list of dusty dates. As the call to prayer resonated, Mehmet escorted me into the building's cavernous nave. Shards of light lanced through the windows, dancing on what Mehmet explained were purple porphyry blocks from Rome, yellow bands of marble from Egypt, and green marble columns from Greece.

Between his describing the complex's history, I shared the story of our journey. On hearing Oxford had travelled to Syria and Lebanon in the 1950s, Mehmet shared my sadness in not being able to follow the First Overland's tyre tracks, recalling his own visits to Damascus, Aleppo, and Palmyra in happier times. Many of the ancient architectural wonders that Mehmet and Tim enjoyed had been deliberately destroyed by Islamic State fighters during their brief reign of ignorant terror just over the border in Syria.

'*Fundamentalism*,' he spat. 'These people claim to know the one true God and will turn the world to rubble in His name. What *nonsense*.'

Mehmet stared up, as if seeing the building for the first time.

'It's impossible to be a fundamentalist in this place. Hagia Sophia shows how our great religions are intertwined, constantly evolving. Look there: Mary and the Christ Child, over there the Orthodox

Patriarchs, and there' – indicating a huge green disk, covered in Arabic script – 'is the declaration of the Prophet Muhammad's greatness. Now our president wants to turn this back into a mosque, stealing it for only one type of believer. Fundamentalism is, sadly, very infectious.'

He sighed, deeply.

'The war in Syria has brought so much death and destruction. I know from history that such conflict can bring progress, rebirth. I'm still struggling to see how this time.'

I thought, guiltily, that while I had followed Syria's tragic implosion through the rolling news, Mehmet had watched it collapse on his doorstep.

'We have four million Syrians in our country, we have accepted more refugees than any other nation as Syria has fallen apart. Istanbul is full of hundreds of thousands of those poor people, many living in the streets, everywhere you look you see Syrians fleeing war. And while we take them in, you Brits worry that we Turks are waiting to flee to London! Your prime minister, Boris Johnson, he tells your people this to scare you, to keep us from joining the EU. His grandfather was Turkish! He should be ashamed of himself.'

I watched rage pass over his kindly face and stood silently with him as crowds of tourists milled around us.

'That is the new religion now, anyway,' he chuckled, pointing to a large crowd by the foot of the Muezzin Balcony jostling for position with their camera phones. Peering over, I could see they were trying to photograph a cat staring calmly across the crowds.

'That is Gli, the Hagia Sophia cat; she has almost 100,000 followers on Instagram!'

I noticed that many of the crowd around Gli were men wearing bloodstained bandages around their heads, exaggerating the strangeness of the scene.

Mehmet explained, 'Istanbul might not be the capital of Turkey anymore, but it *is* the capital of bad hair transplants, cat photos and expensive, painful vanity. Welcome to the future, my friend.'

19

The New Iron Curtain

25 November 2019: Istanbul, Turkey
Expedition Day 93

Shifting the expedition from the Istanbul Hilton was like expunging a band of determined rodents from their den. My grizzled adventurers had taken to luxury; under cover of extravagant goodbyes with the Hilton team, Nat and Marcus completed three loops of the breakfast buffet.

The wrench was exacerbated when I explained that, until we reached London, life would be tough for the expedition. As de facto treasurer, I had the unenviable task of budgeting our accommodation on a rapidly vanishing stash of cash. Delays to our schedule and Oxford's continual repairs had cost us dearly.

Our new ascetic lifestyle began in the town of Edirne, around 240 kilometres (150 miles) from Istanbul, last stop before the Bulgarian border. The only hotel within our new budget was clearly mid-construction, presumably explaining the discount. Picking through scaffolding, we were greeted by a man whose bulging muscles gave the impression of a fleshy cube with legs.

The bellboy's physique was quickly explained by the hotel's unusual artwork, which consisted entirely of heavily oiled men in various states of struggle. Edirne, we discovered, has been the epicentre of Turkey's national sport – *yağlı güreş* or 'grease-wrestling' – since the 1300s. Historically, until a thirty-minute limit was imposed in the 1970s, these greased-up goliaths would grapple for up to two days. The bellboy, clearly a contender to be wary of, hoisted almost all our kit upstairs in one go. We followed into cold, mildewed rooms.

'What a comedown,' said Nat, still defiantly sporting his Hilton slippers.

'At least we're not camping,' I consoled him. We had a tent large enough for the whole team, but it had remained blissfully undisturbed. The 'great camping debate' had raged since Singapore, many of our fanbase online asking why we weren't following the First Overlanders' example by sleeping al fresco.

The easy answer was that as we had planned the expedition to be led by a man in his late eighties, Marcus and I had organized indoor accommodation throughout for fear of being accused of elderly neglect (despite Tim's fierce protestations that we camp where we could), and we had raised sufficient funds for at least a rudimentary roof every night. The honest answer was that I don't imagine we would have coped; moving bed-to-bed day after day was exhausting enough, and after weeks on end of driving Oxford, I challenge anyone to choose differently. In our defence, even the twenty-three-year-old Tim had noted in his diaries that 'any fool could be uncomfortable'. I heartily agreed.

After dinner, we huddled around Marcus's map.

'We're deviating from Tim's route again,' he informed us. 'Rather than looping south-west through Greece, we're taking the direct route north-west via Bulgaria. That would have been impossible in the 1950s.'

In 1955, Bulgaria's new Communist ruler, Todor Zhivkov, was settling into the first of his thirty-six years in charge. Zhivkov's alignment with Soviet Russia placed Bulgaria firmly behind the 'Iron Curtain' foreseen by Churchill. This metaphorical line between Capitalist West and Communist East soon became a physical barrier, through-travel becoming virtually non-existent from 1950 until the collapse of the Soviet Union.

While the Middle East had been open to Tim but too

dangerous for us, the geopolitical tide in Eastern Europe had turned in our favour.

'Welcome to country fifteen, and the European Union!' Marcus chirped, as we pulled up to the Bulgarian border.

'Fortress Europe' was a more accurate description, as I contemplated the towering walls and razor wire ahead. Before us loomed a fearsome barrier constructed recently by Bulgaria to block the hundreds of thousands of people trying to enter Europe illegally each year. As Oxford passed through it and we entered all-new terrain, this time I missed the thrill. I had struggled to sleep last night, Mehmet the tour guide's words weighing heavily on my mind.

In Turkey, millions of Syrians dreamed of a safer life in Europe if they could reach Bulgaria. Countless more from the Middle East, North Africa and beyond risked their lives to reach Europe by land or sea. Thanks to my birthplace, I could saunter through the European frontier that others were, literally, dying to cross.

Four years ago, the eyes of the world turned to a Turkish beach where a three-year-old Syrian boy, Alan Kurdi, had washed up dead. His family were trying to reach the sanctuary of Greece before their overloaded boat capsized. Alan's was one of more than 1,200 deaths that summer, out of over 1 million who attempted the crossing. The heart-shattering image of his tiny, lifeless body symbolized one of our century's greatest crises to date, a crisis driven by a complex mix of war, environmental degradation and desperation that brought out the worst in humanity.

Guiltily I thought of how on the Caspian I had mentally sung the praises of perpetual movement, without acknowledging how my ability to do so was down to the little maroon passport in my pocket. Larry's words about how the world had changed since Tim's journey resurfaced: 'We're more safe today, but less free.' I mentally added a subclause: 'If you're lucky enough to be born in the right place.'

In an attempt to deal with the huge number of people trying to cross this border, in 2016 desperate European leaders signed a deal with Turkey's President Erdoğan, paying Turkey billions of dollars to stop migrants leaving for Europe. It was widely seen as a pretty grubby bargain.

Erdoğan was an increasingly unsavoury partner, whose own brutality against the Kurdish minority in Syria was itself sending Syrians fleeing westwards. Erdoğan had consolidated domestic power in alarmingly authoritarian style since 2016, following an attempted coup that he himself was accused of planning. Now Erdoğan threatened to open the gates at every opportunity, extorting cash and weaponry from the Western powers. I tried to explain this to Nat, although I couldn't quite grasp it myself.

'It hurts your head,' said Nat, trundling through the great steel barrier. 'I'm sure we'll know the truth one day, but by then it won't really matter, will it?'

Nat could be annoyingly wise for a twenty-one-year-old. How much of the Syrian crisis, whose ripples surrounded us, would we remember decades from now? What crises loomed to overtake it?

When Oxford first crossed Europe, plans for a European super-state were accelerating. The 1957 Treaty of Rome kick-started six decades of increasingly close political, economic and cultural union across Europe, with the six original members expanding to twenty-eight. Now, however, the project was entering an unprecedented reverse.

My own country, the UK, was responsible for the sudden change in direction. After a bitterly divisive referendum in June 2016 on its EU membership, the country voted marginally in favour of 'Leave'. Despite the people having expressed their will to exit, three years on Britain was still gridlocked on exactly how to do so. As I neared home, the date of Brexit loomed closer and the political avenues to prevent it seemed exhausted. A snap election scheduled for two days before our planned arrival might throw a final spanner in the works, but the anti-Brexit political parties seemed hard-pressed to defeat the Brexit-supporting Boris Johnson.

As Oxford made her return journey across Europe, the European Union was beginning to shift and crack beneath her tyres. It was a change from Oxford herself falling apart, I suppose.

Bulgaria was a different story. Here at the Union's eastern edge, Bulgaria's 7 million inhabitants had among the highest levels of trust in the EU, many enthusiastically exercising their right to live and work across fellow member-states. Bulgarian jobseekers in the UK had become popular bogeymen for the pro-Brexit British tabloids, ever since Bulgaria's accession in 2007. They painted this as bandit country, its wily inhabitants fleeing their corrupt, poverty-stricken homeland to swindle honest Britons.

Rumbling across Bulgaria's eastern flats, it was hard to shake the stereotype. Bulgaria is the EU's poorest nation, as gloomy Soviet-era buildings crumbling on the roadside attested. Heading north-westwards towards the capital Sofia, however, that impression itself crumbled.

First, we climbed into the Rhodope Mountains, winding through thick forests alongside deep river gorges. The lush greenery lifted my heart after months in the desolate Central Asian steppes. Next, we visited Plovdiv, Bulgaria's second city, claiming to be the oldest continually inhabited in Europe. Its honeycomb streets belied a procession of invaders, whether Persian, Greek, Celtic, Roman, Goth, Hun, Bulgar, Slav, Rus, Crusader or Turk; Bulgaria's rich heritage conveniently overlooked by the Brexit tabloids.

When we arrived at last in Sofia, whose genteel streets were lined with trees aflame in red and gold, the last scraps of the Bulgaria I had conjured in my head were lost. Driving Oxford past the multi-domed majesty of the Aleksander Nevski Cathedral in the evening light left me speechless, and when we finally found our guesthouse tucked above a flashy co-working space, whose users came and went on slick electric scooters, I had mentally to check I hadn't accidentally arrived in a plush suburb of London. Bulgaria still had its problems, I was sure, but it was now light years away from the country Oxford had been forced to avoid back in 1955.

That night, we celebrated Thanksgiving for David's sake, which gave me a convenient excuse to blow the next few days' dinner budget in one go in a cosy Armenian restaurant. As the rich *pelin* wine began to work its fuddling magic, I couldn't help but smile at the dismay with which Lenin and Stalin might have watched our multinational band of travellers toasting our Georgian Jewish comrade on the foundation of the American dream in the heart of Bulgaria. If they weren't so rigid with formaldehyde, I'm sure they'd be turning in their graves.

'We were supposed to be home today,' muttered Nat, leaning on PAC's passenger window.

It was 29 November: by our original schedule, he was right. Instead of the white cliffs of Dover, however, we were only just approaching the Serbian border, and our sixteenth country. The Chinese-border debacle felt a lifetime ago, but its impact was finally hitting home. Even after three months' overlanding, two additional weeks tested those separated from friends, partners and children for perhaps the longest period in their lives.

Larry pointed out that he could be with his wife Simone and daughter Lucy, who were now waiting for him in London, in only forty-eight hours if he drove at full speed without stopping. It made the fourteen driving days that still lay ahead of us seem ludicrously inefficient, but Nat noted how we were due to cover the leg between Serbia and London in exactly the same time as Oxford had in 1955. In a world of swirling change, Oxford at least was a solid, belligerent constant.

By crossing into Serbia, we were once again re-joining her tyre tracks from all those years ago. We were, however, leaving the European Union again, which only intensified a feeling of treading water that had dogged us all that day. A pall of thoughtful silence hung across all three cars.

'Who's the most famous Serbian you know?' I asked Nat, Marcus, and David, in an effort to break the silence.

They were driving with me in PAC that morning as Larry and the Doc formed our rearguard in Enterprise, and up ahead Leo and Tibie were piloting Oxford under an iron-grey sky.

'Novak Djoković,' said Nat, miming a forehand swing.

'Dušan Čarls Simiç,' offered David, who then had to inform his much less cultured companions that Simiç was a Pulitzer Prize-winning poet in the US.

'Slobodan Milošević,' said Marcus, causing a hushed silence in the car.

I had come of age in the 1990s. Milošević's name covered the earliest news bulletins I can remember, and as a child I recall my parents befriending a couple of Kosovan doctors who had been granted asylum in our town, after fleeing the violence in the Balkans. After that, Milošević was popped in my developing brain's 'villain' box, but it was not until studying the collapse of Yugoslavia at university that I truly understood why.

'Balkanisation,' my lecturer had intoned drily on a cold January morning in 2007. 'A largely negative term, describing the process of fragmentation of a larger state into smaller states, which may then be hostile to each other.' We had witnessed the process in Thailand, Burma, India, China and Tajikistan, and now drove through the very peninsula that gave its name to this urge to redraw the map.

When Oxford had last driven through what we now call Serbia, it was merely one part of the Socialist Federal Republic of Yugoslavia (SFRY). After three bouts of fighting between 1990 and 2001, the deadliest conflict on European soil since the Second World War, the SFRY collapsed. In its wake it left seven newly independent countries (Serbia, Croatia, North Macedonia, Montenegro, Bosnia & Herzegovina, Slovenia and Kosovo), myriad atrocities, from rape to genocide, and more than 140,000 corpses.

Slobodan Milošević embodied the aggressive ethnic nationalism that had crippled the SFRY. Milošević strove to carve a 'Greater

Serbia' from the wreckage, putting him on a deadly collision course with the other ethnic groups in and around the Serbian heartlands.

After a decade of conflict, he was finally sent to the Hague to stand trial for the carnage he had wrought. Five years in, Milošević was found dead in his cell after a suspected heart attack. Spared a guilty verdict by death, the spectre of the 'Butcher of the Balkans' still haunts the fractious political settlements that hold the region together today.

However, driving through, Serbia couldn't have felt more peaceful. Hazy mist swaddled low-rolling hills; the air through Oxford's gaps smelled pleasantly of earth and leaf mould. We cruised through countryside so modestly familiar it could have been England in autumn. Only the squat whitewashed houses with terracotta roofs, smoke curling lazily from their chimneys, gave the game away. We were 95 kilometres (60 miles) from Belgrade, and Serbia's thus-far temperate neatness contrasted starkly with my preconceptions.

I remembered being glued to the news in 1999 as a coalition of American, British, French, Italian, German, Belgian, Danish, Dutch, Canadian and Norwegian forces bombarded Belgrade for seventy-eight days. For the second time that decade, NATO's awesome might was unleashed on Milošević to stop his campaign of terror in breakaway Kosovo.[21] Swathes of Belgrade were pulverized by 'Operation Noble Anvil' and hundreds of civilians killed, but the action ended Milošević's barbaric reign.

To save time and money, we stopped only briefly in Belgrade's outskirts before continuing towards Hungary. As the end of our journey neared, our approach to everything – eating, sleeping, driving, talking – became economized and robotic. Despite the powerful tug of home, I regretted our haste. I thought back to the

---

21   Former UK prime minister Tony Blair still remains a saintly figure in Kosovo for his part in nudging NATO into action, with many boys named 'Tonibler' in his honour. His belief in the power of 'humanitarian armed intervention' for taming repressive dictators would lead in part to the Iraq War, and the grisly quagmire that has ensued ever since.

eternally overlanding Karin's words in Uzbekistan about moving so fast you miss the whole point of travel. It was true – I had gained only a surface impression of Bulgaria and Serbia, with few meaningful interactions to provide a window into these nations' souls.

Horgoš, only 4 kilometres (2.5 miles) from the Hungarian border, eased that feeling. Our guesthouse in this sleepy little town had only opened that day, and was still without a name above the door as we lugged our bags through the freshly painted doors. The hotel's owner, Ivan, cheerily whipped dustsheets off tables and began to light a huge fire as we settled into his cosy dining room. Ivan was in his mid-fifties, handsome and silver-haired, with a stocky physique that spoke of a keen athlete now slightly gone to seed. As we devoured a delicious dinner of *sarma*, *duvec* and *riblja čorba* rustled up by Ivan himself, he began to share his story.

'Yugoslavia was heaven,' he announced with a nostalgic sigh, resting his hands on his paunch and rocking back on his chair. 'For twenty years I lived like a king. I was the goalkeeper for the national youth football team, we travelled all over Europe. Can you imagine, all over! Yugoslavia was respected by everyone. Marshal Tito, the president, he balanced all the different national groups in Yugoslavia. He was a very talented man. He was a good Communist, but he hated Soviets. Stalin tried to kill him! But then in 1980, Tito died. Everybody cried. And then, soon after, we went to war.'

As I listened to him talk, Ivan's story reminded me again of those two contradictory forces I could increasingly see were at the heart of all of us – the delight in freedom of movement, and the powerful need to belong. Karin, Coen and David had all expressed it so beautifully, and I realized this journey had brought the tension out more keenly in myself. Suddenly the door opened, revealing a huge bear of a man, stamping his feet from the cold.

'Yannik! Everybody, this is my cousin Yannik.' Ivan pulled out a chair. Yannik settled his enormous bulk, slapping his cousin on the shoulder in greeting.

'I was talking about the war,' said Ivan.

'Which one?' chuckled Yannik, pouring a beer.

'We were conscripted young – eighteen, nineteen?' Ivan continued. 'First, we fought the Croatians, then the Bosnians, then the Kosovans, then the whole damn West. NATO bombed our schools, our hospitals, our monuments. They said it was an "accident". Pah. Now they want us to join NATO! Can you believe it?'

'Things were so much better under Tito,' Yannik added, swilling his beer. 'Then it fell apart. War, sanctions, hyperinflation – prices went up 200 per cent overnight! Once, we all lived side by side; now that's impossible. Croats in Croatia, Serbs in Serbia, and so on. It's difficult, though, we're all mixed up together in the Balkans.'

'So, you're Serbs?' I asked.

'No!' barked Ivan. 'I am a Croat! But for eight generations my family have lived here, in Serbia. So, I suppose yes – you could say I'm sort of Serbian. Only sort of.'

If you could still be considered only 'sort of' Serbian after a *few hundred years* living somewhere, I was beginning to see the crux of the problem.

'And I'm ethnic Hungarian,' said Yannik. 'My family arrived when Serbia was part of the Austro-Hungarian Empire. Horgoš was very diverse once, lots of Germans and Jews lived here before the Second World War, but they were all expelled during that war. We've had much more war since then, of course.'

Ivan nodded. 'But now we've put down our guns and opened guesthouses. When that train station opens again, things will improve,' he indicated a dilapidated building through the window. 'The Chinese have promised to reopen the railway from Horgoš to Budapest. When they do, I hope many tourists will come and go.' I was initially surprised to hear of the Chinese involvement this far west but, thinking back to the scale of President Xi's ambitions we had witnessed on our journey so far, it quickly made sense.

'Until the Chinese come good, the people smugglers are your quickest way out of Horgoš,' chuckled Yannik, darkly.

'Bastards,' Ivan muttered. 'There must be a thousand people right now, hiding in these woods, waiting to slip into Hungary. The smugglers earn fortunes from desperate people. You want to know how I know? Follow me!'

He marched us into the dying evening light, to the rear of the crumbling station opposite. There, scrawled in black spray paint, was written:

HUNGARY €500
ROMANIA €1800
CROATIA €2000

'They can pick from a menu!' Ivan said with disgust.

I jumped. Two dark-haired, bedraggled young men stared from a clump of trees across the abandoned railway line. Seeing I had noticed them, they vanished. All that remained was the uppermost curve of the setting sun, casting a deep orange light on our little group here on the edge of Europe. After a few moments Ivan returned inside, the others following.

Except Tibie. Normally, like me, she was bursting full of questions for the fascinating friends we had made on our journey but had been unusually quiet during Ivan's tale. Now she stood looking downcast and thoughtful, watching the sun sink below the horizon.

'Are you okay?' I asked.

'My dad fought in Ivan's war.'

I didn't know what to say. I'd known Tibie's father had been in the military, but she had never expanded, and out of respect I hadn't asked.

'He fought here in the 1990s. I never knew quite what he was doing, but I remember he was always away. One Christmas, we received a video tape with a Christmas message from him. He was just visible in the night-vision camera, telling us not to worry but that he was very cold. He sent me a Barbie doll he bought from the American camp. It was so sad, that Christmas.'

Tears welled in her eyes. Tibie had been the very image of good-humoured resilience throughout our journey. I was shocked to see her like this.

'I never expected to come here. I never realized Serbia was so nearby, you know? And it's only twenty years since the war ended. It's all so ... close.'

I nodded. Given the Balkans' fractious history, who knew when trouble might spark again. When it did, would the West unite to stop it?

'I guess I should be grateful,' she said, recovering her resolve. 'Only Oxford could have brought me here.'

She was right. If we'd made this journey by plane, we would never have come to this place. The perilous journey facing these desperate people trying to reach Europe on foot would have remained just another news story. Good and bad, Oxford forced us to see the world as it was, before whisking us ever onwards.

We walked back silently to Ivan's fire. Outside, the dark and frost closed in, and the men in the woods began their journey west.

20

La Priorité à Droite!

1 December 2019: Horgoš, Serbia

Expedition Day 99

Crisp frost gripped Ivan's guesthouse, and the sky was so blue it stung my eyes. I was the first awake, eager to set off. At least I'd thought I was first. Turning the corner to our three trusty Land Rovers, I heard snatches of song from Oxford.

'I don't want a lot for Christmas, there is just one thing I need ...'

'Nat, what are you doing?' I asked.

The singing stopped.

'Happy first of December!' said Nat, emerging in his enormous Tibetan camouflage coat and black furry hat. He would have looked menacing but for the red and silver tinsel in his gloved hands. He had been doggedly weaving it throughout Oxford's cabin, creating the air of a fuel-drenched Santa's grotto.

'Where did you get that?' I asked, quietly impressed.

'This hat isn't all I bought in Kashgar's market. Forward planning!'

Slowly the rest of the team emerged, admiring Nat's handiwork. Nat's Christmas spirit was infectious, and soon we were all bopping merrily to Mariah Carey through our now oh-so-familiar car packing routine. Even Oxford refusing to start couldn't dim our joy; the Doc warbled 'Jingle Bells' at the helm as the rest of us heaved her into motion. The beauty of this team, I realized, was that whenever one of us dipped another would rise, dragging the others back to the task in hand.

Waiting to enter Hungary, Nat belting out 'Driving Home for Christmas', I had a sobering realization: it was the beginning of the end for our time together. Six countries, and less than 3,200 kilometres (2,000 miles) remained of our journey. The further west we travelled, the more familiar, and ordinary, everything became.

Weeks ago in Nepal, when Marcus and I had shared the news of our delay, I had bullishly asserted that 'We'll be home in time for Christmas.' It felt silly in the sticky heat of Kathmandu, and in Turkmenistan it seemed as empty a promise as that made to the soldiers who set off to fight in the autumn of 1914. But now it appeared I would actually make good on it.

So why didn't I feel good about it?

Over the following days, I had barely a moment to consider that question. The chaos of our time in Singapore, Malaysia and Thailand returned. We became national news as Budapest welcomed home half-Hungarian Marcus, whose father had fled to the UK in the wake of the Soviet occupation. In Slovakia we were greeted at the Land Rover factory in Nitra by the Slovakian prime minister himself. Next Oxford danced in the glare of countless camera flashes and the bright lights of Vienna's grand boulevards, performing with unaccustomed grace.

Once more, I saw how Oxford's journey had captured the imaginations of total strangers, who shared stories of their previous Land Rover adventures and those they dreamed of making in the future. I saw again how Oxford – that rolling, mechanical patch-up job we had come to love and at times loathe with equal intensity – had become a mirror for others' hopes and ambitions, a conduit for confessions about loved ones who had worshipped these old cars but were gone. Now only the smell of canvas and petrol remained, and they breathed it in deeply.

Not until reaching the outskirts of Baden-Baden, an old spa town in south-west Germany, did I finally have a moment to stop. Our spartan budget had seen us billeted in the guest house of a working convent on the outskirts of the Black Forest. After whipping through five countries in a week I was exhausted. As soon as I saw my single bed with its tired old mattress, I collapsed into it gratefully.

We each had our own little cell rooms, and I realized it was the first time in weeks I had been alone. It felt uncomfortable. For distraction, I read about the place where I found myself, devouring information about a town I'd likely never revisit. I learned that Baden-Baden had headquartered the French troops who had occupied Germany in the wake of the Second World War. The thought that Oxford been here only ten years after Germany's defeat and division by its Allied enemies made me realize quite how old she was. In 1955, Tim had met French border guards still nervously eyeing their German counterparts, and witnessed Munich being rebuilt from rubble.

Today we had streaked through modern-day Europe's economic powerhouse on the famous *autobahns*, mesmerized by supercars zooming past in technicolour blurs. Only the sign for Dachau, where tens of thousands died at Nazi hands, reminded us of the nightmare that once gripped Germany. The world had changed unimaginably since then, and in 2019 another war in Western Europe seemed unthinkable.

As we retraced the First Overland's journey across the world, so much of my time had been spent thinking about the past. Now for the first time in months, I wondered what the future might hold. It was a strange feeling. The expedition, I realized, had in a way suspended time. Each day we woke up together, ate together, drove together, had fun together, bedded down together. Then, next day, we did it again. In this strange, unworldly 'Oxford time' of constant movement, ironically nothing changed. In the world outside people were born, people died, they got jobs, lost them, got sick, or sad, had their hearts broken and mended. We, however, drove ever onwards to our next destination, in an eternal, petrol-filled present. I knew now that this blissful escape from real life was soon to end.

Next morning, Marcus's shaggy head appeared through my door, reading my mood immediately.

'Get up, gloomy guts. The sun is shining, and the breakfast is incredible!'

He wasn't lying – the nuns of Kloster Maria Hilf served a marvellous spread of fresh-baked bread and homemade jams, prepared before morning service. Gentle strains of German song drifted through the corridors, penetrating the dark clouds gathering over me.

'Leopold will give the briefing today,' announced Marcus through a mouthful of jam.

Leo, usually brooding happily behind his camera filming our progress, stepped forward with uncharacteristic gusto, bouncing on his heels.

'*Madames et monsieurs*,' he grinned, 'today we enter the greatest country on Earth – country number twenty-one, la France!'

Nat let out a 'booo', which Leo silenced with a patriotic glare.

Following Leo to Oxford, I chucked him the keys. 'It's only right you take her today.'

I had a sudden flashback to sticky Malaysia, where Leo had first driven this right-hand drive car. It felt like years ago, but this avid European still grimaced every time he had to reach left for the gearstick.

Entering France, it suddenly occurred to me that since Serbia, we had crossed five borders without displaying our passports. Thanks to the Schengen zone, we wouldn't need them until we crossed the Channel. After countless hours at border crossings on two continents, having our papers checked and cars scrutinized, it felt odd to flit between nations without even slowing down. It showed what was possible through concerted political effort: we are not destined to be separated by razor wire.

After a rousing rendition of 'La Marseillaise', Leo peered through the grubby windscreen thoughtfully.

'I haven't lived in France since high school, you know.'

Lost in my own thoughts about the journey's end, I had forgotten how the others must feel, their own journeys winding down. We had all joined the expedition for our personal reasons. For Leo, the journey was a symbolic return after years away from France, the country of his birth. Like me, he was saying goodbye to Myanmar, where he had built a happy life with his partner Angele, using Oxford's journey as an excuse to return home to a country that had transformed in his absence.

'France is hurting,' explained Leo, as we skirted Strasbourg. Three days earlier, on 5 December, Leo, Marcus and I had despondently watched coverage of widespread union strikes across France, some turning violent. The country's transport networks were grinding to a halt, the police and the army were out in force across the country, and Marcus and I feared being trapped in France and having to shift our homecoming deadline yet again. Leo's concern had been more personal.

The cause of these strikes was a proposed reform to the pensions system, Leo informed us, but they were merely the latest wave in a tide of seemingly continuous unrest France had endured since its youthful president, Emmanuel Macron, had ascended to power in 2017. Beating his far-right rival, Marine Le Pen, quite comfortably, Macron had inherited a country deeply divided between his ambitious, reforming vision and Le Pen's desire to turn the tide of globalization, reduce immigration, and return France to an imagined 1950s golden age.

'They should try driving 1950s cars,' I said, massaging my back, 'and see if that dents their enthusiasm.'

Since November 2018, Leo continued, France had been wracked by a series of protests that had rocked the nation: the *Gilet Jaunes* movement. Sparked by a planned rise in fuel taxes, protesters had united wearing the hi-vis vests that all French motorists are required to keep in their cars.

'The car became a symbol ...' Leo tapped Oxford's wheel for emphasis '... of two halves of France that do not understand one another. The wealthy who live in Paris, they don't need cars, so fuel-tax rises are not a problem. For the rest, the poor and those in rural areas, the car is a symbol of independence, of their livelihoods. But then the movement became so much more than cars – it became an outlet for every kind of anger, and right now the French are very, very angry.'

Leo was my first close French friend; through him, I had seen how some of the stereotypes (at least the kinder ones) that we Brits love to hold about 'the old enemy' are wonderfully true. For Leo, art really *was* life, food truly religion. Even in the most remote villages in Myanmar, filming in extreme conditions, Leo would work into the small hours to get the perfect shot, and insist we found the most delicious local food to keep our spirits up.

I had seen his tears of joy when France won the football World Cup in 2018. Together in Yangon we had watched the jubilant scenes on TV that, for a fleeting moment, had healed France's deep economic, social and racial divides; a simple, yet deeply held sense of pride in a national project.

I pulled out Tim's diary.

'Tim said nice things about France, perhaps they will cheer France up?'

'Yes, *continué*!'

I projected above the engine roar: 'The French may be artistic; they may be one of the most cultured and civilized races in the world …'

Leo nodded, approvingly. So I read on.

'… but in one thing they seem to lag behind the Anglo-Saxon races by some thousands of years – this is their habits of hygiene. When one comes to a French public lavatory, one is struck by the fact that in order to achieve the spread and pattern one must assume that the users have swung about at high speed from the overhead light flexes.'

Leo's smile faded.

'My *Eeenglish* is not so good,' my perfectly bilingual companion responded in a thick French accent. 'But I heard "the most cultured and civilized race in the world". Tim is a very wise man.'

After stopping in the Champagne region (for what I would argue were entirely essential reasons), on 9 December we made towards Paris. Foul, black clouds hurled fat drops of rain into the bitter winds whipping through Oxford's cab. Not even the fairy lights and potted poinsettias that Tibie had added to Oxford's grotto could dispel the bleakness.

Nat was back alongside me in Oxford, and Leo in PAC glued to an app one of his fellow citizens had designed to keep track of the strikes. Marcus gnawed his fingernails, worrying whether we would be able to board the car ferry as planned in four days. Thoughts of future movement were quickly curtailed, however, by a distress call from Larry.

'Enterprise calling convoy, Enterprise calling convoy! Enterprise is down.'

In Oxford's rear-view mirror, I could just make out the outline of Larry's Land Rover – a reassuringly constant sight for almost 17,700 kilometres (11,000 miles) – now shrinking into the distance. With a hurried U-turn, we dashed back. Larry, usually pragmatic, looked dejected.

'It's the clutch,' he groaned. 'Dead. I know it.'

The Doc, his co-pilot for much of our long journey, patted Larry consolingly as if standing by a graveside. The truest Land Rover aficionado among us, the Doc knew the weight of Larry's loss. I was reminded anew of the sacrifices the others had made to be here, Larry perhaps above all. He was our crew's oldest member, with a wife and child to care for, and a business he had put on hold.

In Tim's absence, this journey had become a test of personal endurance for Larry – if he finished, he would have an epic *three* London–Singapore overlands under his belt, a feat that would certainly put him in the overland hall of fame. I had often marvelled at his capacity to drive over twelve hours a day without a break. I sometimes worried he might crack with the strain, but in a cruel twist, his trusty steed had broken first.

Fortunately for Larry, since leaving Champagne our convoy had been joined by Sebastian, a wonderfully eccentric French Land Rover fan, who now came to our aid. Complete with beret, round rimless glasses and waxed mustachios, Sebastian looked as if he'd jumped straight out of my school French textbook. For only the second time on our journey a rescue truck was sourced, and our fallen warrior winched aloft. Sebastian knew a garage in Champagne that could possibly fix Enterprise, but it would mean doubling back. It was decided, for the first time in our journey, to split the convoy.

As I watched Larry and the Doc disappear from view, I was surprisingly worry free. It could have been the manic determination in Sebastian's eyes, my faith in the Doc and Larry to solve any mechanical problem, or simply our ability as a team to triumph over any disaster. Whatever it was, I knew we'd overcome. My optimism was rewarded; a few hours after dark, crawling through the gridlocked Parisian traffic, I received a video call from the Doc.

'Alex! We can fix her! We will need to work all night, but we can do it. And look ...'

He turned the screen to show Larry, bedded down on a tiny camp bed in the garage next to his beloved Land Rover.

'You can tell everyone: the expedition is camping!'

'I love Paris, in the winter, when it drizzles ...' sang David, as we both stepped out into the bustling streets of Montmartre. The news had signalled an enormous storm was brewing, but despite the bad weather, I shared David's excitement to be standing in the heart of Paris. I struggled to believe that we were actually here, only the shortest hop away from London and the end of what sometimes had seemed a foolishly impossible challenge.

Over the rich odours of black coffee earlier that day, we had held one of our last morning meetings. Perhaps it was the giddiness of being close to the finish line, but even though we were temporarily a Land Rover down, caught in the middle of the worst transport strikes in modern French history, and facing storms in the Channel that could cancel our ferry, Marcus and I oozed optimism.

Discussing our options, we concluded that – given the strikes and the weather – the car ferry we had booked onto weeks before could be too much of a risk to rely on. We could be stuck in Paris for days and miss our own 'Welcome Home' party, scheduled for 14 December. We made the decision to spend the last dregs of our budget on tickets for the Channel Tunnel as a backup, vowing that even if we had to build a driftwood raft, Oxford at least would hit English soil in four days' time.

Knowing there was nothing left to do but wait for Larry and the Doc, we took PAC and Oxford for a run around Paris. Oxford had last been driving round these streets sixty-four years earlier, her tyres shiny and uncracked, engine sparkling, and her dark-blue paintwork immaculate. She cut a more wizened figure today, but there was no denying the romance of seeing her back on the Parisian cobbles. It seemed the residents felt it too, many honking and waving as we flew by. We were moving with renewed purpose, as we had set ourselves a mission before we left Paris tomorrow.

On a balmy September morning in 1955, the First Overland, barely into their journey to Singapore, had been invited to bounce up the steps of the Palais de Chaillot, deploy their stoves and kettles and – in Tim's words – 'fait le brew-up' in the shadow of the Eiffel Tower for the assembled French press.

'Apparently the sight of six Englishmen brewing tea in the middle of this Trafalgar Square of Paris was just what the French viewers would expect,' Tim wrote. 'It was *vraiment les Anglais*.'

With Leo navigating, we snaked across Paris towards the Eiffel Tower, hoping to recreate the iconic moment. Speeding down Avenue de Wagram, Leo warned gravely, 'This is the most dangerous *rond point* in Paris. Forget everything you have learned about your English roundabouts. Do *exactly* what I say, and we will get through alive.'

Enjoying this Obi-Wan Kenobi routine, I gripped Oxford's wheel, and floored the gas. Ahead, the stuccoed limestone bulk of the Arc de Triomphe loomed ever larger, as did the ten lane, road-marking-free madness encircling it. Our road was one of twelve that were vomiting vehicles of all sizes into the whirling, horn-screeching chaos of Place Charles de Gaulle.

'There is only one rule: *la priorité à droite!*' Leo bellowed as Oxford entered the ring. 'You have to give way while you are *inside* the *rond point!*'

'What?!' I shouted, narrowly dodging a battered Peugeot driven at suicidal speed. Driving on the wrong side of the road always put me on edge, and now this counterintuitive instruction was testing my limits. I slammed Oxford's brakes to let a large Mercedes through, almost forcing a motorbike into Oxford's rear doors. My French was insufficient to grasp the insult blasted through my window.

'Your insurance is probably invalid here, so be careful!' Leo counselled unhelpfully, as I dodged and weaved around the Arc to the opposite edge. Finally, like a comet breaking free from orbit, Oxford screeched onto Avenue Kléber.

I felt I had gained a profound insight into the Gallic soul. Deep inside every Frenchman, as in their beautiful, ordered capital city, is a heart of chaos, a space where the rules no longer apply. It's from here they draw their primal energy to storm the Bastille, chop off royal heads, or grind their country to a halt. And they *love* it.

Up ahead, Eiffel's wrought-iron masterpiece hove into view. A structure that had once been temporary, when it was first built it had divided France's artistic community down the middle. But 130 years later it had come to symbolize the country in which it stood. There waiting beneath it was an even more impressive sight – Larry and Doc, standing alongside Enterprise complete with a brand-new clutch. Flushed with that happy reunion and my successful tussle with the Arc de Triomphe, I approached the same steps the First Overlanders had scaled six decades earlier. I could almost taste the tea. Leo, reading my intent, told me to stop and switch seats.

'This is a job for a Frenchman,' he said. A policeman, toting an enormous machine gun, looked coolly on as Leo edged Oxford towards the pavement. The moment wheel touched curb, six heavily armed officers materialized, bellowing at Leo to stop. The lead officer approached Leo's window.

A conversation in French too quick for me to follow ensued, Leo sharing a picture on his phone. As the officer instructed us to return to the main road, Leo explained.

'I told him this car parked here in 1955. I showed him the proof.'

'And what did he say?'

'He said: "It's not 1955 anymore."'

'How true,' I replied.

21

Homeward Bound

13 December 2019: Brussels, Belgium

Expedition Day 111

'Bollocks,' said Nat.

My eyes cracked open to Nat's phone dimly illuminating the room. He was sat in bed reading the morning news, furry hat enveloping his head, breath misting in the freezing pre-dawn darkness.

'Boris won. We're leaving the EU.'

I grunted, reluctant to move for fear of letting the little warmth I had escape the covers on this bitterly cold Belgian morning. We had detoured here briefly from Paris to take part in a 'Best of British' exhibition at Autoworld in Brussels, an event now deeply ironic in its timing. I was unsure how to feel, but I knew it was a turning point in history, whose repercussions would take years, even decades, to be fully understood. Whatever happened next, the world as I knew it would never be the same.

Through the familiar ritual of washing, dressing and gathering my things, I thought of Tim sixty-four years ago, nearing the end of his own journey across the world. What did he think the future held, back in September 1956? Could he have known that Malaya would be independent only years after he fought to secure British control? That within his lifetime Singapore would be rich beyond compare? That Yugoslavia and Syria would dissolve into bloodshed, or that China would rise from pauper to superpower?

Could he have foreseen Communism's rise and fall, or Britain joining then leaving a 'European Union'? Would he have believed that man would walk on the moon, the world would be connected by a mystical 'world wide web', and that a talking box could let him video call his grandson in Uzbekistan?

Probably not. So, what might someone from the future tell me? How many of my worries today would seem inconsequential? What miseries and marvels awaited sixty-five years ahead? If the decades between the First and Last Overland had proved anything, it was that – whether we like it or not – the great wheels of history will keep on turning, taking us to destinations few can ever predict. I moved to join the team downstairs, lost in thought, before the growl of a familiar engine brought me back to the present.

I stepped out into the crisp winter and headed to where Oxford was parked. The Doc and Nat were readying her for the journey across the French border to Calais, the last 200 kilometres (125 miles) of Europe before we boarded our ferry across the Channel. Alongside them I noticed a hulking, familiar outline I hadn't seen in months. It turned to face me.

'When a Yorkshireman says he's going to do something, he does it,' boomed Adam. 'You must have some Yorkshire in you too, Alex.'

It was the biggest compliment I could have hoped for, besides the fact that this man, who risked a nosebleed leaving York, had driven all the way to Brussels to be with us on our expedition's final leg. He hadn't seen Oxford since putting her on a ship in January, and the joy at the reunion with the car he had gone to such lengths to rescue was written right across his face. It warmed my heart to see it, and him. Whether I was ready or not, it was time to take Oxford home at last.

Checks complete, I climbed in behind the wheel, the frosty leather biting through my jeans. I clapped life into my hands, my left finding the scuffed yellow start button without help from my eyes.

Oxford coughed into life, and a few taps to the gas pedal had her purring. Nat climbed into position alongside me. I waggled the gear stick and steering wheel, as if petting a favourite dog.

Pulling out of Brussels to the E40, the feeling that had been building for days finally hit. It was a feeling of acute, impending loss. In this world of whirling change, Oxford had been a clattering, clanking constant. Despite countless breakdowns, she was always my rock, wrapped in her musk of petrol, grease and clammy leather. She had become a four-wheeled extension of my own body. By the light of her headlamps, I could always see the six feet of road in front, and while driving her they were all that mattered.

I recognized now what drew people like my dad, Adam and the Doc to these machines, pulled the pious of the Series One Club on pilgrimage to Anglesey, or left Larry tearful when Enterprise broke down. Unlike our frail bodies, there was no such thing as a 'write-off' in the Land Rover world. With enough effort and know-how, there was no problem that couldn't be fixed, no lost cause that couldn't be put back on the road. While the clock ticked for our time on Earth, Oxford – and the spirit of adventure she embodied – was in some way immortal. To say goodbye to her, I now knew, was almost to say goodbye to life itself. Tim's face in that Singapore hotel room flashed before me, and now I fully understood how he must have felt knowing his part in this adventure was all but done.

'There's Dunkirk,' said Nat, pointing at a sign on our right. In the distance we could make out the sea, iron-grey and angry.

'Shall we call the little ships?' he said. 'I'd bet my right arm our ferry will be cancelled.'

'Let's hope Boris hasn't closed the Channel Tunnel to celebrate his win, hey?'

After 110 nights of guesthouses, eco lodges, homestays and beach-front shacks, morning sunrises over deserts, mountains, jungles and pristine beaches, the expedition's final overnight was a shabby motel in Calais's ferry terminal. We didn't care. As I blew the last of our budget on champagne and boeuf bourguignon (much to Leo's approval) in a nearby restaurant, I took one last look at my little overlanding family.

Four months ago, some of these people – Tibie, Doc, Larry, Nat – had been total strangers. Go back ten years and I wouldn't recognize a single one. Now, however, this unlikely crew, drawn from six countries and so different in age, background and expertise, were bound together by an experience none of us could forget. I thought of Tim, Pat and Nigel, still friends sixty-five years on. Would our journey unite us for life, as theirs did? I could only hope so.

Nat raised his glass: 'To the Old Lady – Oxford – who we love dearly, and who I'm looking forward to not driving again for quite some time!'

We raised our glasses with Nat to rings of laughter and sympathetic rubbings of lower backs. The only one not laughing was Adam, a small smile playing on his face. He waited for the laughter to subside before giving me a knowing look.

'She'll bring you back to her, just you wait.'

I had lain awake on the covers all night, while the snores of my companions battled the howling wind and hammering rain. When the 6 a.m. alarm finally sounded I was up in a flash, just as I had been on that sweltering Flag Off morning in Singapore. Gone was the well-honed discipline of our morning routine; bags were flung into cars with childlike abandon. The rain had stopped, but the wind more than compensated; we struggled to stand straight for our final team photo before setting off for the ferry. I hurried Oxford through the terminal, the wind threatening to rip the roof from over our heads. But a little gale wasn't going to stop her, not today. She felt alive, invincible beneath my feet.

Nat was in his familiar position alongside me, and Tibie sat in the back broadcasting our final journey to thousands of fans through her mobile phone. I could hear the pings and pops of messages from all over the world; it was bizarre to think of our friends in Singapore, Malaysia, Thailand and Myanmar egging us on in the sticky afternoon heat, or of Alex Fedin in a snow-covered Moscow cheering us over his morning coffee.

I thought of the hundreds of Land Rover fans who had answered our call to welcome Oxford home at a special gathering we had organized just on the other side of the channel, at the port-town of Folkestone. From there we would convoy to London, and the finish line at last. Right now, as I chewed up the final French road, I knew my dad was in his own beloved Series I, charging down the M20 towards the coast, begging it, today of all days, not to overheat. Here in Calais, a phalanx of Land Rovers from the French Dutch Series One Clubs hooted and flashed as we made for the boarding gate. I was still amazed at the lengths to which people were going to be part of Oxford's homecoming.

It was the start of what I knew would be an unforgettable day, and I said as much to Nat, who was hunched over his phone checking our departure time. 'Don't count your chickens. The storm's too strong – the ferry's cancelled!'

We swung about, pointing our seasoned three-car convoy in the direction of the Channel Tunnel. I had wanted to arrive in England by ferry, imagining the famous white cliffs of Dover looming into view, but the tunnel was a fitting way to end our journey. The idea of a land link had still been a pipe dream back in 1955. A Frenchman had not travelled overland to Britain for 8,000 years, and the kingdom's island status had forged our entire national psyche.

Now, after decades of political wrangling and engineering wizardry, around 10 million people a year were shuttled at high speed 75 metres (250 feet) below the seabed. Tim had always been keen to correct when people talked of his London to Singapore 'overland' – his journey had started from the French coast, he observed pedantically. Now thanks to the tunnel, we were finally forging that last link in the chain.

As we sank beneath the sea, nine people and three cars tucked together in a brightly lit car-carriage, I knew it would be that day's last peaceful moment. I pulled my copy of Tim's diary from my bag one last time, and flicked to the end to join Tim finishing his journey on the other side of the world:

> The crossing of that causeway was a moment we had talked about in our Cambridge rooms before we left England, nearly a year earlier. It was a moment which we had talked about throughout the journey – sometimes hopefully, and sometimes as if it were on the other side of the world ... Now it was right underneath us, rolling away as if there had never been any doubt about it at all ... The 'film of the expedition' would here break into triumphant background music.

Perhaps in another universe somewhere, Tim and I were inside Oxford in this carriage together, exhausted and elated, readying ourselves for the final push. Here in this one, however, all I had of him was his trademark looping script. The silence was uncomfortable, so following Tim's instructions, I flicked on 'Jerusalem' and bathed in its stirring verse.

Nat's face appeared in the window. In it were Tim's eyes, Tim's crooked grin.

'Time to go home!' he shouted, punching the air.

A rush of joy filled me as daylight began to flicker in the little square train windows. I had never been so drunk with love for the dull-grey light of England. Pulling onto home soil for the first time in four months, my heart lodged in my throat. We had no time to waste, pointing our wheels in the direction of the Folkestone Harbour Arm, where our families, sponsors and Oxford's fans from across the UK were waiting to welcome us home at last. For the final time, we arranged into convoy, chattered the last into our radios, and pulled into the madness.

More than 200 Land Rovers of all shapes and sizes were gathered, braving the gales and storms. There was honking and hollering, applauding and cheering as we rolled through a crowd worthy of a World Cup-winning team. Pulling to a halt, I stepped out onto the harbour front, and into a crushing hug from my dad. Around me the rest of the team, all looking as startled as I felt, were being swept into similar embraces as they stepped down from the cars.

In among the exuberant mass of friends and family was one small, stooped figure, dressed in a long black coat and matching woolly hat. As Nat stepped out from Oxford on to the tarmacked pier, I watched as it moved towards him with a speed belying its eighty-eight years.

'Grandpa!' Nat shouted.

The mass of flashing cameras turned as one to capture the moment we had all been waiting for. The moment that would bring our story full circle at last. Nat, standing a head taller than Tim, buried his grandpa in his chest where Tim burst into tears. Nat, smiling from ear to ear, held him tighter still, eyes glistening.

A little later, Tim stood on a small stage in front of the gathered crowd, microphone in hand.

'I'm not going to burst into great paeons of praise for what they have done,' Tim said through a microphone.

'I won't do that, because the achievement speaks for itself. But if you'll forgive me a little personal note: if someone had told me when we arrived at Champion Motors on Orchard Road in Singapore in March 1956 … if someone prophetically had told me that sixty-four years later we'd be meeting at bloody Folkestone to celebrate Oxford's return, I would never have believed them.'

The crowd let loose a roar of applause. Tim shivered with the cold, before soldiering on.

'I was meant to be a part of this journey, as many of you know. But at the last minute I quit. Realism overcame ambition; I realized I'd be a risk to the others, and it wasn't a risk I wanted to take.

It was a great, great disappointment. But the fact that a twenty-one-year-old grandson of mine took my place ...'

He paused, overcome with emotion.

'If I sound a bit moved, I am. I bloody am. Thank you.'

After Tim had stepped down from the stage and the crowds had begun to thin, he came to find me, grabbing my arm in a tender grip. There was so much I had thought I would say in this moment, so much I wanted to say after the unexpected way the adventure we had planned together had turned out.

I wanted to say how sorry I was he had not come, but how proud of Nat he would have been at every stage. I wanted to describe to him all the incredible things Nat and I had seen, all the wonderful people we had met, and say how grateful I was to him for that. I wanted to tell him how the world the First Overland travelled through had changed almost beyond recognition, but in so many ways was also still the same.

We were two men normally so easy with words, but in that moment words failed us. Tim held both my hands in his. After a long pause, he said:

'You know, it'll look very good on his CV.'

We both grinned. For now, it was enough.

'But you're not done yet, Alex.' Tim added. 'London is the finish line!'

We clambered back into Oxford as we had done countless times, but this time Nat was squeezed in the middle with Tim – alongside him at last. I could almost hear the rush of memories as Tim ran his wizened hands over her battered interior, but they were memories that now mixed giddily with our own. We pulled onto the M20, a convoy of Land Rovers in front and behind as far as I could see. Finally, a sign to London whooshed overhead: only a few more kilometres until we could apply the handbrake for the final time.

I drove in silence as Nat and Tim talked. There was something different now in the way they were with each other, and I wanted to drink it in. Back in July, when I'd first seen them together, it had always been Nat with the questions, Tim with the stories. Now their roles were reversed. It was Tim asking Nat about the food in Tajikistan and the altitude in Tibet, grandpa asking grandson about the fighting in northern Myanmar and the rains in north-east India. A proud old grandfather enjoying the worldly wise young man his grandson had become.

I remembered how, in the days after my grandad's death, I had envied them for this. But now envy had given way to joy – joy in the part I had been able to play in giving them something I could never have. In now well-practised fashion, I clenched my mind. Whatever the future held, I would remember this.

In just a few hours we were back at the Grenadier pub, by Hyde Park Corner in the heart of London, surrounded by family and friends who had travelled from around the world to celebrate with us. This is where it had all begun for the First Overland on a balmy September day in 1955; and it was here that it would end for us, sixty-four years later on a fresh December night. We ate, drank and danced into the small hours, and I gave my mum the hug I'd been waiting to give her since India.

We had parked Oxford in pride of place outside the nearby London Hilton on Park Lane, whose manager had kindly put up the expedition for one last night. As the team wove unsteadily back to our beds, we stopped to drink in Oxford one last time. She looked more ruggedly beautiful than ever beneath the hotel's twinkling Christmas lights. Struck by the inspiration that so often comes to the incredibly drunk, a tangled web of thoughts I had been weaving since Singapore finally clicked into place.

I now understood what it was about these old cars – and about this one in particular – that drew so many to them. If we humans are born riven by conflicting desires to wander *and* to belong, then what better means of transport is there? For so many people we had met along the way – like Adam, Tim and my dad, who had brought me to the journey's start – a Land Rover was a little capsule of home, of family and of history. They were rich with memories – of youth and of adventures past. The beauty of an old Land Rover was that you could take that deep sense of the familiar with you anywhere in the world. In a Land Rover like this, rich with the memories of those you loved who had driven it before you, you could wander the globe *and* be at home.

I shared my epiphany with Marcus and looked again at Oxford. I took in that little old car who had faithfully carried the First Overlanders across the globe, had been miraculously rescued from her island exile by Adam, and had now transported a whole new generation around the world. Among all the many beloved Land Rovers we had encountered along the way who had – and would – allow their humans to wander with the comfort of home, she was still in a class of her own. Another thought began to dawn.

'Whose idea was our expedition, do you think?' I asked Marcus.

My old friend, who had been living on the same frenetic wavelength for the last eighteen months, didn't let me down.

'I'd say hers,' Marcus answered with a burp.

As we ran our hands across her mottled, battered bonnet one last time, I stopped in shock. Could it be? Surely not. I moved in closer, eyeing a small bundle under her battered windscreen wiper. Unbelievable! I laughed out loud.

Sixty-five years, 19,500 kilometres (12,200 miles), twenty-three countries, two continents …

… and one parking ticket.

I was home.

22

The Last Overland?

1 October 2020: London, England

Nine months later

'The good road ends, as all good roads do.'
Tim Slessor, *expedition diary*

I approached the door of Tim's little terraced house and rang the buzzer, the familiar stub of paper with 'SLESSOR' written in biro taped over the button. In this sleepy little suburb, it was as if nothing had changed since my last visit on the eve of our departure for Singapore.

But everything had changed. I, for one, was now an overlander. When I had last stood here, I was just a wannabe, an apprentice, a dreamer. Now, when Tim opened the door, I could look him in the eye as an equal at last. I had long imagined this moment (think something akin to Frodo returning to the Shire at the end of the last *Lord of the Rings*, yet with more discussion of carburettors), but our happy reunion was taking place under circumstances stranger than either of us could have foreseen.

Larry's observation that the world had become 'more safe, but less free' since Tim's original journey had been taken to extremes. For nearly a year, the Covid-19 virus had swept through the world with little care for the many national borders we had crossed on our road home – causing governments around the world to keep their citizens virtual prisoners in their own homes, for the sake of their own collective safety.

In honour of Tim's iconic journey, and our efforts to recreate it, our expedition had early on gained a nickname – 'the Last Overland'. On returning home, Larry had been the first of many to note the irony of it in light of the global lockdown. Perhaps we really had tempted fate? Over the last few months, the team and I had marvelled at the fortune we'd experienced in squeaking across the finish line shortly before the world's roads closed down to all but essential trade. We all agreed that it would be impossible to recreate our journey today, or in the near future. At last, it seemed, Sir David Attenborough had been proved right.

Here in Britain, unprecedented curbs on personal freedom had been introduced to stem the rising tide of infections. A sense of panic and fear had gripped the nation, and my world – once spanning two continents – had been reduced to a few square metres of south-west London, a daily trip to the supermarket being my only taste of adventure.

Precisely because of his age, Tim's had become even more constrained. The very elderly were particularly isolated from any human contact. Tim was in the highest risk category and to his intense annoyance had been confined to his little flat for most of the year. Besides a few phone calls and emails to exchange our mutual frustration, we had barely spoken. Today, however, was Tim's eighty-ninth birthday, and loosening restrictions had allowed a well-overdue reunion.

As the sound of the buzzer faded, my heart rose when I heard the familiar pad of Tim's clunky boots – a little slower than I remembered? – on the carpeted stairs. At last, I heard a fumbling with the latch.

'Happy birthday!' I said.

The man in front of me looked a little paler, a little more stooped, a little more drawn than I remembered, but the fire in the sharp blue eyes hadn't faded. The familiar uniform of washed-out jeans and oversized blue jumper showed he was still very much in business, even if they hung a little looser.

'Oh, stop making a fuss, Alex. The big one is next year, ninety! Get inside.'

Heading into his sitting room, I was struck again by a sense of timelessness. Almost nothing had changed in here: the same orderly clutter stacked the shelves, Nat's graduation photo beamed from the mantlepiece, the familiar worn-in armchair was ready for tales of adventure, past and future. On the floor, I thought I could still see the scuff marks from where we had pored over paper maps planning our great endeavour. Those countries were no longer a mass of squiggly lines and incomprehensible names, but real places with real people who would live on in my memory for years to come.

'The phone hasn't stopped ringing today,' grinned Tim. 'They must think I'll not be around for the next birthday.'

He must have caught the look of concern on my face at his frail appearance.

'This blasted lockdown, it's been … tough. Bloody boring, bloody lonely. The less you have to do, I find, the more difficult it is to do anything.'

He settled himself heavily into the chair opposite, dust motes dancing in the late-afternoon sun as he caught his breath and collected his thoughts. I'd caught the arch pragmatist in a rare philosophical mood.

'Eighty-nine! It sounds a lot, but life is not that long, Alex.' Sunlight danced on his spectacles as he looked through the window. 'Even if you live to a hundred – there's just so much to do, so much to see.'

It pained me to see my old hero so disconcerted.

'You've seen and done more than most, Tim,' I offered, thinking proudly of the sheer number of incredible places both he *and* I had now seen.

He chuckled darkly.

'You know, before I was twenty-five years old, I'd seen active service, got a degree from Cambridge, driven to Singapore and most of the way back, written a bestselling book and made the first travel series on the brand-new BBC Two. After that, it's hard for everything else not to be an anti-climax.'

Across the room was the familiar old black-and-white photo of the six First Overlanders perched on a log in Turkey, in July 1956. They were only weeks away from arriving home to London. Hatted and bearded (besides Tim, whose sponsorship deal with Remington razors kept him clean-shaven), they looked dusty and exhausted, but undeniably happy as they approached a year on the road.

'Three down, three to go,' Tim said, following my gaze.

'If you could talk to that young man now,' I said, pointing at the young Tim, 'would you tell him to do anything differently?'

'Not a bloody thing,' he answered after a pause. The grin returned to his face.

The conclusion seemed to snap him out of his funk and he heaved himself to his feet.

'Did you know they translated my book into Portuguese? Amazing. I've got a copy here somewhere.'

As Tim rootled in his bookshelves, I noticed the familiar tattered red covers of his *First Overland* expedition diaries poking out from the beneath the coffee table. I picked up one volume, opening the yellowing, crinkled pages to find Tim's familiar biro scrawl. I had taken scanned copies of the diaries on the journey with me, but I hadn't seen the originals since Tim had read from them at the Grenadier all those months ago.

'I never expected anyone to read those bloody diaries,' said Tim with a smile, returning to his seat clutching his pristine copy of *Primeiro Overland*.

I wanted to tell him they had been my constant companion through the journey; how I heard his voice in my ear as I read them again and again; how, when I thought he might never recover from hospitalization in Singapore, his diaries were the only connection to a dear friend I thought I'd lost for ever.

'How is your book going?' he asked.

'I'm struggling with the ending,' I confessed. From the moment I had known Tim was not joining on our journey, I had resolved to write my own account, so at the very least I could share it with him. Luckily, being locked indoors for most of the year had provided ample opportunity.

'Endings are difficult,' he mused. I sensed he was only half talking about my book.

'Are you still going to call it *The Last Overland*?' he asked.

'Yes,' I replied.

'You know I've never liked that bloody title. It's so final, so … morbid! It isn't Oxford's last; it can't be! I know Covid has made the journey we both made impossible for now, but there will be more overlands – there must be.'

His shoulders drooped slightly after the spurt of fire.

'But if it's my "Last Overland" you're referring to, Alex, well you might be right.'

An uncomfortable silence filled the room.

'Are you sad that you weren't able to come with us, in the end?'

'I'll admit I was more than a little disappointed to abandon something I'd dreamed of for so long.'

He paused, before leaning down to the side of his chair and pulling out a large, black ring binder. Large white letters on the front spelled out 'THE LAST OVERLAND: NAT'S DIARY'. I gasped with delight. I'd no idea Nat had been keeping it. Tim flicked through pages filled with photos and Nat's neat hand, a beam of pride crossing his face.

'But the fact that Nat was able to take my place, well, that assuages it all really. He had the time of his life; I'm so proud of him. I often think that I might have dined off that journey for six or seven more years, but Nat – he'll enjoy it for sixty or seventy.'

I watched the grand old adventurer lovingly turn the pages of his grandson's diary. Few grandfathers, I thought, could ever hope to give such a gift to their grandchild as Tim had to Nat. It was clear to me now, however, that Nat had given Tim something even more precious in return. Something that would perhaps allow this restless soul to be at peace with the end of his adventuring. As he flicked through the photographs that Nat had carefully glued in place, I noticed his eyes twinkle with the same delight I had first seen all those months ago, as he pored over maps of the world plotting his next great adventure.

'Your journey will be with him for the rest of his life,' said Tim, looking up. 'Some memories never fade.'

An image of my own grandad flashed in my mind, and I winced.

'I was sorry to hear about your grandfather,' said Tim, sensing my discomfort.

I finally shared the story of my last painful meeting with Harold, and the guilt I'd been carrying for being so far away when he died.

'It was harder for you than him, Alex,' said Tim, pragmatically.

'But what if the same thing happens to me? What if I forget it all?' I asked, voicing the question that, however irrational, had dogged me for years as I'd watched my grandad decline.

Tim paused, clearly pondering about how to respond.

'Well, I'd ask the same question.' He said, looking me in the eye. 'If that is what awaits, would you have done anything differently?'

'No.' I admitted, thinking back to the adventures I had already had, and those I still hoped to make.

'If anything, I'd enjoy it all the more.'

Tim nodded, approvingly.

'I've been thinking, Alex – life often only makes sense when you look backwards. I look back and say, "Shit, you did a lot, Slessor!"'

He looked me in the eye again.

'But more recently I've come to see that it was never about achievement. London, Singapore, whatever – it was about having *purpose*, a shared objective. One that is difficult, but *achievable*. Most importantly, it was having a team you trust to share it with.'

I looked back to the picture of Tim and his comrades, perched so carefree on the log. I noticed now that beside it he'd placed another photo: a near perfect reproduction our team had made of that famous photo, each of the Last Overlanders copying the pose of a First Overlander exactly. I marvelled at the stunning likeness Leo had to Adrian, noticed the unmistakable Slessor eyes and mouth in Nat's face; and as I saw each of them in turn, I missed them all dearly.

But above all I saw eight smiling faces, somewhere between their journey's start and finish, suspended happily for ever in a moment in time.

Epilogue

It was only in the final years of his life that I realized my grandad was a poet. Somewhere on the road, shortly after his death, I wrote this poem for him. If you've been moved by Harold's story, I'd be very grateful if you might consider donating to Dementia UK, who do wonderful work caring for those afflicted, and for those who care for them. Find out more at www.dementiauk.org.

Jaldapara

It's midnight in India, rain dances on tin,
the power's gone out and I half-dream of him.
I walk through his England, his streets and his home,
down pathways he wandered in love, and alone.

Around me his life stitched in silvery thread,
filled with tales from a path only he could have tread.
But as memories faded, the tapestry frayed,
no more crooked smiles, but an old man, afraid.

Now he's free from his prison, soul freed from the flesh,
he stops to look backwards with eyes now so fresh,
at the great grand old father, the brother, the son,
the boxer who battled, some he lost, some he won.

Every thought from a lifetime, of joy and of pain,
they dance all around me like warm monsoon rain.
They flow crystal clear now he's gone through the veil,
to a place where his mind cannot fuddle or fail.

'Do you see me now, Harold?'
'Of course I do, pet.'
The wrinkles start fading and both cheeks are wet.
Two hands meet each other, one gentle, one strong,
it's the end of a parting four decades too long.

'The others will join us, now don't make a fuss,
just put on the kettle we've so much to discuss.
Three daughters who live life in colour and noise,
our family still growing with new girls and boys ...'

Talking long through the night they covered it all,
then they whispered to me all alone in Bengal,
'While one mind may fail, son, please don't forget this:
safe in those that we loved, that's
where we both still live.'

Acknowledgements

The Last Overland was the most ambitious adventure of my life to date. To pull off something on this scale requires an army of people giving their time and energy over weeks, months and years. It's impossible to give credit to all who played their part – small and large – in making it possible, but I'll do my best to name a few.

To those who led the way, the First Overlanders: Tim, Pat and Nigel who I've had the privilege of knowing, and to BB, Henry and Adrian, who I sadly missed, but feel I've come as close to knowing as is possible from this side of the veil.

To Adam Bennett. Your grit, tenacity and no-bullshit approach to life raised Oxford from the ashes and set us on our way. When a Yorkshireman says he's going to do something, never doubt it. To Graeme Aldous, for keeping the flame of the First Overland alight for all those years.

To Marcus, for your friendship, passion and pedantry; Larry, for your wise counsel; The Doc, for your bottomless joy; Leo, for your commitment to your art; David, for teaching with a grin; Tibie, for your unfailing optimism; and to Nat, for just being yourself. Never stop. This story is as much yours as it is mine.

To all the guides and fixers who kept us on the right road, and made us feel at home in every country we passed through: Jerome and the Land Rover Owners of Singapore; Vicky and the Rovernuts of Malaysia; Aleena and the Land Rover Club of Thailand; Will Midwinter; The Land Rover Club of Myanmar; my dear friend Aung Sithu; Rajan Dowerah; Saom and Mr Bunty; Kunda Dixit and Sheilin Tao; Lakhpa; Alex Fedim and Vladimir; Tashmurad; the Land Rover Club of Azerbaijan; Doctor Mehmet,

Cervet and the Land Rover Club of Turkey; Hanna, Tamás and the Land Rover Club of Hungary; the Land Rover Club of France; Sebastien Land-Vintage; the Land Rover Club of Belgium; the UK Land Rover Series One Club; Tony at The Grenadier; the team at the Folkestone Harbour Arm and the many wonderful UK Foreign Office diplomats and officials who smoothed our way.

To the sponsors who made this 'gamble on wheels' a reality: Chee-Pey, Laura, Yen Nee, Jason and Debbie at Singapore Tourism Board; Mitch, Melissa and Stan at AKE; Mark, Tanya, Shih-Hueh and Graham at Klareco Communications; Tom Osborne (who always went above and beyond), Amey, Robin, Joshua, Tim, Mike and all at Land Rover around the globe; Giles, Nick, Neil, Katie and Claire at Bremont; Rob and Charly at Ophir Gin; Tom at Stephenson Harwood; Fiona at Craghoppers; Patrick at Hilton Hotels; Marcus, Dan and Ian at Hagerty; Alan at Dometic; Sasha and Jay at Battleface; Tommy and Andrew at Revolut; Tony Wheeler and the team at Lonely Planet; and to Zoe at Fortnum & Mason. To Krishna, Piers and Robert at the Gurkha Welfare Trust, Ed at Walking with the Wounded, and the whole team at Dementia UK.

Writing this book at times felt like pulling on a thread someone had laid out for me to find. Some days it came easy, others it felt like yanking on a great tangle of knots. Luckily I had the wisest heads to help me through.

To Levison Wood who sat me down on day one (the hardest), distracted and motivated in equal measure, and put a roof over my head for far longer than he should. To Richard Blurton, who did the same; your steadfast patience, generosity, friendship and a glass of wine at the right time will never be forgotten. To Danny McEvoy, whose keen mind was always on hand to help me wrestle this story into shape. To Stu and Gem Webley, and all the team at the Ty Coch Inn, always ready with a kind word and a pint after a long day's writing. To Jascha, for giving me the space and peace to finish.

To the brilliant Keggie Carew and Dan Kieran, who inspired me with their work and reviewed early drafts. To Rebecca Dobbs and Michael Wood for their masterclass in storytelling in all its forms. I learn from you both every day. To Charlie Smith, for your endless enthusiasm and keen eye for design, and to Yasmin Jafar for your eagle-eyed proofing. To Nick Gowing, for your kindness and companionship, just when I needed it most.

To my agents, Jo and Jonathan Cantello at Wolfsong, and to Jo Stansall, Rumana Haider, Saskia Angenent and the whole team at Michael O'Mara. Thank you for helping me to fulfil a childhood dream.

To Kate, Max, Liv, Steph, Ash and Parker for your young hearts and wise heads, and for being as close to family as friends can be. To Melyn, without whom I wouldn't have made it to the start line, and to Emma, without whom I would never have found the finish.

To my brother, Sam, and his family – Rosie, Jack and Charlie – for always saving me a place at their table.

And finally, to my parents, Pam and Roger, who never let me give up. I owe you everything.